# Testimonials

This riveting testimonial should serve as inspiration to us all and to the fact that we can beat diabetes.

**Francine R. Kaufman, M.D.**
Children's Hospital, Los Angeles
Past President of American Diabetes Association
Author of DIABESITY (Bantam, 2005)


James Quander's courageous and well-known fight against diabetes for practically all of his long life has given hope, peace and comfort to victims of diabetes and other diseases, and to their families.

He endured and overcame the pain and suffering of discrimination and segregation without ever compromising his purpose and principles, and he did all this while having a happy family life and a successful and distinguished career. His faith, perseverance and grace have been an inspiration to all, and I am proud to have been his "old Dunbar classmate" and friend.

**Senator Edward W. Brooke**, Washington, D.C.


On behalf of the Board, volunteers, and staff of the Juvenile Diabetes Research Foundation (JDRF), I acknowledge and praise the key role that Rev. James Quander has played in helping raise the awareness of the seriousness of diabetes and the need for "Cure" research. We celebrate him as an "elder diabetes statesman," and for the fine example he set throughout his long life with this chronic, debilitating disease.

**Peter Van Etten**
President and CEO, Juvenile Diabetes Research Foundation


After having read the transcript of the life of Deacon Quander, as a Deacon of African descent, and as President of the National Association of African American Catholic Deacons, I can truthfully say, "The life, struggles and achievemnts of Deacon Quander is a powerful witness and testimony to the ministry of diaconal service, that he consistently demonstrated throughout each phase of his life and ministry."

**Deacon Marvin Threatt, Ph.D**
President, National Association of African American Catholic Deacons

Once again, Deacon James William Quander has made a contribution of himself to the cause of juvenile diabetes, a disease so often ignored. Through his story of courage, struggle, and immense joy, we find a splendid example of a God who has carried him through this disease for at least 80 years. We honor Deacon Quander who also made another contribution to the community during his journey of understanding the meaning of being black and Catholic. Even as a person with diabetes, he was quite aware of his struggle as one of the first black Catholic deacons in Washington, D.C. He respected those who had differing opinions about the black Catholic movement, although we heard (and needed) his sharp critique of some aspects. During his journey, he was in the midst of St. Benedict the Moor parish's first steps to provide Masses that were relevant for black Catholics. This was not an easy task for him but he handled himself with his characteristic courage, endurance and immense joy.

**Jacqueline E. Wilson**
Executive Director (retired), Office of Black Catholics
Archdiocese of Washington, 1979-2002.


James W. Quander was truly a trailblazer and a hero, who demonstrated early in life that juvenile diabetes is not necessarily a death sentence. He challenged those who doubted his determination to survive, placing his trust in God, the old Freedmen's Hospital, the Howard University College of Medicine and the medical staff, who taught him basic survival skills

Diagnosed with juvenile diabetes in 1924, at the age of 6, James Quander refused to let the disease affect his quality of life. Instead, he took control and, with the support of his family and a strict regimen of diet and exercise, he lived for eighty-six happy, healthy and productive years.

James Quander inspired and educated people of all races about living with diabetes. He will always be remembered for his indomitable spirit and his zest for life. He was truly a medical miracle.

In death, he continues to honor Howard by donating proceeds from his life story to the Howard University College of Medicine, to promote diabetic research and education.

**H. Patrick Swygert,**
President, Howard University
Washington, D.C.

On behalf of the Howard University College of Medicine, it is an honor to have this opportunity to make comments in James W. Quander's book, *The Quander Quality: The True Story of a Black Trailblazing Diabetic*. Mr. Quander's biography is indeed uplifting and will be an inspiration for victims and their families and friends who are diagnosed with this disease. Congratulations to both James and co-author, Rohulamin Quander, Esq., for this ambitious undertaking.

Diabetes affects more than 14 million people in the United States — 7 percent of the total population. Moreover, this disorder is 33 percent more prevalent among African-Americans than white Americans. Unlike James Quander, who was diagnosed with this disorder early when he was almost six years old, many people do not know they have the disease; experts call it a "hidden disease."

Although these numbers are cause for concern, thanks to the information in Mr. Quander's book, the outlook for those with diabetes is optimistic. Based on his life's experience, he discussed alternative lifestyles, education, major breakthroughs in research, coupled with religious faith, and family support as contributing factors to his longevity and a happy prosperous life.

Mr. Quander's book imparts an important message to its readers: what you do and how you live your life ultimately counts and influences your long-range health outlook.

Howard University College of Medicine sincerely appreciates Mr. Quander's generosity in donating the proceeds from his and his son's book to the College of Medicine. The proceeds will allow programs in diabetes research and education at Howard University to continue. We thank you.

**Robert E. Taylor, M.D., Ph.D.**
Interim Dean
Howard University College of Medicine

# The Quander Quality

## The True Story of a Black Trailblazing Diabetic

(The Life of James W. Quander)

Co-Authored by James W. Quander
and Rohulamin Quander

Robert D. Reed Publishers • Bandon, OR

Robert D. Reed Publishers
P.O. Box 1992
Bandon, OR 97411
Phone: 541-347-9882 • Fax: -9883
E-mail: 4bobreed@msn.com
web site: www.rdrpublishers.com

Typesetter: **Barbara Kruger**
Editor: **Cleone Lyvonne** ˙
Cover Designer: **Grant Prescott**

ISBN 1-931741-162-X

Library of Congress Control Number 2005927445

Manufactured, typeset and printed in the United States of America

# Dedications

*To John Edward and Maude Pearson Quander,*
*my beloved parents,*
who always had great faith and determination
that I would survive,
despite all dire predictions about my longevity.

*To Charles McDuffy Wilder, M.D.,*
*my first physician and very dear friend,*
*and the medical staff*
at Old Freedmen's Hospital, Washington, D.C.,
who taught me how to become disciplined in diabetic care
and encouraged me to reach out and not succumb
to perceived limitations imposed by my lifelong ailment.

*To Joherra Theresa Rohualamin,*
*my devoted wife of 60 years,*
who loved and cared for me,
nurtured me,
and introduced me to the world.
May she and I have eternal peace – TOGETHER.

Love, James

# Acknowledgments

- Hugh Simmons, M.D., who seamlessly assumed responsibility for my medical care when Dr. Wilder retired from his practice
- Susan Housman, M.D., my physician for the last 15 years, who gave me excellent and attentive care, as she monitored my diabetic health during my twilight years
- The Dunbar High School Class of 1936, my lifelong friends, peers, and confidants, with whom I shared my most fond memories and whose academic prowess likewise spurred me on to "Keep a Pluggin' Away," academically and otherwise
- George L. King, M.D., for his research work as head of the Joslin Diabetes Center, Harvard University, and for writing the Foreword, both symbolic of his interest and dedication to finding a cure for diabetes, by inspiring those who have it, to seek to attain a great quality of life
- Senator Edward W. Brooke, fellow Dunbar High School 1936 classmate, for his being a continuing inspiration to African-Americans everywhere, and for his words of wisdom and encouragement
- H. Patrick Swygert, President, Howard University, for his meaningful words that inspire diabetics and those challenged by adversity, to keep moving forward
- Robert E. Taylor, Interim Dean, Howard University College of Medicine, whose testimonial was both uplifting and inspirational to diabetics and their families
- Francine R. Kaufman, M.D., former president, American Diabetes Association, for her dedication to finding a cure for diabetes and her devotion to promoting improved medical care among juvenile and adult diabetics everywhere
- Peter Van Etten, President and CEO, Juvenile Diabetes Research Foundation, for their dedication to "cure" research and devotion to educating diabetics about how to successfully cope with this lifelong, debilitating disease

- Jacqueline E. Wilson, Director (retired), Office of Black Catholics, Archdiocese of Washington, for her historical perspective on the religious life and contributions of the Black Catholics in the late 20th Century
- Marvin Threatt, Ph.D., President, National Association of African-American Catholic Deacons, for his sharing that James Quander's religious service was a testimonial about the ministry of diaconal service
- Cleone Lyvonne, Editor, always pleasant and helpful, who stayed focused to help us present, in the most interesting manner, a story that begged to be told
- Carmen Torruella Quander, devoted wife and daughter-in-law, our most tirelessly devoted fan, for her support and encouragement at all phases of this effort, as we endeavored to get the story published

# The Quander Quality:
## Autobiography of a Trailblazing Diabetic

## The Life of James W. Quander

# Foreword

It was a privilege to read this autobiography by James W. Quander, who is a pioneer in so many realms. His is a story characterized by integrity, inspiration and wisdom.

As the title suggests, James was a trailblazer in many ways, two of which are: as an African American living in a society that had not yet learned the lessons of civil rights, and as a man with diabetes who came of age in an era when people with diabetes were in, as he put it, "the diabetic closet." These are the threads that run throughout his life, and they poignantly overlap, as he had to negotiate both the challenges of racial discrimination and a complex disease that is difficult to manage.

It took three years for all his symptoms to be diagnosed as type 1 diabetes. It was shortly before his sixth birthday in 1924 when he finally received this diagnosis by a doctor who would become his personal lifesaver. Yet despite the support of his doctor and family, James was forced to live with what he termed the "big secret" for decades, and he did not divulge his diabetes due to the "ignorance and misunderstanding" that the disease generated during this era. It was at the age of 73 that he came out of the closet and out of a life of concealment.

James Quander lived in a time when the technology of rigid glucose monitoring did not exist, and thus the daily managing of diabetes was a time-consuming and inaccurate process. Yet despite these hardships, which are familiar to many who have lived with diabetes for more than 50 years, James Quander was determined to live a healthy and happy life. And he succeeded due to a life of discipline regarding his eating habits, his physical activity and his ability to understand that stress does have an impact on the disease.

James also benefited from the support and love of his family. We know through our research from Joslin 50-Year Medalists (people who have lived with type 1 diabetes for 50 years, a very rare group of people) that support and understanding are as important as physically managing the disease. James Quander lived with diabetes for 80 years; and he clearly recognized that without his family, he would not have been able to manage the many challenges of diabetes.

James Quander's memoir covers a lot of ground. It reflects the painful journey of African Americans to receive equal rights in this country. It also reflects a period of time when diabetes was considered a disability and therefore one did not disclose it on a job application. And it reflects the evolution of diabetes treatment and the inspiration of one man who beat all the odds. What an important legacy for all who have diabetes.

George L. King, M.D.
Director of Research, Joslin Diabetes Center, Boston, Mass.
Professor of Medicine, Harvard Medical School, Boston, Mass.

# Introduction

*The Quander Quality* is the culmination of a life of achievement, bonded to a sober reflection of how my dad, James W. Quander, arrived at a point in his life where he needed to tell his life story. Although the story begins in an ambulance on the way to the hospital emergency room, the fact that he lived long enough to tell the story is itself a miracle.

My dad endured a long journey of physical and psychological disabilities imposed upon him by the adverse effects of a lifetime of Juvenile Diabetes. Confirmed as a diabetic in 1924, shortly before his sixth birthday, the conditions were present but undiagnosed at least three years earlier. Destined to die before his tenth birthday, he defied everyone—doctors, parents, and naysayers—and lived more than 86 years. Yet, despite what some would consider as a lifelong medical "curse," thanks to the determination of his parents, John E. and Maude Pearson Quander, plus the sustained support of Charles M. Wilder, M.D., his first physician, he learned at an early age to confront diabetes head on, and to not only survive, but to prosper and lead a full, productive life.

For years, many individuals, especially from his medical support base and people who had known him since childhood, urged him to tell his story, emphasizing that others needed to know, not just about him as a person, but how he managed to both survive and prosper in the face of so very much adversity. By no means is this a negative story, but it details triumph over what others thought might be a never-ending series of tribulations.

In the course of those 86-plus years, the rich diversity of his exposure took him physically and emotionally to many planes that he never initially contemplated or expected. Born in Washington, D.C., and educated in the then racially segregated Colored Division of the D.C. public school system, he came from a lower socio-economic background. He had never traveled more than 35 miles from home until he was well into his 20s.

Over the course of his eight decades, primarily centered on living an upwardly mobile African-American life in Washington, D.C., he faced both significant and continuing health-related and racial discrimination; discovered the rich history of the Quander Family, documented since 1684 as one of America's oldest black families; was one of the original 16 Roman Catholic Ministers of Service (Permanent Deacons) in the United States, when the church revived the permanent diaconate in 1971; and married outside of the confines of his race's expectations, enjoying 60 years of happy married life.

Inspired by Negro poet Paul Laurence Dunbar's poem, *Keep A Pluggin' Away*, the initial title of this publication was *Keep A Pluggin' Away: How I Survived Juvenile Diabetes For More Than 80 Years*. The title was changed to emphasize the diversified scope of James Quander's remarkable life, a testament to a man who never gave up on the joy of living.

How does someone, who is supposed to die before age ten, tell a life story when he is 86 years old? There is no simple or singular way. Rather, there are a series of experiences, thoughts, and recollections. I hope that as you read *The Quander Quality*, you will appreciate how James W. Quander came to be what he was, and more importantly why he wanted to share this story with others, if for no other reason than to blaze a trail that others might follow as they seek a path to a better life.

This autobiography could not have been written much earlier, as it took decades before he was fully appreciated as an "elder diabetic statesman," someone who should be both listened to and emulated when it comes to creating a pattern of good diabetic health. In his determination to extend the promotion of good diabetic health, he directed that 50% of the proceeds from *The Quander Quality* be donated to the Howard University College of Medicine, Washington, D.C., to promote diabetic-cure research and education about the ailment and how to live a full life in spite of it.

This story is well worth reading, as James Quander's primary objective throughout his life, and as related here, was to send a message of hope and expectation to all persons who suffer from any disability, or who feel despair because of their circumstances. Particularly reaching out to those who are diabetic, he underscores that you can lead a full, happy, and successful life, provided that you adopt a singularly most important tool—DISCIPLINE. Read on and enjoy.

Rohulamin Quander
Son and co-author

# Chapter 1

# This Is My Story

The last thing that I remember was Joherra, my wife of 60 years, saying, "Come on, James, and take this syrup. Please, James! Hold on, the ambulance is on the way." As she valiantly tried to pour the sweet, slippery substance down my throat, while holding my nose, I began to gag. I could not swallow. In my deep recess, I realized that I was choking and subconsciously said to myself, "Is this how I'm supposed to die? To gag and choke on syrup lodged in my throat, administered unwittingly by my loving and devoted wife who's only trying to save me from an insulin reaction?" I cannot remember anything else about that incident.

Next, I saw Papa, my beloved dad, John Edward Quander, who had died in August 1950. He was at the other end of a long tunnel, illuminated with bright lights. His hand was extended, and he said to me, "Come, James! Come to me. You've suffered long enough." In my subconscious, I cried, "Yes, Papa, I'm coming. I'm tired, Papa, and it's been such a long struggle. Come and get me."

I have no recollection of the ambulance or the paramedics, no recollection of any aspect of this event. I relate here only what I was told about the incident. I woke up slowly, still in a cold sweat, covered with several blankets, which seemed to weigh heavily on my frail, thin body. The light was blinding. Was I dead, or was something just shining in my face from overhead?

When I came out of this insulin reaction, my wife was standing there beside me, and said, "James, I thought we lost you. I thought that it was all over." I could barely speak and was so very tired, like I had been through a tough journey on foot and maybe had to swim a part of the way, even though I have only one leg left, the result of diabetic-related poor circulation.

I was so disoriented and could not get my thoughts or words together. I said, "I don't remember anything, except your trying to get that syrup into me." At that moment, the nurse practitioner came into the emergency room cubicle where I had lain on white sheets for the last couple of hours and said, "You really gave us a scare. Your blood sugar dropped to 19. We're going to keep you here for a little while, and then you can go home. This was a really close call." By then my eldest son, Rohulamin, had arrived in the cubicle. He, along with my other three children, had been waiting just outside in the Washington Hospital Center emergency room waiting area.

He looked at my frail and weakened body, took me in his arms and said, "Dad, this was a really bad one, a close call. I think it's critical that you write your life history as a juvenile diabetic because you have much to tell; and with severe insulin reactions like this, you can't have too many of these and survive. You've just got to tell your story, to share it with the millions of others who need to know how you've lived successfully with this ailment all these years. Yet, you're still here, despite what has happened on too many occasions already. Let me interview you, and let's write this autobiography together, while we still have time. O.K.?"

I agreed, and now you are reading the work product of that incident, the night I actually brushed with death—again.

Consideration of when I was going to tell my story has been floating around for decades. Several of my doctors have commented through the years that they had never treated someone who has survived Type I Juvenile Diabetes for so very many years. They encouraged me to write my life story, to share with others how I have lived with this ailment for these 80 plus years, in hope that other diabetics, especially Type I Juvenile Diabetics, and their families, could understand that, as challenging as it may be, it is really possible to live a long, fruitful, and happy life, despite the physical, medical, and psychological challenges that are inherently associated with this ailment.

Although the symptoms of my ailment were present since I was three years old, I was not officially diagnosed with Diabetes Millitis until early 1924. My parents did not initially recognize frequent bedwetting, great hunger and thirst, and periods of light-headedness in the early 1920s as symptomatic of the ailment. Since bedwetting was typical for young children, they simply suspected that maybe I was just a little delayed in growing out of it. That I was hungry and thirsty all the time was greeted with, "James certainly has a good appetite, but he just doesn't seem to gain much weight." My dizziness was most probably caused by widely fluctuating blood sugar. However, in the shadow of my loving parents who had very little formal education, it would take a major health incident in the spring of 1924, just about the time of my sixth birthday, before my parents finally realized the magnitude of what was occurring, and that I really was very ill.

By the age of ten, Papa (John Edward Quander, 1883-1950) was orphaned and left to care for a younger sister and brother. His mother died first, and having left school and joining the work force at age nine to help support the family, he only completed two years of formal education in the rigidly segregated Maryland of the late 19th Century.

Mama (Maude Pearson Quander, 1880-1961) was from Walterboro, South Carolina. She too had little formal education there, although she pursued a night school education at the Armstrong School in Washington, D.C., after she and Papa married in 1905. Neither of them really understood much about Diabetes at that early time, only that their fifth child had the ailment, and in all likelihood, would not live beyond ten years of age. I am getting ahead of the story for now.

I was born on Friday, April 19, 1918, at 662 Acker Street, N.E., in Washington, D.C. It was a bright sunny day in the spring when many of my extended Quander and Pearson family members and the neighbors, some of whom were themselves former slaves or first generation descendants, were just feeling the warmer weather of springtime. Beginning to stir about in the neighborhood, they were busy meeting and greeting folks that they had not seen since the prior fall. Acker Street, N.E., ran for only one block, between F and G, and Sixth and Seventh Streets, all main thoroughfares. Undoubtedly it was one of those streets in Washington, D.C., of which there were many, where the original large rear yards of the white residents who resided on the outer, main streets were cut through to make smaller streets and smaller houses in the rear to create housing for blacks, especially in a town where restrictive racial covenants limited the places where colored folk could live.

All of the residents were "colored," the racial term that we used then to describe African-Americans. For ease in understanding me, I will interchangeably use the terms "colored," "Negro," "Black," and "African-American," as the situation and context warrant. But in 1918, in Acker Street, living among a diverse cross-section of persons of African descent, we were universally called "colored" among ourselves, and likewise referred to as such by the few white persons with whom some of us came in contact.

Acker Street was a microcosm of the colored community of the day. It was not a residential street for the upper class blacks, most of whom lived closer to Howard University or in Georgetown. Still, we had our share of teachers, preachers, Pullman porters, federal government workers, common laborers, domestic workers, and the like. Virtually all of the women were housewives, except for a few teachers, and those that were not housewives were generally domestic workers for white families.

I was born the fifth of six children, delivered by Dr. Wilder, in the front bedroom of our circa 1880 house. Even though Dr. Charles M. Wilder did not graduate from the University of Pennsylvania Medical School until the following year in 1919, it is believed that he was the one there at my birth. It was a common practice for medical students to act as "midwives" during this era.

His father, Dr. James Wilder, a graduate of Howard University College of Medicine in 1888, had been our family physician, and between them, they delivered all five of my siblings and me. Later, when I was diagnosed with diabetes, Dr. Charles M. Wilder would remain my physician as he developed an interest in treating diabetes among the colored residents of the District of Columbia. I became one of his prime medical charges: he wrestled with trying to save me, and at the same time, chart a way for me to have a decent quality of life.

I learned to love that man and owe my life to him. He taught me not only what diabetes is, but how I could learn, through self-discipline and careful planning, to live a full life as close to "normal" as possible. As well, he was a soul mate to Mama, because his mother was also a Pearson from the same general area of Walterboro, South Carolina, that my mother came from, although we were never able to verify a specific family connection.

Looking for answers to why I was cursed with such a lifelong, debilitating ailment, I once asked my mother if her pregnancy with me had been difficult, and whether she had any indication prior to my birth that maybe something was not medically right. Answering "No!" she added that I was the fifth child of six, and there was nothing about her pregnancy to distinguish me from any of the other children. Laughing, she said, "If anything, I was a little embarrassed to be having a child at my age. But I was even more embarrassed when Kitty was born." Although she never volunteered how old she was when we were born, I later figured out that she was two weeks shy of her 38th birthday when I was born and 41 years old when Kitty was born.

While I do not personally recall much of our actual life on Acker Street because we moved away from there in 1922, just after my fourth birthday, I have many "after-acquired accumulated memories" of living there based upon the constant past recollections and conversations with Quander and Pearson family and friends who spoke of the community that characterized this time in our family's history. As a result, I really do recall much of what life was like while living on that street.

First of all, there are a significant number of descendants of families that lived on Acker Street with us in the 1920s that are still living there, more than 80 years later. The house we lived in seemed large, but now, in retrospect and in driving past it occasionally just to look at it, it was actually quite small. Papa rented the house for several years while saving to buy our own house.

The dining room and kitchen were both on the street level and were the biggest rooms in the house. Access from the street, which is called an "English basement" entrance, was directly into the dining room, proceeding back to the kitchen that had a corrugated tin ceiling, a very popular ceiling material at that time.

The second level, which for some reason was called the "first floor," had two rooms, a parlor in the front, which we used only on the occasion of visitors, and a back room, which we used as a bedroom. With three boys, three girls, and both parents in such a small house, we needed all the room that we could get. As well, what I call "Maude Pearson Quander's way station" was in full operation as relatives from South Carolina came and went with some degree of regularity—always to find a ready bed, food on the table, and a warm welcome at our home whenever they came through. And some of them came through rather often.

I never heard one single word of complaint from Papa about all of the people, some relatives and some not. Having lost his mother in about 1890 and his father in 1893 (at ten years of age), he was left to care for his younger brother and sister. Even though he had a large number of Quander relatives, including several uncles and one aunt, he still felt particularly close to Mama's people, most all of whom were very cultured, some educated, even bordering on being aristocratic, but almost all mulatto people from Walterboro, South Carolina.

We had good neighbors, too. Mr. and Mrs. Maurice Corbett were the dearest of friends. Mr. Corbett took a liking to my father, taught him basic mathematics, and helped him improve his reading skills. Papa was as smart as a whip, with a quick analytical mind. With Corbett's aid, Papa dramatically improved his reading and writing skills. He learned to do enough mathematics to later be able to successfully operate his own business and then eventually secure a federal government job. Mr. Corbett's wife, Elvira, whom we called "Mamee," was my mother's best friend, for whom my sister, Ruth Elvira, was named. She was also Elvira's godmother. Their daughter, "Mildred," was my first sweetheart.

After the Corbetts and we each moved away from Acker Street, my parents' deep and abiding friendship continued until all four of them died. Other families who lived in the street were the Whitmans, whose daughters, The Whitman Sisters, danced professionally on stage; the Roys; the Hargroves; the Tillmans; Rev. White, pastor of a large Protestant church; Catherine Fletcher, who was my sister Cora's godmother; and C. Beatrice Culver, who used to remind me regularly that she remembers my mother being pregnant with me.

While Mama stayed home and kept house, Papa worked at the Center Market, which fronted down the middle of Pennsylvania Avenue between Seventh and 14th Streets, N.W., with the rear of the market located on Constitution Avenue, N.W., running the length of several of the same numbered streets. The market was closed and torn down years ago, replaced by federal buildings, the most famous of which is the National Archives Building, which houses the Declaration of Independence, the Constitution of the United States, and the Emancipation Proclamation, among other historically significant documents.

Originally working as a vegetable and fruit laborer, he entrusted himself to Mr. Merrick and became one of his most valued colored employees. Working for Merrick for several years, Papa secured jobs for several of his younger cousins who relocated to Washington from Upper Marlboro, Maryland, in the early part of the Twentieth Century. Over time he became one of Merrick's primary vegetable men.

Through the years, and as our family fortunes increased slightly, Papa opened his own small fruit and vegetable stand and earned enough money to feed not only a family of eight, but also a significant amount of other relatives and family friends who routinely came to visit. In some cases they took up residency for months, or even years at a time. By the time he eventually lost his own business due to the Great Depression, Papa had been working at the Center Market for almost 40 years—initially as a laborer, then for Merrick, then for himself, and later as a vegetable and fruit man for the District Grocery Store system.

Not only was he loving and kind, he was also extremely generous and routinely brought home fresh fruits, vegetables, and sometime meats that were being discarded at the market. There were several widows or other people who were either out of work or did not have any money to buy groceries in the neighborhood, both on Acker Street, and later on 17th Street, where we would later move. They routinely depended upon John Edward Quander's kindness when he collected still usable, but discarded produce—potatoes, greens, meats—and dragged it home on the streetcar, sometimes even by the bushel, to distribute. Mama was a great cook and was able to take this discarded food that was often soft, bruised, or past its prime for salability, and create something truly magnificent.

I did not know it then, nor did she or Papa, but this was a diabetic food preparation training ground for both of them. I was already a sick child and was about to become even sicker. Had they not had the determination to save me, had she not been able to prepare the type of food that my debilitated health required, I would not be writing this autobiography today, 80 years later.

Despite the debilitating effects of diabetes, which would soon present itself and set the tone for the rest of my life, I had a very good childhood. My parents believed in celebrations. Every birthday was celebrated, and all holidays were special. At Christmas the house was beautifully decorated, the kitchen smelled of magnificent aromas of fresh baking, and friends came to call and stayed a long, long time to enjoy Mama's fruitcakes, pound cakes, eggnog, and homemade wines, which she set into fermentation the prior summer. Coming from a Southern culture where the slaves' food supplies had been limited, she learned from her mother, Hannah Fraser Pearson, how to pickle or make preserves out of watermelon rinds and cucumbers, to make her own relish, hot sauces and mustards, and to can all varieties of fruits and vegetables.

In the dead of winter, when certain food items were not generally available in our then less than mobile society of the 1920s, we had freshly canned peaches, tomatoes, and other beautifully preserved items on the coldest days. Despite Prohibition or any laws restricting alcohol intake by children, I always tasted her homemade blackberry wine and peach brandy all year long. Some of these recipes I still have, passed down through the family over more than 100 years.

Unquestionably, the single most vivid recollection that I have of my entire childhood was the day that I got scalded. Although the incident occurred more than 80 years ago, in 1922, shortly before my fourth birthday, I remember it as if it occurred only yesterday. I was playing by myself, running back and forth. I was wearing a little white dress shirt with a hand-tied bow tie, which was fashionable at the time, complemented by navy blue trousers, and Buster Brown shoes. Why I was so dressed up at the moment of this incident escapes me.

Grandma, Hannah Fraser Pearson (c.1839-1926), was sitting at her sewing machine. An outstanding men's tailor, she made several outfits for me, including what I had on that day. Freed at birth by her father-master, Frederick Fraser, Walterboro, South Carolina, mother of 14 children, and widowed in 1890 by the death of my grandfather, Willie Pearson, she had come to live with us in her later years.

A little bit of a woman, she was wearing her traditional "uniform," i.e., a stiff-collared, cuffed, long-sleeve white blouse, which drew up around her neck making her look very stern, although she was not; a long cotton or woolen skirt, depending upon the season; and a mid-length apron across the front. At the time of the incident, she was past 80 years of age, and her long white hair was plaited into two braids, which she usually piled on top of her head.

As she sat at her foot-operated sewing machine making a new suit for one of us, as a silly little child, self-entertaining, I suddenly darted away from running in circles playing with a toy, and crashed with full force into my older sister, Elvira, then age eight, who was transferring a swinging-handled iron kettle of hot boiling water from the stove to the sink, intending to pour the water onto some rice she had in a pot. As I knocked the kettle out of her hand, and before the pot hit the floor, I was scalded from just below my neck to my right elbow and let out the most blood-curdling scream imaginable.

In a reflex action, Grandma's arms popped open, and I flew into the safety of her wide skirt, wailing, screaming uncontrollably, and writhing in pain. Grandma, Mama, and Elvira all knew that I had been badly burned, but in the excitement of the moment, no one knew where. Thinking quickly, Grandma took her sewing scissors and immediately cut off all of my clothes down to my underpants while Mama brought butter from the icebox. Grandma rubbed me from head to toe in butter while Mama telephoned for Dr. Wilder to come immediately. Had they known better in those days, she would have rubbed me down in ice to slow the burning sensation. We had a telephone before most of our neighbors did, and they occasionally made or received calls at our home. Why Papa felt the need to have a telephone as far back as 1921, I really do not know for sure, but it came in very handily that day.

Elvira, realizing what had occurred and how it had happened, almost went into shock herself. She was numb with fear and could not quite bring herself to realize that I alone had caused this terrible accident, and that there was nothing she could have done to prevent this tragedy. Without warning, I had suddenly darted in her direction. At age eight, it was traditional for a young girl to begin domestic responsibilities. Learning to cook was one of those tasks, a task that she mastered quite well.

In 1922, doctors still made house calls. Dr. Wilder closed his office and rushed over to the house. By the time of his arrival, I had gone into post-trauma shock and passed into unconsciousness, in which state I remained for two full days and part of a third day. The burn would later be diagnosed as a traumatic, third-degree burn of the right upper arm to the elbow. It left a permanent, keloided scar that the doctors opined could not be removed or corrected by skin grafts because of the fear of infections. When I regained consciousness on the evening of the third day, I was in my parents' big bed in the front bedroom on the second floor. During the three-day wait, my mother and grandmother never left my side. As well, Papa, who had to work during this crisis, called home several times per day inquiring whether there had been any change in my condition.

My right arm was wrapped in huge gauze, which Dr. Wilder and my mother and father changed regularly. He taught them how to change the bandage, underscoring his fear that infection might still set into this badly burned arm. Of course, since I had not yet been diagnosed as a juvenile diabetic, the potential magnitude of an infection was not yet realized. He also prepared them for the reality of their child sustaining a permanently scared upper right arm. Each time the bandage was changed, Mama, Papa, or Grandma gently rubbed a salve onto my burned skin, which remained extremely tender, and was already showing the early signs of permanent scarring. While I have managed to block the additional details of my life as a three-year-old burn victim out of my mind, I recall my fourth birthday party held within a couple of weeks after the burn incident.

The party was in my parents' bedroom. I was tied to the bed posts to both keep me in the bed and to restrict the range of my movements while in the bed. The room was beautifully decorated with multicolored balloons, streamers, and other decorations everywhere, including different color tissue paper adorning the bed and the room. It seems that Mama and Papa just opened up to the neighborhood and let all the children in.

They were laughing, playing, shrieking at the top of their lungs, and Mama and a couple of the neighbor ladies kept saying: "Don't shake the bed!" "Stop rocking the bed!" "Get out from under the bed!" And with each shake of the bed, I felt a pain in my bandaged arm. How do you control a bunch of three- and four-year-olds confined to an upstairs bedroom at a birthday party? I still have not figured out that one.

We had a great time, with me tied to the bedpost and their playing all around and under the bed. After everyone sang a loud and raucous *Happy Birthday*, the gifts were opened, and Mama served vanilla and chocolate ice cream and her famous yellow cake with coconut icing. This too was my favorite cake, and she made it often. Oblivious at the time as to where my health was headed, I ate ice cream and two pieces of coconut cake to my heart's content. It would be one of the last times that I freely took in this combination of sugar without sustaining some type of negative side effects.

Although it is inconclusive whether the traumatic burn and the associated post-traumatic syndrome played any significant role in the soon-thereafter onset of juvenile diabetes, some of my doctors have at least observed that the shock to my young body may have caused certain sudden imbalances in my body chemistry. Still, it would be quite a stretch to conclude that the burn incident caused diabetes, and no medical person has ever said such.

In September 1922, at the age of four and a half years, I started all-day school—kindergarten in the morning and first grade in the afternoon. Today we would consider this arrangement as quite unusual, but Logan School administrators allowed it. Going to school all day was a major life-change experience for me. With my mother at home, I liked the idea of being able to stay home with her. But off I was sent to Logan School, located at Third and L Streets, N.E., the local elementary school to which the colored children in the neighborhood were sent. In retrospect, I was too young, hardly prepared to start school at the time, and going for the entire day made it even more difficult.

Unlike today and to the best of my knowledge, there was no strict enforcement of any age-appropriate guideline standard to control when a child could start school. If the guidelines existed at the time, they were not enforced with regard to me. With the exception of my younger sister, Catherine, born in 1921, nicknamed "Kitty," all of my other siblings were in school. I was carted off, too, taken in hand by my older sister, Cora, who was born in 1911.

Interestingly enough, we no longer lived in the Acker Street neighborhood. My father bought a house in Northwest, and we moved to 1913 17th Street in 1922, sometime after my fourth birthday party in April, but before school opened in September. Cora wanted to graduate with her class, so each morning she took the streetcar from 17th and U Streets, N.W., to Third and H Streets, N.E., and we walked the final block to school. She wanted company, and my parents selected me.

Logan was not a bad experience. Despite my being enrolled for only one year, I made several new friends there, children who generally lived in the neighborhood, but not necessarily on Acker Street. My parents never let me wander about the neighborhood unsupervised, so naturally I did not know many children from the neighborhood that we had just vacated, other than an immediate Quander family which also resided on Acker Street, the children of my parents' friends, and the nearby neighbors' children.

# Chapter 2

# Discovering That I Was a Juvenile Diabetic

Young children often wet the bed at night. However, my case was an exception. Shortly after we moved to 1913 17th Street, N.W., between T and U Streets, in the area the colored call, "Strivers Row," I started wetting the bed on a regular basis. It was not an occasional thing, but a prolonged bedwetting that occurred with such frequency that my parents became concerned. Was it because I was fearful, having been sent to school at such an early age? I was just four years old. Was there some psychological problem, which they did not understand, that created or contributed to this medical anomaly? I am certain that they had no clue that maybe there was a serious medical problem.

Initially, they tried the usual remedies of nothing to drink after dinner; no watermelon, evening servings of fruit, or other known diuretic foods; and making certain that I go to the bathroom each night just before I recited my prayers. Intermittently, that effort worked, but only partially. After I made a step or two of forward progress, I would quickly lose my momentum and slip back, having periods of bedwetting that occurred almost nightly.

We were a large family of nine, including Grandma, living in a small, three-bedroom house. I always shared a bed with one of my brothers, either Joseph P. or John E., Jr., and both complained that they did not want to sleep with a little brother who wet the bed every night. It was not funny. Mama bought rubber sheets to prevent any more urine getting into the mattress, further creating an already wet smelly situation. Before they caught onto the frequency of the bedwetting, the mattress was really reeking. My siblings laughed and generously poked fun at me, having not the slightest clue that I was gravely ill with an out-of-control, life-threatening illness.

The only solution that worked was to wake me up at 3:00 a.m. and lead me to the bathroom. Papa worked at night and was not at home, so Mama or one of my older siblings would set the clock. That worked, but at what price. No one wanted to get up at that hour every morning, and catch me before I made a mess of everything.

With the 3:00 a.m. routine becoming a haphazard part of our daily lives, the situation seemed to improve and the magnitude of the problem was temporarily forgotten. We were focused on settling into our new home, and my bedwetting problem was not appreciated as the symptom of a more serious problem. We had been renting at Acker Street, but when Papa's Uncle Edward Quander decided to sell his small rental property, he offered it to his nephew. Papa paid $3,000 for the house in 1922, which the family owned until 1952. In 2003, with state-of-the-art amenities, that tiny house, located in the gentrified, trendy, historic Adams-Morgan neighborhood, was resold for well over $400,000.00.

According to constructing permits located for erecting the house, it was built in about 1881 when that part of town was being developed in the post-Civil War era. Not unlike Acker Street, it lacked indoor plumbing. One of the first things Papa did was to take a portion off the back bedroom and have a bathroom installed. This was our first indoor bathroom. Acker Street had an outhouse, too, which I remember visiting in the dead of winter. There would be no more of that, thank God.

After completing the school year 1922-23 at the Logan School, it was decided that I would continue my education at the Sumner-Magruder Elementary School, the neighborhood school for colored children. The school was really two adjacent buildings, with the lower grades housed in the Magruder building, and the upper grades (fourth, fifth, and sixth) housed in the Charles Sumner building. William B. Magruder was a former mayor of the District of Columbia, while Sumner was the abolitionist United States senator from Massachusetts.

The buildings were located on the corner of 17th and M Streets, walking distance and much closer to where we now lived. Besides, Cora had graduated from Logan with her eighth grade class the prior June, and there was no reason for me to continue going to Logan. I was her company on the streetcar, but now she was in senior high school.

My teacher, of whom I was deathly afraid, was Miss Dyson. As the year progressed, she tagged me as too immature to advance to the third grade. Eventually, she transmitted that message to my parents, both of whom were relatively naïve in such matters, and of the widely held opinion that the teacher's word should not generally be challenged. She told them that I needed to be a little older so that I could better adjust to my appropriate age peer group. They accepted that opinion, and I was retained in the second grade for another academic year. Fortunately, it was not a big deal. I had been enrolled in a kindergarten-first grade program at Logan at age four and a half years, and now, at age six years, was probably among the youngest children in my class. Maybe I was too young for the third grade.

There was one big problem, however. This was the era of corporal punishment as a part of the daily classroom routine. One day Miss Dyson, angered by one of my fellow classmate's disrespect, raised her hand and with full force went to slap him in his face. Expecting the blow, he ducked, and I caught the full force of the blow intended for my errant fellow classmate right in my face. The evidence of all five of her right hand fingernails dug into my flesh leaving me literally and figuratively scarred, humiliated, and embarrassed—all because of someone else's misbehavior! She went to her grave still owing me an apology. When I told my parents the source of my injury, and how it occurred, they never said a word to Miss Dyson about the incident. Perhaps, they were intimidated.

Fortunately, my second time around (1925-26) second-grade teacher was Martha Winston, who later became an outstanding principal in the District of Columbia school system, as well as a personal friend in later years. I did not know it then, but beginning with her, I formed lifelong friendships with many of my future teachers. Despite the horrendous experience of being denied our equal rights as American citizens, if there was anything good about the old racially segregated system, it was the microcosm in which all of the elements of the colored society were right there in your neighborhood.

Your teachers, doctors, lawyers, ministers, domestic workers, laborers, government workers, and other role models were all residing among each other, forced into confined areas due to institutionalized racism. As the years progressed, several of my teachers would be neighbors, or attended Saint Augustine's Roman Catholic Church where we worshipped, or otherwise were highly visible in the community. We could not help but form bonds, and with my personality and respect for older people, it was inevitable that I would align with several of these teachers for life.

While never really under control in early 1924, just about the time of my sixth birthday, the bedwetting cycle started up again. Once again the middle-of-the-night bathroom routine was re-instituted. I overheard my parents one day discussing me, with Mama saying, "John, there must be something wrong with 'Jimsen Weed' (my nickname), because he's too old to be still doing this." Papa agreed and said, "Let's get in touch with Dr. Wilder and see." Within a matter of days after that, things really fell apart.

It was during the Easter season. Both my parents and all of us were devout Roman Catholics. Mama converted from being a Presbyterian and was already Catholic when she met my father while residing as a roomer in his cousin's house. Papa was from Upper Marlboro, Maryland, a colored Catholic enclave of long standing. We always went to Mass on Sunday. Because Papa worked at the Center Market at night, he was used to being up very early in the morning and generally attended 6:00 a.m. Mass on Sundays. Mama went to a later Mass and was active with the Ladies Auxiliary of the Knights of Saint John, one of the few national-level Catholic organizations that accepted Negroes as members, although the individual chapters of the organization were all segregated by race.

My siblings and I generally went to Sunday school after the 9:00 a.m. Mass. Often we would pass by our cousins' or friends' homes and parade to church as a group. St. Augustine's was then located at 15th and M Streets, N.W., just two blocks from my school. On this particular Sunday morning, I was not feeling very well. I woke up extremely tired and irritable. Although I told Papa that I really did not feel up to going to Mass and Sunday school, being from a strict Catholic home, not feeling well on a Sunday morning was simply unacceptable. The entire household was emptied out on Sunday mornings, and everybody had to go to Mass. My constant protestations fell on deaf ears as Mama hurried me along to get ready so that I would not make the others late.

After breakfast, I managed to drag myself along, but essentially I was in a daze the entire time. I paid no attention to the Mass and had no idea what the Sunday school was about that day. Mrs. Jackson, the Sunday school teacher, who would later become my fifth grade teacher at Sumner, asked me more than once, "Jim, is anything wrong? You don't seem to be yourself this morning." All I recall saying was, "I'm so tired! I'm so very tired!" I could hardly wait for Sunday school to end so that I could go home and get back into my bed.

As we headed home with me in tow to both Cora and Elvira, the other children were laughing and playing along the way. It was a beautiful spring day, and the flowers were showing all the signs that they were approaching full bloom. But all of that was a haze. And when at last we reached the 1900 block of 17th Street, each step that I took was a milestone. My energy level was gone, and I just did not know if I was going to make the last few steps to my front door.

Finally, we got to our front yard, and as my siblings ran on into the house, I collapsed onto one of the two forest green park benches that we always sat on in the front yard in the evenings. There was no air conditioning or television then; and being neighborly in an era when there was very little crime, it was common for us to sit in the front yard as a family, or to converse with the neighbors or passersby, while waiting for the Good Humor Man to come with his ice cream wagon. Eighty-six years later, those two park benches remain a part of our family history, heirlooms, which I still sit on in my backyard.

I just could not move and relished the fact that I was home—at least almost in my own room, in my own bed. As my siblings entered the house without me, Mama and Papa, who were in the kitchen, the place where more time was spent than in any other room, immediately noticed my absence and inquired concerning my whereabouts. Cora replied, "He's sick, outside on the bench." Papa scrambled and rushed through the dining room and up from the English basement to my aid. I heard him calling, "Jim, Jim, are you all right? Son, are you all right?" I answered, "Papa, Papa, come get me. I'm too weak to get up. I can hardly move. Come get me."

Mama, who was not one known to ever get excited, set all of that coolness aside and came running right behind him. She shouted: "What wrong? What's wrong? Oh, my baby is sick, he's sick!" Both she and Papa knelt down in the yard to attend to me. As she looked me over, I could see the concern in her face as she said, "Jimsen is too weak to even walk." She had given me the love name of "Jimsen Weed," referring to a plant that grew wild in the American South. And years later on her deathbed in 1962, she would still be calling me that name, "Jimsen Weed."

Papa scooped me up and carried me to my bed where Mama took my clothes off and put my pajamas on. At last I felt safe and comfortable, at home in my own bed, in my own room, with both my parents at my side. Although it was late Sunday morning, Papa immediately called Dr. Wilder. He was at church, and because there were no beepers or cell telephones, he could not be reached initially. A message was left, and Dr. Wilder called in the early afternoon and came by shortly thereafter. When he examined me, he again related to my parents that I was of small stature and underweight for my age, physical aspects which he had previously noted on prior occasions. Once he was given the most recent history of what had been occurring—bedwetting, weakness, excessive thirst, and occasional dizziness—he surely knew or strongly suspected that he was being confronted with a case of Type I Juvenile Diabetes.

He said nothing to that effect to either my parents or to me but told them, "I'm going to arrange for James to go to the lab tomorrow morning for some tests." The next morning, Monday, I was feeling fine, as if nothing had occurred the day before. Still, Mama got me ready, and instead of heading to school, she took me up to the lab, which was around the corner, in the 1500 block of U Street, where they ran a battery of medical examinations. Before we left the house, I said, "But Mama, I haven't had any breakfast!" She replied, "Jimsen Weed, Dr. Wilder said you have to fast—nothing to eat or drink since last night's dinner."

Exactly what they did that morning, I do not recall in detail, but medical staff there repeatedly stuck me with needles as they collected several blood samples. Although I received the standard childhood inoculations at the prescribed intervals, those scheduled medically mandated medications were nothing compared to this experience. As a child of five years, I was frightened, cold, and hungry, indeed uncertain what was happening. My sole comfort was that Mama was with me, and her presence was all the sustenance that I needed.

The results of the lab tests were sent to Dr. Wilder, who then called Mama and Papa to come into his office. Because I was the subject of the medical conference, I too attended. There, Dr. Wilder explained to my parents and me for the first time that, based upon the blood sugar and urinalysis results, I was confirmed to be suffering from an ailment called Diabetes Mellitus.

He explained further that the ailment was caused by an inability of my body to break down its sugar intake due to a malfunctioning pancreas (the organ which creates needed insulin), a necessary component for the body to properly digest the sugar intake from food and the natural sugars that are stored in the liver, all of which sugars are periodically released for the body's sustenance. I do not recall him referring to my ailment as "Type I Juvenile Diabetes" as that term seems to have emerged in later years, after medical science gained a better understating of the ailment and separated it into Type I (Juvenile) and Type II (Adult Onset) diabetes.

Then he took me aside, although my parents were there listening, pretending that only he and I were present. Looking me straight into both eyes, he said, "Jim, you have a very serious illness, and we don't have a cure for it yet. But the doctors are working on it, and maybe there will be a cure very soon. But in the meantime, you and I are going to work together as a team so that your condition doesn't get any worse. But you have to promise to do what I tell you so that it won't get any worse. Do you understand me?" Although I still was not sure what was happening, I nodded my head in the affirmative. What had been present for perhaps as long as two years was now medically confirmed. I was a Type I Juvenile Diabetic. Exactly what that meant, I still did not have a clue.

I doubt that my parents did either. My parents, Maude and John, were good, basic people, both steady as rocks, and relied upon by the neighbors both on Acker and 17th Streets as people that others could confide in when they had personal problems. Papa was also a marriage counselor, not by formal training, but by reputation. Many couples, young and old, sought his wise counsel to discuss problems that they were facing in their marriages. "Mister John," as he was affectionately called, gave wise counsel that saved or improved many domestic relationships.

Still, despite Dr. Wilder's explanation, I doubt seriously if they fully appreciated the great health risk that diabetes posed to me, even though they learned early on that there was no cure for the ailment, and that juvenile diabetics often did not live very long. I was never present during any conversations in which Dr. Wilder advised my parents how virulently destructive diabetes was to the body, and that it was doubtful that I would live much beyond ten years of age. Only later did I learn from my older siblings that they had overheard my parents discussing my health situation and sharing their determination to prove Dr. Wilder and the medical community to be wrong on this prognosis.

I can say truthfully that never once did Mama or Papa ever let on to me that they believed that I was not going to make it. Instead, they decided that they would do everything within their human ability to provide me with a quality of life equal to that of my two brothers and three sisters. It was 1924, the Roaring Twenties, good economic times. Papa had branched out to open his own fruit and vegetable stand at the Center Market, and he was able to get the freshest of locally grown foods there that Dr. Wilder prescribed as necessary to build up my weight and overall health.

And Mama, being the cook that she was, there was nothing that she could not fix to appeal to me. Dr. Wilder had a nutritionist at Freedmen's Hospital prepare a juvenile diabetic diet, relatively low in carbohydrates, which focused heavily upon proteins like lean meats and beans. Mama followed the dietary directions to the letter. I did not yet realize it, but she was creating an atmosphere of strict personal self-discipline that would serve me throughout the rest of my life. Because she learned to make the prescribed foods so appealing, those normal temptations to steal food and eat something that would later create a problem eventually dissipated.

As well, Papa would walk up to 18th Street and Columbia Road to the one bakery that we knew of that baked gluten bread, a special low-carbohydrate bread then prescribed for diabetics, which, in light of so many other bread options, has largely fallen out of favor in currently recommended diabetic diets. It was my regimen to eat several slices of it per day. Not having a car, he would trudge up there several times per month to get the bread to assure that I always had it.

Pig insulin had just been recently introduced for human use and was still experimental in the minds of many. Despite my serious condition, Dr. Wilder initially preferred to attempt regulating my diabetes with a strict diet to see how I would respond to that effort. Alternatively, if that regimen was less than effective, then he would direct that I take insulin injections. And for the next several months, we tried to get this new thing called "diabetes" under control.

My parents and I did not yet know that Dr. Wilder had gained an increasingly favorable reputation in the Negro community as a diabetic specialist. This was an era when virtually all physicians were still family practitioners, and highly developed specialties and practitioners were not yet a common part of the wider practice of medicine, as least not in our racial community. Following in his father's footsteps, Dr. Charles Wilder maintained and expanded his father's turn-of-the-century medical practice in Washington, D.C.

My parents had no understanding at the time that diabetes was a particular problem in the African-American community, at least in part the long-term result of poor nutrition. Too much fat pork, not enough green vegetables, too many starches, and too high a sugar intake were all factors that surely contributed to the high presence of this condition in our racial communities. As well, this had to have been a problem that was exacerbated by slavery and its long-term physiological and psychological effects. Not only was diabetes the side effect of overall poor health, the lack of education on the proper diet was a major component as people needed information on how to eat and how to properly fix foods to minimize or eliminate certain health-related conditions.

Many of these sick people were drawn to Dr. Wilder and seemingly populated an entire wing at Freedmen's Hospital, founded in 1868 to treat the then recently-freed slaves. The hospital is now a part of Howard University, founded in 1867, and continues to provide quality health care for patients suffering from diabetes and its effects. It would be to this same adult ward that I would eventually be admitted for treatment on several occasions for my own diabetes-related complications.

His mother being a Pearson, like my own mother, Maude Pearson Quander, and being from the same general area surrounding Walterboro, South Carolina, we always assumed that we were distant relatives, although back in that day, no effort was made to make the exact connection. Once we checked only a generation or two and found no instant commonality. His Pearson family was very white in color, mostly quadroons and octoroons, now generally discarded racial identification terms left over from slavery that emphasized how little African and how much Caucasian blood ran in your blue veins.

The bluer the veins, whiter the skin, and straighter the hair, within the colored society that was Washington, D.C., at that time, put you at the top of the social and economic scale. My own direct Pearson family members were generally not as fair in complexion as Dr. Wilder, being more cinnamon or café au lait in complexion, yet very aristocratic in their conduct and bearing. By today's standards, some might criticize them for "mimicking the white man" in terms of how they conducted themselves. Regretfully, the whole system was off base. It created hurtful self-segregation within our own African-American communities; and in the process, venues for self-hatred and widely practiced discrimination between people of African descent, based upon some artificially created color bar.

The white man has told people of African descent for generations that their black ancestors were of little to no value and their contributions minimal. Many of us endured that brainwashing to the point of virtually rejecting everything that was associated with blackness, Africa and the American South, embracing instead whatever standards the white community established for beauty, achievement, and success.

Consequently, the Pearson-Wilders, who like my mother were South Carolinians, were in a position—due to their looks, color, education, and social status—to operate at the highest level of colored society in Washington, D.C. If they desired, many of them could have left this side of the color line and passed for white. However, my mother, Maude Pearson Quander, was never a part of that society. She was also very light with soft, almost-straight hair, Semitic looking actually, the granddaughter of the Caucasian master, Frederick Fraser, of Walterboro, and his favorite slave, Mary Ellen Lee. Not a physical beauty, Mama routinely poked fun at herself by saying, "I'm ugly, just like Mrs. [Eleanor] Roosevelt." And like Mrs. Roosevelt, Mama was genteel and polished. She had very little formal schooling by the time she left Walterboro in about 1890 and came to live in Washington, D.C. Later, as an adult with six children, Mama, and her sister, Aunt Ruth Pearson, would enroll in night school at Armstrong High School, founded in 1902, to help the colored residents of the District of Columbia improve upon their basic reading, writing, and math skills.

Although both of them knew basic reading and writing before Armstrong, they each greatly increased in their self-confidence as a result of being enrolled there. Still, they had so much refinement, the result of good home training and exposure to a small, but focused upper crust—white and black—in Walterboro. As they said in those days, "They knew how to do."

Mama's father, Willie Pearson, Sr., also from Walterboro, and rumored to be descended from African royalty, was light brown, nothing near white in appearance. For that reason, although some of the near-white Pearson-Wilders would deny that there was any connection, Dr. Wilder always maintained that he still thought that there was some distant relationship.

Dr. Charles Wilder, over time, ceased just to be the family physician. He and his wife, Jennie Taylor, who taught at the Dunbar High School, became true friends of my parents and me. His father, James Wilder, had been the family physician before him.

Papa, on the other hand, was orphaned at ten years of age, left to care for a younger brother, Charles, and sister, Sally. His other sister was literally burned to death in a fire in the front yard in 1887. Papa, who was only three or four years old at the time, never forgot any of the lurid details of that incident. He was a brown-skinned man, but not really dark in complexion. And if he ever had any hair, I never saw it: he was bald from my earliest recollections. He did not come from any sophisticated background that I was ever aware of; but in later years, I came to realize that our Quander family's history was so distinguished that it is recognized as one of the oldest consistently documented African-American families, with documents dating back to 1684, and oral traditions extending back to the 1660s in Charles County, Maryland.

Now that I was learning about diabetes and came to understand that Dr. Wilder had developed a specialty in treating diabetes, I came to love him as a second father. After my own father, John Edward, and my older brother, Joseph Pearson, Dr. Wilder became my third and lasting male role model. He told me that I needed to strictly adhere to my diet, and wanting to please him and show that I both respected him and loved him, I really set out and tried to strictly align myself to his food and nutritional guidelines.

Today, as I pen these words in 2004, 80 years after my diabetes was medically confirmed, I can truthfully assert that Dr. Wilder's message to me of the need for strict discipline in food and personal behavior is the key to how I have lived, and am still living, a wonderful life.

# Chapter 3

# My Introduction to Insulin

Despite Dr. Wilder's explicit directions to my parents concerning my strict diet, and my dedicated efforts to adhere to the prescribed food program to please both my parents and my doctor, things went very badly. First of all, as a child of six years, it was extremely difficult to be so strict in governing my food intake. Mama was such a good cook that from the beginning I cheated on eating and would deny that I had stolen a piece of cake, a soda, or some other sugar-laden or otherwise proscribed item of food.

I lied repeatedly to all of them. Mama would say, "Jimsen, did you cut a piece of cake?" I would say, "No, Mama, I didn't." Papa would note that the ice cream was less than he recalled just a couple of hours ago and would ask me, "Jim, have you been eating ice cream? You know that's not on your diet, don't you?" And I would deny it repeatedly. Further, whenever Dr. Wilder came to visit, either socially or medically, he would always ask me if I had been "good." We all knew what "good" meant. Naturally, I looked him straight in the eye and denied any dietary violations. I knew that these little denials were lies and routinely confessed them to my priest in the confessional, promising Jesus Christ that I would do my best not to either commit the prohibited food violations in the future, or to lie about it afterwards. But at that time in my young life, my best efforts never worked out, and the truth always came out—with a vengeance.

The stores did not sell diabetic-friendly foods in those days; such products did not yet exist in the 1920s. For diabetics, and especially me as a young diabetic, the road was extremely difficult, and eternal vigilance was the price that had to be daily paid if I as a diabetic was going to sustain any meaningful, lasting quality of life.

As a young and impressionable child, I remember hearing and being terrified at the thought that if my blood sugar got too high, as it already had done on a number of occasions in the recent past, then my blood would turn to syrup and my circulation would be cut off. According to what I was told and sincerely believed, next I would have great pains in my legs and arms, and the doctors would cut all of them off. It was not just a thought or a dream. My parents in the context of a promise related it to me.

I was fearful of that, but at age six, almost seven, and still new to the ailment, I did not begin to appreciate that what I probably thought was merely a scare tactic actually contained many kernels of truth. Only later, well into adulthood, did it dawn upon me that I might lose one or more limbs directly related to diabetic circulatory problems and conditions adversely affected by the inability to control my blood sugar and keep it within certain confines. Only as a young adult did I come to fully realize and understand that the adults with whom I shared the diabetic ward at Freedmen's Hospital in Washington, D.C., in the 1920s and early 1930s, with me usually as the only child on the ward, had lost one or more limbs due to diabetes-related complications.

Opened in 1868 to accommodate the medical needs of free blacks and the recently freed slaves, Freedmen's Hospital was the only all-black hospital in the rigidly segregated Washington, D.C., of this era, although most of the other hospitals did have separate colored wards where African-Americans in need of hospital stays were accommodated.

For the most part, to say that my diabetes was "under control" was an oxymoron, as it never seemed to be really under control in this era. I was six and seven years old, on a strict diet, and largely restricting myself to that diet, but there were problems galore. As a result of my occasional, but mostly weekend recklessness of stealing food and denying it, Mondays were often very difficult.

My blood sugar levels were higher on Mondays than any other day of the week, and on too many occasions even approached a glucose level of 500. As well, because my blood sugar was so high, I had to urinate frequently. The colloquial term for this condition was "spilling," a situation in which the body is attempting to dump the excess sugar that is passed off in the urine. Unfortunately, spilling creates its own adverse effects: the loss of too much liquid causes an unquenchable thirst, dry throat, sustained weakness, and occasional dizziness.

Early on, Mama got into the daily routine of fixing a totally different menu for me. Typically, while everyone else had smothered pork chops, rice, lima beans, homemade hot bread with plenty of butter, and ice tea for dinner, I would have a small portion of baked chicken, a baked potato, and a lettuce and tomato salad, gluten bread, and Saccharin-sweetened ice tea. For dessert, which we ate almost every day, Mama would have freshly baked chocolate cake or some delicious fruit concoction with ice cream, all of which I was forbidden to touch. I would be served Saccharin sweetened Jell-O or tapioca, both of which I learned to love and still eat with regularity today. Despite Mama's best efforts and with my reputation for wanting to eat all the time—another diabetic symptom—I remained a food thief and would steal every chance I got.

I was only fooling myself and paid a big price—three periods of hospitalization at Freedmen's Hospital for diabetic-related complications by the time I was ten years old—all caused by my eating indiscretions. Freedmen's Hospital became my second home and my sustained hope for survival as time and again I found myself there in a ward filled with African-American adult males, many of whom gazed upon me with obvious expressions of pity for my condition. They were all much older than I was and suffering the debilitating effects of the ailment. Each of them knew well, perhaps far better than I, what was in store for my future as a diabetic. People have often asked me why I was not placed at Children's Hospital instead. I was Dr. Wilder's patient, and because he was increasingly recognized as a diabetic specialist (in addition to his family practice), he wanted me in a hospital where he had full, unfettered privileges and a caring staff that would monitor me closely every day. That degree of attention and caring was probably not as available in a segregated hospital where colored were tolerated and Negro doctors were looked upon as less fully qualified.

During each of my hospitalizations, I stayed at least a full week while staff worked to bring my diabetes under control. Because there was no medical insurance when I was diagnosed with diabetes, and such programs did not even exist in that era, every medical cost was borne by my parents. I missed time from school each time. When I returned, Dr. Wilder always sent a note to my teacher explaining to her that I had been under his care.

I can still vividly picture my second grade teacher, Martha Winston, standing in front of me while reading the note and then looking down at my inquiring face and saying, "Well, Jim, you're back now. And young man, you have a little catching up to do. But it will be okay." Dr. Wilder's notes never said what I was being treated for, and until this life story, I have never so openly revealed to anyone the nature of my illness or reason for any of those periods of hospitalization.

Ward Eight was all male. I remember the Ward number so well because the head nurse on the ward, Ruth Freeman, was so very beautiful, both physically and as a person. Even I as a young child less than ten years old, could not help but notice. Physically she looked more like an East Indian than a typical colored American female. She had the most beautiful brown skin, keen features, and black silky hair. I learned early in life that African-American women come in all sizes, shapes, and colors, and she was a good example of that. Years later she would rise to the rank of major in the U.S. Armed Forces during World War II.

The following year and one other time thereafter, I returned to Freedmen's for my second and third diabetic complications-related hospitalization. These two times I was on another ward, and the head nurse was a Miss Boston, who, like Miss Freeman, was most caring of all her charges on the ward and kind to me.

I learned very early that diabetes and its suffering were then considered to be "The Big Secret," something that was not discussed with anyone outside of the immediate family. While some individuals must have figured out what my problem was, they did not get that information from me. The negative attitude that some people displayed towards diabetics in the 1920s was not unlike the discrimination openly expressed against people with AIDS in the 1990s. Trying to explain to anyone in 1924-25—that diabetes was a systemic, hereditary ailment, and not an airborne illness or a sexually transmitted disease—was pretty hopeless in certain circles. So the better thinking of the era was to maintain the condition as "The Big Secret."

I would later be exposed to overt discrimination by several of my classmates and their friends, as it occasionally got back to me when events were ongoing, that someone had said, "Don't invite Jim Quander. There's something 'wrong' with him." That same attitude would be an albatross that I repeatedly had to bear through much of my entire life. As my peer group grew older and more mature, I expected them to be more educated, open-minded, and understanding; and indeed most of them were. However, in a few isolated instances, these supposedly educated people became less so.

In the spring of 1925, around the time of my seventh birthday, April 19th, I was introduced to insulin injections during the first of my many periods of hospitalization. Earlier Dr. Wilder decided that I should not go onto insulin injections and told my family and me that he wanted to see if we could control my diabetes by diet. Despite our best efforts, and I have to admit that I really tried, my occasional theft of forbidden foods predominated, and the diet alone option did not work. Things got out of hand and could not be brought back into alignment easily.

On that day, when Dr. Wilder was making his hospital rounds, he came over to me, leaned over my bed and said, as if this was a conference between two age contemporaries, "Jim, you and I have to have a medical conference. I told you earlier that you have diabetes, and that we would have to closely regulate your diet. Well, that's not working. Now we have to do something else." He then explained to me, in terms that I could understand, how the sugar in my blood was not being absorbed properly into my body's digestive system because the amount of insulin that my body should normally produce to act as a sugar-digesting agent was insufficient. Instead, my body was either not producing insulin, or it was not producing enough of it. Therefore, I would have to replace or supplement the deficiency with daily insulin injections.

While I sat on the side of my bed in ward eight, with my legs dangling because I was too small to touch the floor, with several adult diabetics overhearing his words but saying nothing, Dr. Wilder took me to another world. He had taught me the year before exactly how to conduct a urinalysis and to evaluate my blood sugar, and as I matured into the ailment, I would learn more and more about how and why diabetes existed, and what I needed to do to carefully monitor myself.

I had become pretty proficient in holding a test tube on a clamp filled with a pre-measured small amount of fresh urine, a designated amount of clear mid-blue Benedict's solution, commonly called "copper sulfate," plus some water, then cooking the entire solution over the kitchen stove or a Bunsen burner for several minutes to determine my blood sugar level based upon the color results. If the concoction did not change color, no measurable amount of sugar was spilling into the urine, meaning that either the blood sugar level was "normal" or low enough not to be of concern.

Unfortunately, in those days there was only a system for measuring high blood sugar but nothing that I am aware of to determine if the sugar level was too low. As a result, there was always the danger that no indication of sugar spillage into the urine might be an indication of an impending insulin-related diabetic shock due to low blood sugar.

If the urine blood sugar test color result was green, there was an indication of some spillage of sugar into the urine, but not too much. If it was bright orange, the blood sugar spillage was higher. If it was red, the spillage was significantly too high. If the color passed from red and went to maroon, the spillage was the highest and most dangerous, and if not brought down quickly, could lead to permanent damage to a number of body systems. I used a color chart to facilitate determining my blood sugar levels, evaluating whether the sugar content was negative, 1+, 2+, 3+, 4+, etc., and each numerical assessment was tied to the color chart. The chart was one of my most useful tools as a juvenile diabetic. In later years some conveniences would facilitate measuring blood sugar levels, and no one was happier than I when copper sulfate tablets appeared on the market, which eliminated at least a portion of having to measure ingredients as carefully in order to get the most accurate reading.

High blood sugar meant that the sugar in the blood was also syrupy, thick, and sticky. The more that it became and stayed that way, the more it clogged the body's systems, most typically the blood system, which markedly reduced circulation. This is a simplified explanation of what frequently happens to diabetics, resulting in extreme pain due to a decrease in blood and systems circulation, followed by bypass surgeries and even amputations of the body's extremities.

What was "normal" blood sugar for me was adjusted over the years as my body chemistry changed with maturity. My median of 100 glucose level of "normal" was gradually adjusted upward several times during this decade, to a new "normal" of 140. At this earlier time, wherever the blood sugar reading was, my initial sole remedy was to address it through eating the proper foods.

Now Dr. Wilder was singing a different tune. For the first time, he explained to me the rationale of why I now needed to take insulin more than once per day. My condition was too erratic and could not be controlled through diet alone. Although he always knew that I was a little food thief, despite my steadfast denials to that effect, he never confronted me on it, other than to say, "Now, Jim, you aren't stealing are you?" He would drop the subject after my steadfast, "No, Dr. Wilder! I don't steal!" This was his way of reminding me what my responsibilities were, teaching me to be disciplined with regard to my food intake and variety. Being so young, I did not yet fully appreciate what he was doing. Still, the lecturing was slowly getting through, and I was weaning myself from those forbidden food items.

By the time of my first hospitalization in 1925, my medical condition had deteriorated badly. One hour I was urinating frequently and spilling high sugar content. A few hours later the opposite condition presented itself, i.e., extremely low blood sugar levels that caused me to break out in cold sweats and experience weakness, sustained thirst, and dizziness. I would become somewhat disoriented, too, although still not akin to some of my later critical, life-threatening experiences as an adult diabetic.

Having concluded his "medical conference" with me that day, Dr. Wilder then assembled all of the necessary medical implements and proceeded to both explain and demonstrate the proper use of the injection needle, syringe, a bottle of insulin, alcohol, and the cotton swab. He showed me exactly what to do and how to hold and connect everything for the best results. He then incorporated my prior knowledge on conducting a blood sugar evaluation from urinalysis results, and he explained to me that the amount of insulin that I should take at a given moment depended upon the urinalysis results garnered from the test as measured by the color chart. Despite all of this information and technique, it would still prove to be anything but exact. I still experienced many problems incidental to injecting too little or too much insulin, guided by what the test results indicated.

It was about dinnertime, and based upon the result of a recent blood sugar test that the nurse had run, he let me figure out exactly how many units of insulin I should inject. Confirming that my very first self-determination calculation was accurate, he watched me, at age seven, complete the process myself.

First I cleaned the needle, syringe, and bottle containing the insulin. The diabetic industry started using the metric system at the outset, and it still does. After making cubic centimeter unit calculations in advance, measured by the metric quality markers on the side of the glass syringe, and based upon the blood sugar results, I gently shook the refrigerated insulin. I then inserted the needle and syringe into the rubber tip of the bottle and held everything upside down to draw the purified pig insulin from the bottle. Next, I cleaned my upper left thigh with the alcohol-laden cotton swab and injected the cold medication into my flesh. I felt the prick of the sharp needle as I injected myself, and likewise, I felt the cold medication as it entered my body. Both of these experiences would dissipate in their significance as I became accustomed to the multi-times-per-day practice.

As Dr. Wilder prepared to release me, we had the same heart-to-heart talk that he gave me in December 1924 as the Christmas holidays were approaching. He knew how great a cook Mama was: his and his wife's feet were under our dining room table with some regularity. He said, "Jim, I'm getting ready to release you soon, so you can go back home and back to school, but you've got to promise me that you will follow everything that I've told you. Stick exactly to your diet and take your insulin each and every day, without fail. Otherwise, you'll be right back here again, and maybe next time you won't be 'so lucky.'"

My first insulin was U 20, a weaker strength that I took in larger qualities twice a day. Later I moved to U 40, and now am at U 80, three times per day, which is much stronger but with lesser quantity at each injection. By way of explanation, "U 80" means 80 units of insulin strength, per cubic centimeter (cc). All of the needle syringes were made of glass, and relatively delicate, so I took great care not to drop them. Later in my diabetic history I was also introduced to taking one dose of NPH per day, a longer effect but slower acting insulin. NPH maintained a certain level of insulin in my blood system at all times, a desirable situation which helped to curb wild fluctuations, although they still occurred, only less frequently.

As a result, injecting myself with needles two and three times per day, both my thighs and arms have become lumpy. Now I inject directly four times per day, but into my stomach. While this seems to work better, now my fingertips are sore from testing my blood sugar four to five times a day.

I wasn't sure what Dr. Wilder meant by "so lucky," but at that moment, I resolved to do much better, and set a new tone for my future behavior. Although I still fell off the wagon a few times, I can truthfully state that I was a much-improved person, even at the young age of seven. I was coming to appreciate already that the key to "controlling" diabetes, if ever it can be controlled, rests with self-discipline, and learning to listen to your body. Never mistreat the condition by eating the wrong foods or engaging in diabetic unfriendly behavior—drinking alcohol on more than an occasional basis, using illegal drugs, a lack of rest—all of which will adversely affect you, whether the next day or several years later.

From that day forward in 1925, until my sight began declining in 2000, now more than 75 years later, other than when I was hospitalized, no one, and I do mean NO ONE, had ever injected me with insulin. Not my parents. Not my wife of 60 years. Not any of my subsequent treating physicians. I have been totally self-sufficient when it came to my insulin injections, and at times, depending upon my blood sugar levels, I have injected myself up to three times per day—twice in the morning, and once in the evenings, when necessary.

Because of my long period of independence, my becoming dependent in recent years is a source of concern. Becoming partially disabled due to a right leg amputation just below the knee, further enfeebled by diabetes and now a slowly-advancing case of prostate cancer, I wondered what the future held should my condition further deteriorate. Surrounded by all of my family— wife, four children, and ten grandchildren—in my mind, none of them was trained or equipped to begin administering insulin to me. But then, just as I quickly absorbed the process while sitting on the side of the bed at Freedmen's Hospital in 1925, several of them learned how to do it, and since 2000 have been my caretakers.

Back at home, Mama and Papa stuck to the strict diet regimen given to me by the Freedmen's Hospital staff dietitian, a special assortment of foods expressly recommended for diabetics, including some helpful hints about how best to prepare the food for the maximum nutritional value. By today's dietary standards, my 1925 prescribed diet seems archaic, but it was based upon medical and dietary information then available. Of course there were no specifically manufactured fat-free or sugar-free products like today. Extra vigilance was the key.

To determine food intake amounts, my parents and I had two basic options. We could weigh everything or we could use measuring spoons and marked cups to determine portion size by weight and volume. We never used a scale, and very quickly Mama and I learned to measure the quantity size by experience, and did away with all of the measuring devices. Still, and despite all of the measuring, things would still go astray, medically. Physical and psychological stresses always play a role in diabetic health, and no matter how strictly I adhered to the dictated medical regimen, blood sugar levels could skyrocket one moment, and insulin shock with concomitant low blood sugar levels could result at some time shortly thereafter.

As always, the objective was to avoid hypoglycemia (insulin reaction or insulin shock), which could occur if there was too much insulin in my body system in proportion to the amount of blood sugar. If the blood sugar dropped too low, and "too low" varied during different phases of my life, an insulin reaction would occur, and have to be offset with a quick infusion of sugar into my system, usually sweetened orange juice or hard peppermint candy.

With Papa's access to fresh vegetables, fruits, and meats, Mama prepared everything according to the diet instructions. Although I called them "special foods," in reality they were regular foods, but not necessarily what we, as colored folk living in a segregated society, would normally eat. For example, my diet called for a routine serving of eggplant, broccoli, and cauliflower, things that relatively few of our racial group seemed to eat in those days. Other foods directed were a variety of beans, cabbage, okra, plus a daily serving of white potatoes, the latter of which is a surprise to many, since potatoes are high in carbohydrates and increase the blood sugar so dramatically, and are expressly deleted from many diabetic diets today. Even now, I eat several servings of white potatoes, seemingly with no adverse blood sugar side effects

All of this food was fresh and prepared daily by Mama, including lettuce, tomato, and cucumber salads. To this day, tomatoes are my favorite. I can eat them in any way they are prepared, including just biting into one, eating it whole like any other fruit.

It was a comprehensive diet, and recited breakfast and lunch suggestions. Breakfast included eggs, oatmeal, cream of wheat, and oranges, whether whole or in juice form. Little to nothing was known about cholesterol in those days. I ate at least two eggs per day, and even now have never had a cholesterol problem. Chicken, fixed in a non-greasy way, was the mainstay in the meat area. Occasional small portion servings of beef and lamb were allowed, but not pork, because of the fat content. Yet I routinely ate moderate amounts of bacon and ham, and never had a problem. However, neither of those meats was listed on the diet. And of course gluten bread, made especially for diabetics, was a central part of the menu, as well as other coarse grain breads. Quickly it became apparent that Mama was cooking two separate menus or at least something extra for me, a practice that my wife would later adopt. Although we often ate the same things, my siblings frequently complained that the universal menu that Mama prepared for a particular meal was too bland, and that they wanted something different.

Being African-American, chitterlings, pig feet, various kinds of rice, and heavy gravies and sauces appeared, indigenous cooking from Mama's Walterboro, South Carolina, birth. As we sat to the dinner table, I would be eating from my limited, but tasty offering for the evening, while the rest of the family would be eating something else entirely. I realized quite early that an occasional spoon of chitterlings or a pig foot added to my plate did me no harm. Such was also the usual case with occasional small portions of other so-called "forbidden foods."

Not having a really good understanding of why Mama was routinely making a separate menu for me, my sisters Elvira and Kitty often had something negative to say about me being spoiled, or called me Mama and Papa's pet. While I initially tried to slough off their barbs and not to let them get me down, as life progressed, and we all grew into adulthood and older age, sadly they continued to maintain that point of view, which became very counter-productive to us as adults. It would literally drive a wedge between us, as they seemed to have little to no understanding or appreciation for how sick I was as a child, and that only through sheer determination, of which self-discipline was a major part, did I manage to survive this long. For a child whose prognosis was likely death before ten years of age, I have survived to live into my mid-80s, while both Elvira and Kitty are now dead.

Cora, my older sister, born in 1911, was the exact opposite. She was always very attentive and solicitous, concerned about both my physical and mental health, and fiercely protective. She did not suffer Elvira or Kitty's criticisms gladly and never lost faith in me or her belief that I would survive this illness. Fortunately, my two brothers, Joseph and Edward, also subscribed to Cora's point of view.

Mama continued to bake fresh breads at least once or twice a week, and I continued to eat it, with a modest amount of butter on each roll. I never suffered a negative side effect from eating them either, and concluded early on that it was entirely possible to eat certain things that were very tasty, prepared fresh, and not suffer any negative side effects because of diabetes. It seemed that at last

I was learning how to be disciplined in my eating, yet at the same time to enjoy food.

She became a master at fixing no sugar, low sugar, or artificially sweetened with Saccharin desserts. One of the most delicious desserts was her homemade applesauce. Papa would bring home the old apples, which would be discarded because they were bruised or past their prime, and getting soft. And Mama would work miracles, cutting and mixing different varieties of apples together, producing a no-sugar-added applesauce, just the right amount of fermentation, a tinge on the tongue, and highly digestible.

I had trouble keeping the others in the family away from my applesauce, and would point them to the cake or pie, and away from the applesauce. I know now what they felt when I stole food from them, and then denied it. They did the same to me, but since there were several of them, and only one of me, I readily knew that they were stealing my desserts.

There was no Sweet and Low or Equal then, so the choices for artificial sweeteners were limited. To the best of my knowledge, Saccharin was the only available artificial sweetener. I could add it to my coffee, tea, or anything. In addition to always putting it in her Jell-Os and tapioca puddings, Mama added Saccharin to different types of custards, and even ice cream. Fresh fruit like peaches, strawberries, and berries, topped with non-sweet custard, was also my dessert staple.

I never believed that Saccharin caused cancer, as the health officials would later assert, because as much of it as I had used for over seven decades, if it did cause cancer, I would have been one of the first to contract it. I was delighted to see that Saccharin was put back onto the market in 1999.

It was in this same 1925-26 time frame that I learned to do certain things for myself. Mama taught me how to operate the ice cream maker, and how to also make the ice cream mix to put into the canister. We took turns cranking the canister, rotating the mechanism as it churned through the wooden bucket packed with ice and rock salt. This churning process made the ice cream curdle, and then harden. Quickly I became so proficient in the operation of this device, that I would make two batches, one right after the other.

First, I would make a batch for the entire family, using sugar and sliced fruit, and then immediately make another batch for myself, this time again using fresh fruit, but sweetening it with Saccharin. Although we had no freezer in those days, we did have dry ice, and were able to preserve the ice cream for at least 24 hours, if not longer.

Dr. Wilder did not want me to miss too much school, especially since I was already repeating the second grade. Although he never specifically told me to keep my diabetes a secret, my parents frequently did, and I did just that. I never told any of my teachers or fellow students at Sumner-Magruder school that I was a diabetic, although children are very perceptive. I am certain that several of them knew that something must have been "wrong," or if not wrong, then at least "different" about Jim Quander.

But as noted above, the prejudice against diabetics in that era was akin to HIV and AIDS now. Many people did not want to be around you, and were quite open in stating their feelings. Further, children can be exceedingly cruel, as they have not yet learned discretion and how to keep certain impressions, whether accurate or not, to themselves.

We had no cafeteria at Sumner-Macgruder School, so I had to take my own lunch every day. While the other children brought sandwiches, Mama always fixed me a full meal for lunch. The portions were commensurate with my age. In 1925-26, there were no plastic containers, no Saran Wrap, not even microwaves. Transporting lunch to school and keeping it from spoiling was a challenge, but everything was prepared and packed to be eaten at room temperature, except for hot soup in my thermos.

The school did not have a stove or an icebox that I was ever aware of, and even if they had both of them, there were no prepackaged diabetic or dietetic packed meals that I could simply heat and eat. There was nothing available. Fortunately, times have certainly changed for the better. All diabetics in this country now have so many conveniences available to them, to make it both healthier and easier to live a long and successful life with diabetes.

Mama proved to be more than up to the challenge. Based upon the diet directives that she was given to follow, coupled with her good judgment, she had everything under control and packaged to prevent spoiling or leakage. She functioned with the aid of small, reusable tin cans, wax paper, and thermos jars, all neatly placed in a lunch pail, ready to be eaten at room temperature.

While the other children ate peanut butter and jelly sandwiches or yesterday's meat leftovers, I had lettuce and tomato salad, chicken salad or boned chicken, string beans or broccoli, or some other green vegetable which had been drained of its juices prior to packing, gluten bread, a piece of fruit, which was most often an orange or two, and some crackers for dessert. The children always noticed, and were inquisitive about why I ate this type of lunch every day. I never really gave an answer, other than, "This is what my mother made for me."

Quite frequently there were food treats at school that included things that I could eat. The mothers formed a food committee, and being mostly housewives, it was easy for them to execute on their plan. Knowing that school lunches were bland, and realizing that it would be nice to provide some variety for the children, several days per month the committee fixed hot lunches and brought them to the school. These were more elaborate than any lunch that most children would bring, and included entrees just off the home stove, since most people lived in the immediate neighborhood. Mama made certain that she was on the food committee, to assure that the menu for that day included foods that I could eat. This type of special lunch menu saw me through both elementary and junior high school. Later, when I was in high school, I sometimes ate the food prepared by the cafeteria staff, although I continued to bring my lunch from home for the most part.

But despite these best efforts by my parents and me to keep my diabetes under control, once we thought we reasonably had it under control, inevitably something would go wrong, and my health would suddenly deteriorate, causing me to miss school for medical appointments or to be placed back in the hospital for another week or more. As my body changed relative to normal growth, both my diet and insulin intake would be adjusted to accommodate. But even these modifications often caused adversity and put my diabetes into an out-of-control status as my body valiantly struggled to adjust to the changes.

Since I had not directly heard any conversations between Dr. Wilder and my parents to the effect I was not expected to live to be ten years of age, I did not then fully appreciate the depth of their concern each time I became seriously ill. Further, it did not help Mama and Papa to have me so sick, especially since my older brother, John Edward, Jr., Papa's namesake, had just recently died in 1924 from tuberculosis complicated by severe epileptic seizures. He was only 15 years old. They, and especially Mama, were already depressed about the loss of Edward and were still mourning his death. The likelihood that they were also going to lose me, too, was more than they could bear at the moment.

Dr. Wilder was very committed, and pledged to Mama and Papa that he would do everything he could to keep me alive, and to assure that I would live "as normal a life as possible." It was to that objective that I was unwittingly steered, to put me in a place where I could take care of myself, and be disciplined enough to stay on my diet, despite all of the wrong food temptations that would surely present themselves later in life, when I alone would be making food choices.

# Chapter 4

# Discipline: The Key to Living Successfully as a Diabetic

Although my parents were always concerned about my long-term success as a diabetic and hoped only for the best, they also realized that I should not be unreasonably pampered. The world at large would not stop to take into consideration that I was a juvenile diabetic and had special health, food, and medical needs. We had no maids or cleaning help. Realizing that I needed to be given a level of personal responsibility, at an early age, my parents assigned me house chores to handle on a regular basis each Saturday morning.

Dr. Wilder told my parents and me that getting proper exercise, stretching my limbs and muscles, and keeping the blood circulating were the keys to a diabetic's continuing favorable health. While people tend to think of exercise as playing some type of sport, my exercise routine came from another direction, and it worked just as well.

As each house chore responsibility was added, Papa would say, "Now, Jim, this used to be done by Cora, or Elvira, but now I'm assigning this to you." And with that, I was gradually given the responsibility for keeping major portions of the house clean. Papa worked all night at the market, lifting, pulling, and pushing heavy sacks or racks of fruit, vegetables, or meats; and when he came home in the early morning, he was tired. The last thing he wanted to do was clean house. And while Mama was home and kept house, she had angina and a heart murmur, which regularly made her weak and put her in the bed, sometimes for days at a time. As a child, many times I was fearful that I was going to lose her due to heart problems, but ultimately she lived to be 81 years old and died in 1962.

By the time I was seven, several of the chores had been reassigned to me. I was given the responsibility of cleaning the first floor (the English basement entrance level), which included the dining room, kitchen and pantry; and the center core area, where the spiral staircase led up to the second floor; and the staircase leading between the first and second levels. On the second level, I maintained the living room parlor and front porch and steps, all located on that level. Eventually my little sister, Kitty, was assigned the rest of the second floor, including the back bedroom and the hall area between the two rooms, both bedrooms on the third floor, and the bathroom.

We always had so much company coming through the house that the areas of my responsibility received hard wear. Although Papa was an orphan, the Quander family was still huge, and family members dropped by routinely, quite often without calling first. Being left alone to fend for himself and his two younger siblings, as Papa grew older, several of his cousins came to realize that he was a wise man, full of wisdom. They regularly sought his advice and counsel on any number of subjects and received good common-sense-based advice, despite his limited schooling.

As well, from Mama's side, connected family and friends were regulars. Heading to or from New York, they would stay for days, causing me to give up or share my bed more frequently than I care to recall. Mama found herself cooking morning, noon, and night. Naturally, it fell to Kitty and me to make certain that the house got straight, and it stayed that way. While Saturday was the official housekeeping day, occasionally we were pressed into chores on a weekday, just after school, because someone was coming for dinner, and manual attention was needed to spiff up.

When I got a little older, Papa added more responsibilities: the trash collection, keeping both the front and rear yards cut and cleaned, and sweeping the sidewalk in front of our house. The yards were small, and having watched him many times, I knew how to operate the push lawnmower and the hedge clippers. In those days, unlike now when we have better conveniences and timesaving devices, we did a lot of manual scrubbing, waxing, and polishing. I scrubbed the kitchen floor on my hands and knees and dared anyone to enter it so long as my floor was still wet. Some of these chores could be rotated and were not done every week.

I learned to spread paste wax in a thin enough coat that it would dry quickly, and then I would bring the hardwood floors up to a nice shine. I became so proud of myself in seeing a clean floor, a shining piece of furniture, or clean windows; yet I had not the slightest clue that this regimen was physical exercise which burned off the body's stored sugar.

Papa never neglected to give me a little money for my services, initially averaging about $2.50 per week, which was not bad for the late 1920s, and in the Great Depression of the 1930s. As I got older, he raised my payment to $5.00, although not each time, since he too had lost his business in this era of economic chaos. He knew that he was not obligated to pay me; but orphaned at ten, with two younger siblings to support, he had been working since he was about nine years old, and he knew what it was to want. He was determined to reward me for my efforts, even if the remuneration was small. After several months of this arrangement, he began referring to this money as my weekly allowance, which kindled my entrepreneurial spirit, although I did not yet realize it. This same pattern and spirit continued essentially all the way through college; and as I grew older, I became more proficient at recognizing and capitalizing upon it.

Later, in the junior high and senior high school years, I got up at 6:00 a.m. on Saturdays, got the chores done, and was ready to head to the Howard or Lincoln Theater in time to catch the live stage show and big-band matinee or a movie. I knew clearly what my obligations were and never challenged Papa on it. My home priorities came first, and if my chores were not done, there would be no 12:30 p.m. matinee or early movie. We lived at 1913 17th Street, N.W., between T and U Streets, N.W., so getting to the U Street theaters on time was never a problem.

U Street in those days was nicknamed both "Strivers Row" and "Black Broadway," because most of the major entertainment centers for colored Washington, D.C., were located on U Street, or one block away. Besides the famous Howard and Lincoln Theaters, both of which featured major big-band groups, we also had the Booker T., named for Booker T. Washington; the Republic; the Dunbar, named for Paul Laurence Dunbar; and the Hiawatha, the latter of which currently houses that other great cultural icon, Ben's Chili Bowl, which opened in 1958.

There were also many high-quality nightclubs located on U Street or close by. One such establishment was the Republic Gardens. Another was the Crystal Caverns, now called the Bohemian Caverns. As well, a famous third destination site was the Lincoln Colonnade, located on V Street, N.W., directly behind the Lincoln Theater. The Colonnade could be accessed from either U or V Streets. There were also numerous smaller clubs in the immediate area as well. This was the era of Prohibition, and although I was still too young to drink alcoholic beverages, everyone knew that despite the legal ban against alcohol, if you wanted a drink in a U Street club, you could easily get one.

The vibrancy of life along U Street brings back a particular memory of our wind-up Victrola, and large 78-RPM phonograph records collection. While many people in that era still did not have a Victrola, we did. It was one of my greatest pleasures to wind it up, play the records, and dance. Despite several negative attitudes held about dancing, and despite Mama's utilitarian Presbyterian background (although she later converted to Roman Catholicism), we were always allowed to dance. As a young child, I danced and danced. Perhaps that was the beginning of my history of getting so much exercise, which would later prove crucial to my survival as a juvenile diabetic. Both dancing and house chores were important components of our family routine. Of course there was no dancing on Sundays, the Lord's Day.

After Kitty (born in 1921) and me, there were no younger siblings to pass the chores down to. Cora was living in New York much of the time, and Elvira got married at age 15 and briefly took to dancing on the stage. My brother Joseph (we called him "Pearson") was in college in West Virginia, and my other brother,

John Edward, was dead from the effects of tuberculosis. Although Mama and Papa took in our older, orphaned cousin, Alberta Gaines, to live with us, the great bulk of the chores still rested upon Kitty and me.

I noticed one key aspect of my diabetic ailment, particularly after all of the work around the house had been completed: the scrubbing, waxing, and polishing always left me feeling quite good, flush with energy, and ready to have fun.

Despite the strict regimen of my daily diet, I often relaxed that cycle on Saturday afternoons. At the movies I would treat myself to typical theater foods. They sold hot dogs, different types of cupcakes, popcorn and Crackerjacks, candies, ice cream, soda –everything for a nickel apiece. And for these few hours, I would partake of all of it, just in moderation. And I do not recall ever having any adverse side effects from these treats. I had finally learned that I could have occasional food treats that were not on my diet, so long as it remained occasional, and the portions were small. Come Sunday, though, it was back to the usual diet and Mama's good home cooking.

As I grew older, and attended to my own health needs more independently, I realized and appreciated that one of the keys to successfully living with diabetes is to exercise discipline and control in all you do—food intake, alcoholic beverage intake, amount of exercise, and getting plenty of rest. My diabetes has never been "controlled" in the true sense of the word, as it flipped out of alignment with some degree of regularity, and routinely did so for the greater part of the last 75 to 80 years. But once I learned to engage in all activities, and especially food consumption, in moderation, all of the diabetic-related adverse incidents likewise became less severe.

Look at it this way. While I eventually lost my right leg in January 1995, in my 77th year, due to poor circulation and diabetic neuropathy (nerve damage), I am convinced, and so are my doctors, that had I not exercised great discipline for all of the prior decades, I probably would have lost that leg perhaps as much as 15 to 20 years sooner. Exercise and discipline surely made a difference in the quality of my life, not the least of which was personal and independent mobility.

However, being so disciplined and self-reliant for so long also created another side effect, i.e., it made me leery and somewhat distrustful of others. As soon as they learned that I had diabetes, my parents underscored that this was a family matter. I was not to tell anyone about it, and never to discuss it with anyone, not even within the family. It was to be our "Big Secret"! I was perfectly content to follow my parental directive and never told anyone of my ailment. However, keeping the "Big Secret" was often a challenge, given the natural curiosity of children, some of whom continued to question my lunch menus, or wondered aloud why I had been absent from school so often and for sustained periods.

While I cannot now recall (after 75 years) the incident that prompted my response, I vividly remember telling a couple of my classmates, "You're not my friend!" after they said or did something related to my diabetic condition that hurt me deeply. I was eight or nine years old, and in the third grade at the time. From that day forward, I noticed certain attitudes of indisposition towards me. Perhaps the indisposition was even there before then, but I was too young to really know what was happening. Here we were, all African-American children, seven, eight, and nine years of age, living in a rigidly racially segregated environment, and I was being further discriminated against.

This negative experience—this feeling that was difficult to actually put my finger on and say, "There it is—discrimination!"— was to be only the first in a long line of continuing insults, most often visited upon me by my own fellow racial group, since this is the only group of people that I routinely came in contact with during America's apartheid era.

Without fully realizing it or intending it to happen, slowly, but concertedly, I withdrew. I had a "Big Secret" and was determined to keep it. I was deeply hurt by some classmates that I initially thought were my friends, only to find out otherwise. Fortunately, as the years progressed, some of these same classmates matured and realized that we are not all the same, and were different from the beginning. With this maturity came a different and far more positive attitude and disposition towards me. Indeed, I am happy to say that many of them are now my dearest friends and close acquaintances, although in a few instances, it took literally decades to cultivate this favorable relationship.

Did these young classmates form these opinions themselves, or get them from their teachers or parents? To this day, I still do not know. All I know is that I observed certain behavioral patterns, mostly on the playground and in the classrooms, and could no longer confide in or trust them, because some of those same young people had done me in. If I was going to survive, and I was determined to survive, I would have to make it on my own. While obviously some of them must have concluded that there was "something wrong" with Jim Quander, I kept my counsel, and never revealed my "Big Secret"—Jim Quander was a juvenile diabetic, and he might not live to be ten years old.

I became a recluse, staying mostly in the house. In the summer months, I became an avid reader and would average reading one complete book per day. The libraries were not segregated, and use was not restricted. During my weekly visit to the Mount Pleasant library branch, located at 16th and Lamont Streets, N.W., I would gather my week's reading supply each time. I struck up a friendly relationship with the head librarian and staff, none of which names can I recall. The head librarian, a lovely Caucasian woman, would see me coming through the door and say, "Jim, I've pulled some books off the shelf for you to look at." To facilitate my selection, she would proceed to explain a little about each of the books that I was not already familiar with. Within a short time, books became my truest friends. Despite my very young age, among the books read were *Call of the Wild, All Quiet on the Western Front*, and various stories about the old Wild West.

After I followed this routine for a few summers, I drew the criticism of Mrs. Fannie Taylor Broadus, my sixth grade teacher at the Morgan School, who complained to Mama that I was reading "adult-subject" books that were too advanced for my age. When I returned to school in September 1929 and was asked what books I had read over the summer, I related the story line of a love story that contained sexual overtones, which caused Mrs. Broadus to quickly shut me up. Despite my self-imposed reclusion, I was far from isolation, as the steady stream of company at the house did not cease. I formed relationships with older people, some of whom were aware of my diabetes since my parents had confided in them. As well, many of these visitors had children whom I was friendly with, who accepted me as I was—in my own home. They would not see me ill, nor at school or absent from school, and as such, would have no questions or display hurtful attitudes towards me.

I bestowed my love on my two dogs, Peggy, a German Shepherd, and Teddy Boy, a mixed breed. I cared deeply for them, walked them several times a day, fed them, cleaned up after them, gave them their baths, and routinely got them inoculated. Papa and Mama rarely had to remind me to attend to any chore related to Peggy and Teddy Boy. Diabetics are better off by keeping active, and I had two loving animals to care for who unconditionally loved me in return—and showed it. Having an animal to care for was a central way to keep physically and mentally fit, active, and gave me a reason to live.

With the exception of the last few years, when I was suffering severe circulatory, mobility, and nerve problems, I have always kept a dog or even two. In my young married years, we even had cats. I highly recommend that diabetics have animals to shower their time and attention onto. In addition to showing your love, caring for animals also relieves stress, which many diabetics tend to build up and retain, especially due to the frustration of trying to successfully live with this ailment, including other people's negative dispositions towards you.

Negative ideas about diabetics can come from anywhere, including within your own close family, too. I was seven years old and had not been too long introduced to taking daily insulin, using the techniques that Dr. Wilder had taught me while sitting on the side of the bed at Freedmen's Hospital. One of my relatives, Mary Brown Diggs, Papa's favorite first cousin, was the cook/housekeeper for Mr. Justice James C. McReynolds, a long-term member of the U.S. Supreme Court. Visiting the house one day, and upon observing me measuring my insulin dosage, cleaning my thigh, and then injecting myself, she blurted out, "Huh! I'd rather be dead before you would get me to do that for the rest of my life!"

I had never seen my father that angry in life, either before or since that incident. He was furious and blinded with rage. Looking her straight in the eye, he yelled, "How dare you! You don't say that to a child! This is just a little boy seven years old. And you can drop dead! And furthermore, get out of my house!" He actually ordered Cousin Mary out of his house, and as he was almost pushing her out the door, he said, "If you're going to be talking that way, you're not welcome here."

Considering that he loved Cousin Mary dearly, just like a sister, I was shocked by the level of his emotion. I too had an emotional attachment to her and considered her as my very dear cousin; but when she showed her ignorance and hurt me in my own kitchen, I was emotionally scarred for life.

I was only a child, and perhaps she did not feel that she owed me an apology; but eventually she and Papa repaired their differences, and she came back into his good graces, once again his closest first cousin, his soul mate at times. Although I was deeply hurt, I recovered and knew that she loved me. While she never said, "I'm sorry, Jim!" her subsequent acts of kindness and consideration, including inquiring about my health and bringing foods that I could eat, sustained our relationship until the day she died in 1961. She meant no harm by her insensitivity and indiscretion when she let her mouth run away from her and get her in trouble in the process.

Years later she would be a part of my wedding day celebration, a celebration of a new life-achievement milestone for a kid who was supposed to be dead by age ten. But we all learned a lesson that day in 1926, i.e., that you can never tell where ignorance and misunderstanding concerning diabetes and its proper treatment will come from. Will it be from a close family member, a friend, or a stranger? Most of my negative and even positive diabetic-related experiences have come from family and friends; as strangers will probably not comment, or if they do, many of them are more educated about what you're going through, and their comments are more attuned to understanding you.

Respectively, as I look back upon my early life as a juvenile diabetic, I am left with but one conclusion: my disciplinary pattern at that early time was the key to my still being here to tell this story—more than 75 years later. Further, I owe so much to Dr. Wilder who got me started in the right direction.

I always wanted to please him, and to have him tell me at examination time, "Jim, you are really doing well." I always made it a point to try hard and do the best that I could. I had no idea at that time, being between eight to about eleven years of age, that in being so strict about my diet and habits, keeping a written record of my food and insulin intake, as well as three times each day testing my urine and interpreting the results of my daily urinalysis, I was in hard training, setting a disciplinary course for myself from which I have never deviated. As well, I learned in this same period how to say "No!" and to pass up food items that would be tempting to most people, even diabetics.

By the time I graduated from elementary school, and with the help of my parents who made certain that I had available foods that I could eat, I was rarely tempted to eat foods that I knew that I could not or should not have. As well, I had learned to eat in such moderation that the occasional piece of cake or occasional ice cream with sugar would be only when I already knew that my diabetes was in line and my blood sugar was sufficiently low enough for me to handle it without problem. In other words, the temptation to violate my diet was finally gone, and it has remained "gone" pretty much ever since.

Even though there were at least three hospitalizations before the age of ten, and days here and there when I was absent from school; and despite my insulin dosage having to be constantly monitored and adjusted to accommodate my body's changes as I grew, I was diligent about attending school. I was a very good student in elementary school and graduated from Morgan Elementary School in 1930, at the age of 12 years, with most of my Sumner School class.

Washington still being the rigidly segregated Nation's Capital City that it was, in 1929, the Board of Education decided to convert the previously all-white Morgan School to all colored, as the neighborhood demographics had changed. With little prior notice, most all of my rising sixth grade Sumner classmates who lived in the 17th and U Streets, N.W., area, including me, were summarily transferred to the "new" Morgan School, from which we subsequently graduated in June 1930, the first class of colored to graduate from that school.

Despite being in the initial graduating class from Morgan, I have always identified with the Sumner-Magruder Elementary School, the place where I completed the second through the fifth grades, and later, in 1940, would be invited back to be the commencement speaker to the sixth grade graduating Class of 1940.

# Chapter 5

# Junior High School: A New Challenge

After graduating from Morgan Elementary School in 1930, I was assigned to attend the Robert Shaw Junior High School, located at Seventh Street and Rhode Island Avenue, N.W., in the heart of the Shaw neighborhood. The school building formerly served as the old William McKinley High School; but as the neighborhood demographics gradually changed from white to colored, a brand new McKinley High School was built for the white on a grand overlook of the National Capital City at Second and T Streets, N.E. They abandoned their old building in 1927, and the discard, renamed as Robert Shaw Junior High School, was given to us. Both the school and the local community were named for Captain Robert Shaw, the Caucasian Civil War hero who led the 54th Massachusetts Regiment during the War Between the States, and the many colored Americans who fought under his leadership.

As far as many are concerned, although others will certainly disagree, Shaw was rated as the top junior high school for colored children in the District. The highest-ranking students were generally sent to Shaw where the teachers prepared their seventh, eighth, and ninth grade charges for the rigors of high school, which in most cases meant preparation to attend The Paul Laurence Dunbar High School, the first all-academic high school for colored in the United States.

In September 1930, I was enrolled in Shaw Junior High School and immediately reunited with several of my Sumner School classmates from whom I was suddenly separated in September of 1929, when the Morgan School was converted to all Negro.

Shaw was a totally new experience for me. I was used to being quite sheltered, staying in the same classroom all day, and having a small group of steady friends and associates. Now, I was suddenly thrust into a totally new environment, one that was significantly far from home, which was also a great concern to my parents in the event that I became sick at school.

There had been a few occasions in elementary school where Mama was called and told to come to Sumner and get me because I was not well. She always got there very quickly and took me home immediately, where I was sometimes kept for a day or two while my diabetic side effects retreated and my strength returned. Now with me located three times the distance as before, taking two streetcars each way in the morning and again in the afternoon, everyone became alarmed.

Dr. Wilder stepped into the picture and told my parents that in his professional judgment, I should be transferred from Shaw and sent to the closer Garnett-Patterson, another junior high school, also located in the Shaw District. We lived on 17th Street, N.W., just off U Street, and Garnett-Patterson was located on the corner of 10th and U Streets, just seven blocks from our home. It was located approximately the same distance to our house as Sumner-Magruder, only in a different direction.

So after only about three weeks at Shaw, I was transferred to Garnett-Patterson, and in retrospect, I realize that this was a golden opportunity. I cannot say that Shaw was a more challenging school academically because I was not there long enough to evaluate and compare. As well, I was only 12 years old and not professionally equipped to make such a determination. But I do know this: Garnett-Patterson proved to be the right placement for me in so very many ways that I have no regrets. My report cards and routine placement on the semester honor roll for academic achievement verified to me that I was in the right place.

Not only did I meet new people, I made many lifelong friends during that three year period, many of which relationships endure to this day. And the friendships were not limited to just the peer group. The teachers were just wonderful and showed their concern for us in such a way that is no longer a part of the educational fabric of this country. In certain respects, the harsh realities of racial separation in all phases of our young lives in Washington, D.C., in 1930 also had a silver lining. The teachers, who were themselves the victims of racial discrimination in the society at large, were a group determined and dedicated to preparing us for whatever life laid ahead, including providing us with a quality education that we could use anywhere. Despite stereotypes and preconceived notions that African-Americans in the 1920s, 1930s, and 1940s did not go to college, most everyone at Garnett-Patterson would eventually go to college and graduate.

Although largely unrecognized by the white community at that time, the segregated educational system provided by the Colored Division of the District of Columbia Public Schools was one of the top educational systems in the United States. The test score results, as well as the college acceptances to Ivy League Schools, and subsequent professions attained, repeatedly verify my assertion.

Nowhere else in the United States was there such a concentration of highly educated and formally trained colored teachers than here, in the National Capital City. With the presence of Howard University, Miner Normal School (later Miner Teacher's College), and the federal government, there were more colored college graduates in Washington, D.C., than anywhere else in the country. And with career opportunities severely limited due to racism, the options for this highly qualified group were likewise greatly limited.

Other than teaching in the D.C. public schools, generally the only professions for college-educated colored graduates at that time were clergy, medicine, law, or federal government service, the latter of which career option most often restricted the colored employee to positions in the post office, the government printing office, or as messengers. Still, it was federal service, and a steady job. Many college-trained, degree-holding African-American men supported their families, bought homes, and educated their children from the relatively good wages that the colored were paid from these professions or in government service.

It was in that community and cultural atmosphere that I was sent to Shaw Junior High School in September 1930, and three weeks later was transferred to Garnett-Patterson. While I do not now recall the details, my diabetes was out of control for a couple of weeks, with erratic blood sugar and insulin reactions, just about the same time that school was opening. As is the case so often for diabetics, there was no physiological reason for this problem. Dr. Wilder attributed it to stress related to my now being in junior high school, with more independence and self-reliance. As well, there were uncertainties associated with my totally new surroundings.

Stress and emotions often wreak havoc with diabetes. Over the decades, I have experienced this erratic diabetic fluctuation on many occasions, sometimes for unknown reasons. But fortunately, this particular period of blood sugar fluctuation did not require hospitalization. I worked closely with Dr. Wilder, watched my diet even more carefully, and adjusted my insulin intake to correspond with my blood sugar level indications, as reflected in my three-times-per-day urinalysis—before and after school, and at bedtime. With the self-discipline that I had developed and maintained since about the age of seven or eight, by the time I reached junior high school, I was sufficiently disciplined. I had no real fear of losing my ability to control what I ate, in terms of frequency, portion sizes, and content.

From this point forward, although I am certain that it was more subconsciously planned than actively undertaken, I set into a routine of being a normal 12-13-year-old in the seventh grade. I took all of the standard academic courses including Latin, English, math, and science, without any difficulty or restrictions; and I found time to also participate in a number of extracurricular activities, including the Latin and math clubs. In the Latin club, we discussed all sorts of interesting Roman history topics. In the math club, we engrossed ourselves in mathematical discussions and problems. It was this combination of activities that began to build my personal self-confidence. My club activities, as well as my roles in little theater, were the great opportunity that I needed to showcase myself. Still, I did not then realize or appreciate what was occurring.

We performed many different plays in junior high little theater. Among them was "Robin Hood." I vividly recall being one of the men in Sherwood Forest, wearing a green costume with tights, and singing a duet with William "Dubb" Bullock, a classmate. He later became a medical doctor, and the brother-in-law of Walter Washington, the District of Columbia's first elected mayor in the Twentieth Century. I cannot recall the name of the song, but it was really a debut for me. Several classmates complimented me by telling me, "Jim, I didn't know that you could sing."

From this single exposure, I received several others and eventually routinely sang solos in little theater. There were also several non-school-related singing events, which I quickly took advantage of. This was the era of vaudeville, and most everything was music related, both in school and independently. I entered a number of those competitions, and although I never won any high level prizes, it was the sheer enjoyment and the attraction of the theater that helped me feel more outgoing than my health condition would otherwise indicate.

One of the songs that I sang in this 1930-31 era was *When I Take My Sugar To Tea*. It went like this:

> *When I take my Sugar to Tea*
> *All the Guys are Jealous of Me,*
> *And I never take her when the gang's around.*
> *When I take my Sugar to tea,*
> *All the guys are jealous of me,*
> *So I never take her when the guys are around*
> *When I take my Sugar to tea.*

And another song that I sang solo during this era was *Sweet and Lovely*:

> *Sweet and Lovely*
> *Sweeter than flowers in May*
> *And she loves me*
> *There's nothing more I can say*

*When she's in my arms so tenderly*
*There's a thrill that words cannot express*
*In my heart the song of love is calling me*
*Sweet memories, tenderly*
*Sweet and lovely*
*Sweeter than the rose in May*
*And she loves me*
*There is nothing more I can say.*

There were several other songs that I sang, too. Prior to this time, I taught myself how to tap dance, based upon seeing it in vaudeville shows and watching other people do it. My sister, Elvira, had a friend, Nettie Tilghman (Burt), who was a great dancer. She was especially good in tap dancing. Nettie was about 16 or 17 years old when I was about 11 years old. She could really dance, and everyone knew it. She visited the house regularly and one day started to tap dance. I secretly harbored being a great dancer, and since about ten years of age while still in elementary school, I had regularly danced with a broom, or alone. One day, I simply jumped into her tap dance routine in the kitchen. The rest is history.

After that day, I felt both invigorated and vindicated as a dancer and entered several additional amateur shows. Sometimes I entered as a singer, sometimes as a dancer, and at other times as a tap dancer. There were competitions all over town, sometimes to live music and sometimes using a phonograph and a record. But my highlight as a young boy, maybe ten or eleven years of age, was when I tap danced on the stage of the Lincoln Theater. When my son, Rohulamin, asked me if the house was full that day, I responded: "Well, there were people there!" To me it made no difference, because Jim Quander was there, and I was up on the stage in my own world.

Although there was an appreciation in the colored community for the arts, the appreciation was very limited. Most African-Americans were just beginning to come into the American mainstream, and many of my generation still had not yet achieved that level in the society. By the 1930s, several of the oldest members in the society had been slaves in their youth. As their numbers rapidly decreased, many of their adult children and grandchildren were beginning to experience the full effects of the Great Depression, which took full effect in the early 1930s after the collapse of the stock market in 1929.

As President Franklin Delano Roosevelt and Congress sought to reverse the collapse of the American economy and to get people back to work, several organizations were created, generally known by their alphabetic acronyms, such as N.Y.A. (the National Youth Administration) and W.P.A. (Work Project Administration). Both entities were founded in 1935. NYA's main objective was to keep young people in school, and by offering incentives to stay in school, including a few dollars to encourage that objective, many of us stayed in school who otherwise would not have been able to do so.

WPA had a related goal, i.e., to get Americans back to work. WPA focused on the arts and had several components. Perhaps the best known was the Federal Writers Project, which interviewed thousands of former slaves in the 1930s to get their life stories on paper before they died.

Less well known, but no less important, were the Federal Theater and Federal Music Projects which paid professionals, and even some who were not at that exact level of competence, to teach students the arts. This played out in school dramatic and comedy productions, musicals, and little theater of all dimensions. Our teachers were being paid to teach, and we were being paid to learn. Nothing could have been better, and I still cherish those days.

Although my participation in little theater started while I was in junior high school before the NYA and the WPA were created, this activity continued all the way through college. What had initially been a volunteer extracurricular effort on the part of my teachers now became paid part-time positions to train singers, dancers, musicians, and playwrights under the WPA program. The federal government's efforts during the Depression to get people back to work was successful, and the NYA program became a forerunner of the current work-study program, which likewise is designed to pay students a stipend for staying in school, as well as helping to relieve some of the pressure on the job market.

Because of peer pressure, it was not easy being a male dancer in the early 1930s. The perception was that boys did not dance, at least not on the stage in a theatrical manner. And for African-American males, the pressure was even more pronounced. Some of your own classmates would talk about you behind your back or call you names. Many of the parents were indisposed to associating with theater people, assuming wrongfully, that they were a fast and wild bunch.

While there is good and bad everywhere, within the black community, and being just a couple of generations from slavery, the focus then was strictly upon academics. So many people of Washington, D.C., society at that time were very narrowly focused, and there was no room for anyone who was thought to be riffraff or of no account. That ugly head of discrimination would rear its head many more times in my life, and it was particularly ugly during my high school era, but more on that later. Jim Quander was always a loner, and known to be such. So their attitudes and comments meant nothing to me. I ignored the negative attitudes and just kept moving on.

Eventually, it all worked out, and some of the same contemporaries who were too shy to dance or made fun of me were the same ones who complimented me in later life, saying, "Jim, you really didn't care, did you? You set your own tone and pace and didn't let anyone else tell you that you couldn't, and we admired that in you."

I never won first place in any competition that I entered, only honorable mentions and recognitions for participation, but that was fine with me. While it would have been nice to win a first place, my focus was on being active, and maybe one day being eventually recognized as a performing art talent. Many young kids today have no idea that dancing vaudeville at the Apollo Theater in New York, or at the Howard and Lincoln Theaters here in Washington, was all the rage in the 1920s, 1930s, and 1940s; and that it was also a great opportunity for many local talents to showcase themselves and to be discovered.

For me, these opportunities were all an integral part of my diabetic discipline. The routine of singing and dancing provided a release of stress, and the discipline to balance schoolwork with extracurricular activities was a great chance to get needed exercise—whether it was energy spent in walking to practice or calories burned while dancing. The end result was the same: Jim Quander's diabetes was under control.

One particularly interesting experience was in English. On at least three separate occasions, my eighth and ninth grade English teacher, Mary Delaney Evans, had to be away from class. With permission of Walker Savoy, the principal, she left me in charge of the class with instructions to teach the class according to the lesson plans that she had prepared for her periods of absence. I was her star pupil and had the respect of both her and the class. Almost 70 years later, several of my classmates still fondly recall those occasions, emphasizing that, unfortunately in the context of current school-related behavioral problems, this arrangement would never work in an inner-city public school today.

Progressing in my junior high experience, I never lost sight of the fact that I was a juvenile diabetic, or assumed that there would be no problems in the future. As I had learned during my elementary school era, I always carried hard candy in my pockets or book bag, just in case I felt an insulin reaction coming on, or some problem related to low blood sugar. And I needed to eat that candy on several occasions during this period.

Of course my first line of defense against diabetic-related problems was food. Continuing in the same tradition that my mother started when I was in elementary school, my lunches continued to be full meals. Only this time, the children were not as curious as before. Several of them had been to elementary school with me and already knew what to expect. As the children got older, they too ate more diversified meals. Several of them brought last night's leftover dinner to school for lunch, and there was a full cafeteria in the Garnett-Patterson building, which served a pretty full meal as well.

My standard lunch was food that could be briefly kept at room temperature. It typically consisted of meat, most often chicken, a green vegetable, a lettuce and tomato salad with mayonnaise, a slice or two of gluten bread, and a piece of fresh fruit. Despite the lack of refrigeration, the mayonnaise never spoiled or created a problem. And besides, in those days, I don't think we even realized that mayonnaise should be refrigerated after the bottle was open to avoid a food poisoning problem.

Despite my best efforts, I still had problems. The first insulin incident occurred in Ruth Gordon Savoy's seventh grade math class as I was preparing to take a math exam. I just could not get myself together, and seeing that, Mrs. Savoy said, "Jim, You're an 'A' student, so come back later and take the exam." I took her advice, left the classroom, and after taking some candy, felt better. I never told her what was wrong with me, and I doubt that she knew that I was a diabetic. Remember, this was in the era when diabetes was still the "BIG SECRET," and keeping it such was paramount, seemingly at all costs. Perhaps what occurred that day could be best described as a sudden drop in blood sugar due to anxiety-induced stress. As well, this same situation occurred sporadically while in high school and in college.

The second incident also occurred in math class. I was in the eighth or ninth grade, and the year was 1931 or 1932. It was in algebra class, and I had been studying hard the night before for a major test. My teacher was Irene Miller Reid, the daughter of the famous Howard University educator, Dr. Kelly Miller. When it was time to take the test, I was seated in my regular seat with my pencil in my hand, but had what I would describe as an "out-of-body experience."

Mrs. Reid came over to me, and seeing my dazed state, inquired with, "Quander, are you all right? What's the matter?" I looked up at her. She appeared fuzzy to me. I was able to reply and said, "You know, I just can't get myself together. My mind is perfectly blank, really blank. I've forgotten everything that I've ever known." She obviously realized that I was ill and may have suspected what the problem was, but she did not let on.

I was one of her very best students, so she said, "Quander, something is wrong. You don't have to take the exam today. You go home and go to bed, and come back and take it tomorrow." I took her advice, collected my things, and left the classroom. By then, the whole class was abuzz with, "What's wrong with Jim Quander?" No one really knew, except perhaps some of my closest friends, most all of whom were also neighbors in the Seventeenth Street area. They kept my secret.

As soon as I left the classroom, I took a couple of pieces of hard candy and headed to the principal's office for permission to leave school. As I headed out the door of the school building, and onto U Street to go home, I was already starting to feel better, but I remained lightheaded for the next several hours. When I arrived home and told Mama and Papa what happened, they both told me that I had done the right thing by not taking the exam and by coming home early. These were not the only two incidents like this which occurred while I was in junior high school, only the most vividly recalled.

One of those same type health-related incidents would later occur in college in the presence of the same Irene Miller Reid, who by then was a member of the math faculty at Miner Teacher's College when I arrived there in 1936. By then I believe that she had figured out that I was a Type I juvenile diabetic and subject to insulin reactions, although she never let on that she knew. In later years, as I would see her out socially, I told her that I was a juvenile diabetic and had suffered with it since I was about four years old. By the expression on her face, I could see her mind working as she thought to herself, "Ah ha! I thought so!"

# Chapter 6

# Coming Into My Own

Most everyone has fond memories of their high school years. I was no exception, but my high school was truly a different place from most. The Paul Laurence Dunbar High School was one of the most outstanding high schools in America—public, private, or parochial. I do not just mean *one of the most outstanding black high schools in America*. It was modeled after the old Boston Latin High School where the emphasis was strictly upon high academic achievement and the classical approach to education.

Not until high school did I really come into my own. So often young people are shy, retiring, and afraid of what everybody else will think or say about them. I was no different, but learned at an early age—really too early to be burdened with carrying the baggage of being a juvenile diabetic—that people's support for you is fickle and lasts only so long as they feel that you have something to offer. But in order to have that "something," you have to reach out to them, as they likewise reach back to you.

Since I was such a loner, it still amazes me that I really became so actively involved during my high school years, 1933 to 1936. Now 68 years later, I understand and appreciate that the physical exercise and effort associated with forcing myself to reach out, and the rewards of diversity that became a part of this effort, are what has sustained me these seven decades.

A quick overview of the 19th century D.C. educational system for Negroes is helpful at this point. What started in 1851 in

Washington, D.C., as a tutoring class founded by Myrtilla Miner, a Caucasian abolitionist teacher, for the benefit of young African-American girls, germinated and expanded in several directions after her death, including the establishment in November 1870 of the Preparatory High School for Colored Youth in the basement of the Fifteenth Street Presbyterian Church. This provided the only opportunity for preparation of leadership among the colored people of the nation's capital who had recently been freed from slavery and who were being guided by friends of the abolitionist tradition to develop their utmost potential.

Many whites objected to the idea of creating an all-academic, classics-based high school for colored children. They felt that a trade school would be better to teach trades like shoe repair, farming, blacksmithing, plumbing, etc. The idea of training a cadre of blacks for university was alien to this hostile group. They still did not believe that descendants from Africa possessed sufficiently intellectual skills to pursue college, let alone handle difficult subjects and graduate, many with honors.

The idea of maintaining and expanding an educated, intellectual class of African-Americans persevered; and in 1891, a new building was erected on M Street, between First Street and New York Avenue, N.W., to house the classical curriculum high school for Negroes. Not named for a person, it was simply called "The M Street School," which name served until 1916. In that year, a new high school building was constructed at First and N Streets, N.W., and named for Paul Laurence Dunbar, the outstanding African-American poet, who was an intimate friend of Orville and Wilbur Wright, and in whose newspaper in Ohio, Dunbar finally received a steady ear for his poetry. One of his poems, *Keep A Pluggin' Away*, has been my motto and inspiration throughout my life, and it was considered for the title of this autobiography.

There was much opposition to Miss Miner's determination and efforts in 1851, but she persisted. After her death at a relatively young age, but in continuum of her legacy, the Miner Normal School was created in 1876. Three years later, it became a part of the Colored Division of the D.C. public school system committed to training teachers for the burgeoning group of free people of color who were pouring into the national capital city in this later

Reconstruction era. Later still, and as a result of Congressional action in 1929, the institution would be re-titled and accredited as Miner Teacher's College, a lasting tribute to the great contributions and sacrifices that Miss Miner made on behalf of young African-Americans.

Some of the most outstanding graduates from Dunbar and its predecessor-named institutions include: U.S. Senator Edward W. Brooke, who was in my class of 1936; Elizabeth Catlett, artist; Mercer Cook, Ambassador; Col. West A. Hamilton, military; and William H. Hastie, federal judge and governor of the U.S. Virgin Islands.

Based upon my excellent academic record at Garnet-Patterson, including graduating with honors, I was selected to attend "The Dunbar High School," as we called it. There were other Dunbar high schools around the country, but the one in Washington, D.C., had acquired a reputation that was unequaled; and for that reason, we practiced our perceived superiority with a vengeance, and not a little bit of pride, arrogance, and self-discrimination.

Into this mix was thrown a fifteen-year-old James W. Quander, juvenile diabetic. It was at least a little traumatic for me to enroll there. Not only was I entering a new academic environment, I was conscious about both my height and weight. In September 1933, I was all of five feet, three inches, and weighed a paltry 105 to 110 pounds. Most everyone else, including many of the girls, towered over me and weighed more, sometimes nearly twice as much. Even now, in my old age, I am only five feet and six inches tall and weigh about 120 pounds. For many diabetics, getting the weight off is a problem, but for us juvenile diabetics who never were able to gain weight, the opposite is frequently the problem.

Some years ago I saw a picture of myself taken on Easter Sunday morning in 1930 wearing my new Easter outfit, standing in front of the family home at 1913 17th Street. N.W. In the photo I am wearing "stovepipe" pants, which are hard to describe to anyone today, since that male fashion has never returned in America. They were primarily pants that came down a little below the knee and were gathered at that spot. My otherwise exposed, skinny legs were covered by long socks, but they still looked like two pipes hanging beneath shortened pants. Stovepipes were great for riding a bicycle, as there were no pant leg and cuff to get entangled in the chain. I guess that was a main reason for creating this fashion statement in the first place.

Looking at this old photo, I was appalled at how thin I was—a string bean. My son, Rohulamin, upon seeing the picture for the first time, exclaimed, "Dad, look how thin and small you were." All I could say was, "Yes, look how thin I was, how really thin; and short, too."

But once I arrived at Dunbar in September 1933, many of my fears dissipated quickly, as the environment was both familiar and challenging. It was familiar because so many of my prior schools chums were there, some that I had not seen since elementary school. But it was also a great transition, being more adult in focus, and academically demanding.

I did not know it at that early stage, but as a result of the Dunbar experience, I bonded with several of my teachers and began forming lifelong relationships that would endure until these teachers' own respective deaths. This too was a side effect of the Dunbar experience, as well as the effect of racially segregated Washington, D.C. Segregation and restrictive covenants on housing literally forced the Negroes into certain neighborhoods, and in many instances, these same teachers were also our neighbors.

When I enrolled in the 10th grade, I was assigned to take the standard academic subjects for tenth grade—English, geometry, Latin, chemistry, and physical training. Later, when I entered the 11th grade, I dropped mandatory Latin and switched to French as an elective. I tackled everything, gave it my best, and did extremely well.

Dunbar was the high school for the best and the brightest. It was where Washington, D.C.'s "Talented Tenth," as W.E.B. DuBois called the upper class colored people in America, sent their children. Undeniably it was a school for the children of the doctors, lawyers, teachers, and preachers: their parents had achieved as much as the white society would allow them to in those days. But Dunbar was much, much more, too.

Despite any negative images that the school might have garnered for its reputation of catering to the children of the privileged, including the unfortunate subject of color discrimination within our own ethnic group, Dunbar was a place where good students, young people determined to succeed and achieve, could readily do so, despite their complexion, family background and history, and economic status.

Dunbar attracted everybody. Although the better connected were naturally in a more-favored position to assure that their children got into Dunbar than those who lacked those affiliations, the academic record of the potential new Dunbar student was the real barometer for acceptance, regardless of everything else. I, James William Quander, was not privy to any connecting network. Papa, who was such wise counsel that even far-better-educated people sought his advice, was totally orphaned at age nine or ten. Having to work to support his two surviving siblings, his wise counsel and good reputation belied the fact that he was only able to complete two years of formal education.

Mama came here from Walterboro, South Carolina, in 1890, when she was ten years old, and likewise had little formal education. Like Papa, she too was most ambitious and enrolled in night school at Armstrong High School to improve her reading and math skills. Neither of them could be found on the Washington, D.C., social register.

But they had smart, focused children, and four of the six of us— Joseph, Cora, Catherine and myself—all attended and graduated from Dunbar. I had brains, and everyone knew it; so there was no real doubt in the minds of my Garnett-Patterson teachers that I would go anywhere else other than Dunbar High School. There were only three high schools for Negroes in Washington, D.C., at the time.

Armstrong High School, created in 1902, while offering an academic program, was more focused on teaching its students trades and was far more manually oriented. While many of its graduates did attend college and do well, it was not the strong academic institution that Dunbar was, and it was never created to be a direct competitor.

In 1928, the business department of Dunbar was separated into a different institution, Francis Cardozo High School, the third created high school for colored. The highest percentage of its graduates entered federal government service as clerks, typists, messengers, printers, and other jobs that were "reserved" for the colored in that era, although many of its students also earned college degrees.

Even today, the previously racially segregated Dunbar High School is still recalled as one of the most outstanding public high schools in the United States—black or white—for the pre-1954 school desegregation era. Undoubtedly, this statement is surprising to many who had no prior knowledge of Dunbar's legacy. During the segregated era when children and school faculty were separated by race, a black-operated institution not only survived, but it prospered in the racially divided atmosphere that was Washington, D.C., at the time.

A much better understanding emerges once you realize that the faculty was topnotch, second to none anywhere; and during the general era of my 1933-1936 tenure there, at least five of them had Ph.D. degrees—yet they were teaching in a high school. This situation was a pervasive side effect from rigidly-enforced racial separation, which transcended the academic community. It also prevented otherwise outstanding individuals from being selected for career positions for which they were eminently qualified. Our graduates went to Harvard, Yale, Amherst, the Seven Sisters Colleges, and the best of the historically blacks colleges and universities, including Howard University in Washington, D.C., and Morehouse College and Spellman College, both in Atlanta, Georgia.

I learned early that I had to operate in a certain way, if I expected to function as a juvenile diabetic. This routine called for not only a strict diet but also a lot of physical activity and exercise. I got a lot of both by keeping myself constantly busy. The walking, playing sports, performing in theater, newspaper routes, and grocery deliveries, plus working in so many summer jobs during my Garnett-Patterson Junior High likewise prepared me for my very active Dunbar-era life, and subsequently affected everything else that I have ever done.

When I was a young child, my parents were concerned about my short stature and light weight. I never seemed to grow as fast as the others, and I could not keep my weight on. In later years, my smallness would prove to be a blessing. As well, the rigorous exercise that Dr. Wilder permitted has proven to be a major blessing in my later years, and a tribute to my longevity. The pace was set then, and I have kept active ever since, although my movements are now considerably restricted.

Because of the enforced segregation in Washington, D.C., including the denial of ready access to the legitimate theaters in downtown, beyond academics Dunbar became a hub of extracurricular activity in itself. We were treated to the best and most famous in the show business world, both black and white. They came to us, and we were acculturated as a result and set our own standard for active little theater and vaudeville because of whom we had seen on our own Dunbar stage.

This was long before the cries of Black Power and Afro centricity, and there was a conscious effort to emulate many of the white actors and actresses in style, manners, and in the selection of repertoire. This point is easily verified by a reference to our programs from theater productions, concerts, and commencement exercises. The classics and traditional white composers were favored and much preferred. In significant measure, we were the grandchildren of slaves, and many of our grandparents simply wanted to forget everything they ever heard about Africa and knew about slavery. A measurable percentage of them actually pretended that this institution never existed.

Because of the national legacy that Dunbar and its predecessor educational institutions had established and maintained, many of the students, including some in my own peer group, were from among the privileged classes, i.e., the Talented Tenth, about which W.E.B. DuBois, Booker T. Washington, and others spoke. Although I was not a part of that persuasion, there was a significant sense of superiority among many of us.

During my three years at Dunbar, and as a part of our acculturation process, the school sponsored a number of field trips. I rarely subscribed because of my parents' concern that the change in routine might cause me to have a stress-induced insulin reaction, that I would not be able to explain to anyone what was the problem, or how to address it. While I regret missing these opportunities, the school was visited by several professional show people, including Shakespearean actors Maurice Evans and Gertrude Lawrence, and many prominent Broadway or vaudevillian stars, who, when they were appearing on the stages of Washington, would come and give us a lecture and perform one-act plays or other entertainment venues that they were appearing in, in downtown theaters, which we were either prohibited or restricted from attending.

Sometimes we would use the school auditorium, and at other times it would be a theater in the round set up in the gymnasium, with all of us drawing up to the guests who were speaking in the center of the circle. One day Lady Astor visited. I remember her well because she seemed uncomfortable around educated people of color. I surmise that the only black folks she had previously come in contact with were domestic servants. Her awkwardness in our presence was an inspiration in reverse. Not only did she anger me, but I was inspired and determined to show white folk that I too was intelligent, could think, and did not need to be either talked down to or patronized.

While I assume that she meant well, after she left, I distinctly recall one teacher telling us, "You're Dunbar students. We're training you to be future doctors, lawyers, and educators. We're not training you to be anybody's maid." In that context, Lady Astor's visit in the name of theater had a silver lining, despite the insulting tone. We saw through this experience and realized that, although we were still in high school, we were probably already better educated than she.

Shortly after I graduated in 1936, Ingrid Bergman, the Swedish actress, visited Dunbar. She was very much a civil rights activist in her day. A native of Sweden, she was appalled at the treatment African-Americans received in our own country, and spoke out about it on several occasions. When the whites told her, "Miss Bergman, you don't understand," she retorted to the effect that there was nothing more to understand, other than the fact that the colored Americans were not given fair treatment and access, and that that conduct by whites against blacks had to change. When few others were doing anything comparable, she spoke out against segregated theaters and racial discrimination. Her efforts contributed significantly to the eventual breakdown of segregated facilities in Washington, D.C.

Others who came to visit were Freddie Washington, the famous actress of color, who starred in *Imitation of Life*, and Nina Mae

McKinney. Although his appearance was controversial and caught negative publicity in the press, we were also blessed with Bill Bojangles, the famous tap dancer. Walter Smith, our principal, did not relish Bojangles's presence at the school and allegedly acted very insultingly towards him.

While the exact reasons for this rude attitude and behavior are still not particularly clear to me, it was widely believed that Bojangles's being unwelcome was in part due to both his very dark complexion, and the fact that tap dance style, a throwback and reminder of slavery, was not appreciated as a sophisticated enough art form to be represented on the stage of "The Dunbar High School." Insulted to his face, Bojangles was reported to have said, "Well, I'm not going to pay any attention to that man [Mr. Walter Smith, principal], because I make more money in a month than he does in a year."

Years later, in the 1940s, also after I had graduated, when Hattie McDaniels came to Dunbar shortly after her having been the first African-American woman to win an Academy Award for playing a mammy in *Gone With the Wind*, Mr. Smith's attitude was quite different. She was welcomed with open arms, and her very black complexion did not appear to be of noticeable concern.

But it was also at Dunbar where, despite my distinguished academic achievements, I was discriminated against and would eventually be denied my single greatest academic goal— membership in the National Honor Society. I was 15 years old when I entered the 10th grade. My reputation as a good student, a singer, dancer, and entrepreneur had preceded me. When I arrived, I fell right into the same routine. Academics are what it was all about, and I saw this as my opportunity to really distinguish myself. It was also the first time in my young life that I made so many of my own life decisions, rather than relying upon Papa, Mama, or Dr. Wilder to guide me in the directions they wanted.

Long before Dunbar, I had been told that I was not supposed to do certain things because of their fear that I would sustain an injury or wound that would not heal, or a life-threatening infection. With that warning, a part of my daily life for all of my then ten or eleven diagnosed diabetic years, I was tired of "being good."

Swimming was a mandatory, graded activity at Dunbar. Almost the first thing Dr. Wilder told my parents and me was that I could not take swimming because I might catch something. Besides, he said, the pools were not very clean. Further, I distinctly recall his telling me that he did not want me to have an insulin attack at the pool, due to stress and high anxiety, and that if I had one, I could easily drown. Since no one knew that I was a diabetic, and they did not know of my condition, they likewise would not know what to do for me. Need I say more? He succeeded in scaring both of my parents into absolutely forbidding me from taking swimming.

Likewise, although ROTC was mandatory, and the annual citywide drill competitions for the Colored Division were the highlight of the year, at the request of my doctor, I was excused from ROTC as well. When I asked Dr. Wilder why he would not let me join the corps, since it was not for war itself, just drilling and competition, he said, "Jim, I can't have you out on the field after school, rolling around in the heat, dirt, and mud during some of those military exercises, because you might get hurt or get an infection. And besides, those scabbards and blades that they use can be dangerous. If you got cut by one of them, it could be fatal."

"Get infected! Get infected!" That was all I ever heard. I was devastated. Although I was not all that hyped up on the military, being a ROTC cadet was a part of the academic and extracurricular rigor at Dunbar. The girls seemed to be especially attracted to the guys in uniform, and that opportunity was being denied to me. Several of my classmates, being observant, asked me why I was not enrolled in either swimming or ROTC. I dismissed their queries by noting that my doctor had me excused for health reasons. While most of them let it drop based upon my answer, a few were persistent and inquired further.

I never told them the truth: I kept the "Big Secret." While most of them probably did not know what I was experiencing, a few of my closest friends did know and inquired no further. Members of this latter group were primarily my closest friends, several of whom were also immediate neighbors around 17th Street. Their parents were often family friends as well.

For the first time, I directly confronted my parents and told them that I had decided to take gym class, despite anything that Dr.

Wilder or they had to say about it. And surprisingly they did not object or try to persuade me otherwise. In fact, within a day or two, Mama and Papa took me downtown to pick out my basketball shoes, and subsequently they saw me in my gym uniform on several occasions. Dr. Wilder did not know, and they never said any more about it. Case closed!

It was a new feeling of independence. I had made a decision for myself and was living with it. My parents did not object, contest, or counter me. They supported me in this decision and applauded my efforts to be just a regular guy. The boys and girls took gym separately, and my gym/basketball class had several of my lifelong associates in it, including Samuel McCottry, Vincent Brown, Leroy Dillard, Nat Dixon, Norbert Gillam, Highwarden Just, Joseph Dwyer, William "Dubb" Bullock, and Charles Pinderhughes, to name a few.

Although many of the guys had previously played basketball in junior high or on the neighborhood playgrounds, Perry Jacobs, our gym teacher, taught us the fundamentals of basketball and good sportsmanship. We were young teenage boys, many of whom would later be inducted into the National Honor Society before graduation, and eventually be distinguished in medicine, law, religion, education, small business, banking, government service, plus other professions. As well, many came from distinguished families. Just to be a "regular guy," and not always forced to the sidelines for health reasons, was an exhilarating experience for me.

While I never became a basketball star, largely due to my short stature, I learned the game well and routinely played it at gym time and on the local playgrounds with the neighborhood guys, increasing both my visibility among my peers and personal self-confidence. The same was true for baseball and horseshoes, both of which I routinely played, mostly in the late afternoon or long evenings before dark. All of them were typical teenage boy activities for the mid 1930s pastime when there was no television, air conditioning, or shopping malls to distract us.

# Chapter 7

# Eyes Wide Open

Not all the discipline in the world could have prepared me for what happened in November 1933, just two months after I had enrolled in the 10th grade. Suddenly I came down with Scarlet Fever and had to be hospitalized. It was a serious illness, quite often fatal, and there was some question whether I would survive.

I came down with an extremely sore throat and reddish blotches appeared all over my body. Areas of my skin loosened, and some of it eventually peeled and fell off. I had to be hospitalized and remained in the colored ward at Garfield Hospital for two weeks, further quarantined from the other patients because of the contagion. By the time I was released to go home, three or more weeks had passed, and Dr. Wilder felt that I should wait until February 1934, before returning to school.

It was at about this same time that I changed doctors. Dr. Charles Wilder had always been my savior and good friend. He delivered me at birth and explained to me just before my sixth birthday what it meant to be a diabetic. It was he that told my parents that I might not live to ten years of age during my first diabetic hospitalization period in 1925. But in rapidly failing health, he passed me off to his younger associate, Dr. Hugh Simmons, who would remain my doctor for the next several years, providing an uninterrupted medical continuity for my care.

Like Dr. Wilder, a significant portion of Dr. Simmons's medical practice concentrated on treating diabetics. In those days most doctors were general practitioners. Although Dr. Simmons's specialty was cardiology, he also focused upon the significant number of diabetics in the colored community. In his later years most people would refer to him as a diabetic specialist rather than as a cardiologist or general practitioner.

I lost the entire semester and the academic credits for my math, English, Latin, everything, and from all appearances would never be able to graduate with my 1936 high school class. That was a lonely period in my life because, aside from not being able to deliver my newspapers for much of that time, I was also confined to the house. But, once the contagion passed, I received visitors. Several of my classmates came by or telephoned to see how I was doing. I also arranged to tutor two elementary-level children, Jean and Agnes Gray, after their school. Their mother, Sarah, was a dear friend of my parents, and based upon medical assurances that I was well past contagion, she was not fearful of Scarlet Fever infections for her daughters.

By February 1934, I was well-rested, fully recovered from Scarlet Fever, and ready to go back to school. I had two options. Since the D.C. public schools' curriculum was structured to include both February and June graduations, I could pace myself a little slower, and graduate one semester later, in February 1937. Or I could accelerate myself, attend summer school, complete everything, and still graduate with my class in June 1936. Because I already knew many of the people in my 10th grade class even before I enrolled at Dunbar, I elected the later, but more stringent option.

At the time I temporarily dropped out of school, I was earning all "As" and "Bs" in each of my subjects, a tone that I set and maintained throughout my high school career. I wondered whether I would be able to maintain that level of commitment and focus in February, after losing the entire semester due to an illness. Once I decided that my goal was to graduate with my class in June 1936, despite my having lost the entire semester of September 1933 to January 1934, my plan of action became clearer every day.

Because I was so disciplined in my daily life, and especially in my self-handling of my diabetic condition, I managed to put my agenda and plans into little boxes in my mind. Getting focused and staying that way was not too difficult. I roared back to school in February 1934, and was eager to tackle whatever academic life offered.

I did extremely well that semester, and again earned all "As" and "Bs," a trend that I started at the outset of high school, and never varied from, earning only one "C" from an advanced math class. I had always told my children that I earned only one "C" grade in high school. Whether they believed me or not, my assertion was verified when my son, Rohulamin, while researching for this book, obtained my high school transcript, which verified my statement. Sitting there very lonely and isolated was the one "C" grade that Mr. Ulysses S. Bassett gave me in Algebra. There was also a major "rest of the story" about that class and that grade, which I will tell you about later.

In addition to the French, Latin, math, and debating clubs, I was also involved in several theater productions. My particular favorite activity was the French club, monitored by Mary (Molly) Gibson Brewer Hundley, my French teacher. She also would become a dear lifelong friend, someone who my wife and all four of my children would get to know and admire. Later in life, she would also introduce us to Lillian Evans (Madame Evanti) Tibbs, the first African-American female world-class opera singer, who had to leave this country and tour Europe, in order to become famous. Madame Evanti later became a regular visitor to our home.

Mrs. Hundley took me to the "Church of the Presidents," the historic St. John's Episcopal Church, located on Lafayette Square, directly across from the White House. We referred to the church as, *L'Elgiese de la Presidents*. Attending there was neither a Dunbar nor French club activity, but a separate cultural activity.

There they had planned activities and a community of people who wanted to speak French. Despite this being such a racially segregated town at the time, there did not seem to be any problem among these people, most of whom were foreign born, that I was an "American of Color," as we were generally called.

In fact, the situation was just the opposite. They wanted to know about Americans of Color, as so many incorrect stereotypes had been conjured up about my race. Not coming in contact with many brown-skinned people, they would ask me questions like,

"Do you have a flush toilet in your house?" The answer was "Yes!" "Were your parents slaves?" The answer was "No, but at least three of my grandparents were slaves." They were thirsting for knowledge, and with Mrs. Hundley and me generally being the only persons of color there, they had no one else to ask.

I could never have convinced them that Mrs. Hundley was a descendant from African slaves. Her fair skin, straight hair, and features were such that no one ever would have initially thought that she was a Daughter of Africa. She, being a member of the distinguished Syphax Family and a direct descendant from Martha Washington through George Washington Parke Custis, President George Washington's step grandson, her appearance led the French speakers at the church to immediately assume that she was of some racial ancestry other than African-American. Although she probably could not have passed for white, her complexion, sophisticated manners, and fluency in French, having studied annually at the Sorbonne, gave no indication of her racial identity.

These gatherings were held on Sunday afternoons. I made certain that I ate adequately before I went, having learned that I could never rely upon their light refreshments to tide me over until I had a full dinner. Besides, the French cookies, cakes, and sweet drinks they served would wreak havoc with my diet and discipline, if I partook. My standard reply to an offer of something to drink became, "No, thank you. I'll just have a glass of water."

Throughout most of high school, I kept the two newspaper delivery routes that I started while in junior high school. Other than working around the house, delivering papers was the first sustained job that I ever had, and I maintained one or both routes for the greater part of ten years. It was the *Washington Post* in the morning and the *Evening Star* in the afternoon. Even when I let the *Post* route go, I generally kept the *Star* route. Both routes were not too far from the house, further downtown in the Sumner-Magruder school area, around Seventeenth and M Streets, near the Mayflower Hotel and the National Geographic headquarters. The area was much more residential then than it is today.

To deliver the *Post*, I arose at 4:30 a.m. daily, dressed and collected my papers and had them delivered by 6:00 a.m. Returning home, I usually found Papa awake, having come in from his work at the Center Market where he worked the night shift. He usually got off about 5:30 a.m. Mama was an early riser, too, and she would fix a full breakfast for him and me. Before breakfast I would bathe, test my blood sugar the old fashioned way using the Bunsen burner, and then take my insulin, regulating the amount depending upon the blood sugar level. I would be off to school by 8:00 a.m., walking the 25 blocks to school in nice weather, or catching the streetcar on U Street just a half block from the house.

On the weekends, and especially in bad weather, Papa helped me make my paper deliveries. The Sunday paper delivery was especially demanding: the Sunday paper was always significantly larger and heavier than the weekly, and it took longer to deliver. During a significant portion of this era, I was also obligated to deliver both the Sunday *Post* and *Star*, which made my job all the more demanding. I still vividly picture Papa on a typical cold and snowy early February morning, pulling the sled in the snow, rolling up and locking the papers into "Tomahawks," as we called them, and throwing the papers up onto the front porches, as we plodded our way through darkness and early morning light. Despite his bowlegs, heavyset frame, and rheumatoid condition, he never complained once. And we grew personally closer because of it.

To my entrepreneurial expansions of delivering newspapers and groceries, I added a totally new dimension in the summers of 1934 and 1935. Cora, my sister, had been living and studying nursing in New York for a few years. While there, she sold ice cream from a street vendor cart that someone made for her. It was a cute, boxy cart, not dissimilar to a big baby carriage. Several times she told me how much money she had made in New York pushing the cart in selected New York neighborhoods during the hot summer months. Now that she had returned to D.C. and brought the cart home with her, she suggested that maybe I should take up the trade. She showed me exactly how to do it and where to get wholesale ice cream.

Seeing this as a good opportunity to earn a significant amount of money in the summer, I agreed. At the outset, I did not realize that this opportunity would prove to be a lifesaver in many respects. My academic counselors had advised me that in order to graduate with my class in June 1936, I would have to take summer school classes. Otherwise, I could slow the pace and graduate in the February 1937 class, since they did have half-year graduations at that time. I elected not to do the latter, as it would place me into a class cycle outside of my immediate loop of friends and associates, some of whom I had been in class with since my two-in-one kindergarten-first grade enrollment at Logan School where I started school in 1922.

I elected the summer school option, followed by my selling ice cream daily. The Great Depression was on. The summers were long and hot, and there was no air conditioning. This situation seemed just right and ripe for me. As a young entrepreneur who had already established himself by selling newspapers and delivering groceries, selling ice cream would be my third job. I had not reckoned the amount of walking involved in selling ice cream on the street. Nor had I fully considered just how hot it might be on certain days, where I would go in the event of a sudden rain shower, and most importantly what adverse impacts my working in the streets and pushing a cart would have upon my diabetic condition.

I discussed the idea with Dr. Simmons. He told me that the keys to good diabetic health, in addition to my daily monitoring of my food and insulin intake, were getting plenty of exercise and keeping a sufficient amount of bodily fluid in me. He said, "James, I don't see anything wrong with this. It's up to you, and knowing you as I do, I think that you will tackle this just like you have tackled everything else. Give it a try. If it doesn't work out, no harm is done."

Looking back, what still amazes me is how I was disciplined enough to keep all of the juggled balls in the air—outstanding academic work, assigned household chores, two newspaper routes, occasional Saturday grocery deliveries, singing and dancing, plus math, debating, Latin, and French Club activities. As well, in the summer months, I also took on additional jobs. No one could ever say then, or now, that Jim Quander was lazy.

From time to time, I temporarily gave up my paper routes due to academic demands, but I always went back to delivering them. There was a high turnover, and I was deemed to be one of the most reliable delivery boys either paper had. My self-discipline, cultivated by years of strict adherence to my diabetic diet and scheduled monitoring, inculcated me to them, as someone they could depend upon. Every time I worked for a few months and left, they would beg me to stay and conclude our communication with, "You'll be back. We're looking for you." And, invariably, including throughout my college years, I went back and resumed delivery of one or two newspaper routes for several years.

The added convenience of having a big, flat, wide paper wagon was not lost on me. It immediately gave rise to my entrepreneurial spirit to deliver groceries from the supermarkets in the area. This was during the Great Depression, but I could easily make about $7.00 to $8.00 on Saturdays delivering groceries to customers' homes, most of whom either had no cars or lived in the immediate area but needed help in ferrying their packages home.

And while my diabetes has never fully stayed under "control" in that sense, this routine and the physical exercise associated with it seemed to work well. My doctors were always concerned that I was doing too much and might collapse under the regimen of such a tight schedule. Dr. Wilder often said, "Now Jim, are you sure that you're getting enough rest? It seems to me that you're wearing yourself out with too much *going*." But assuring both him and my parents that I could handle everything, I kept going and was psychologically conditioning myself to always be disciplined in monitoring my health as a diabetic and in remaining focused.

His associate, and my new doctor, Hugh Simmons, seamlessly picked up where Dr. Wilder left off. By this time, Dr. Wilder's health had declined and he was no longer my active physician. He subsequently died on November 27, 1935, at age 41. Acquainted with what I was endeavoring to do, Dr. Simmons urged me on by adding that most importantly, I needed the best walking shoes I could find, shoes that would also allow my feet to get adequate airflow. I was to only wear white socks, since the dye from other socks might rub off. His parting words were to always keep my head covered on hot days to avoid the heat and intensity of the direct sun.

I was in heaven. Although I did not have to, I bought myself a completely white everything. It was a white button-down shirt, white trousers, white shoes, and heavily padded white socks. My hat was a wide-brimmed straw helmet, with a headband inside. This allowed the air to circulate around my head but kept the sun off my head and neck. It worked perfectly.

I was told on more than one occasion that it looked like I was wearing a jungle outfit. While some people were honest in their assessment, others obviously only intended their remarks to hurt. And I had to figure out which of these people were which. I regret that I never took a picture in my uniform. It would be a treasure today.

To assure that no blisters or bruises developed upon my tired feet, I washed and inspected them every night, applied foot powder to keep them dry and Vaseline to keep them supple. Around the house everyone was teasing me about how fastidious I was over a pair of feet. But deep down, they all knew why I was doing this, and respected my effort.

Other than my sister, Cora, who kept her counsel, neither my parents nor my friends realized that during certain summer weeks, I netted an average of between $40.00 to $45.00 per week from sales of Dixie cups, frozen icicles, Popsicles, and chocolate-covered vanilla bars. For the Depression years in 1930s dollars, this was a lot of money.

Layering and packing everything into my insulated pushcart, I set out and sold for five to ten cents a piece. While ten cents was not cheap in 1934 and 1935, on a hot day an ice cream hit the spot and I was much in demand. Despite the abundance, I was not tempted to eat the ice cream because I knew how disciplined I had to remain if I was to succeed in this opportunity. While I usually stayed on the street until I was sold out, occasionally, I would eat some and always considered it to be a treat. But I never lost sight of my goal—to keep my diabetes under control—and I knew that too much sugar intake was inconsistent with that objective.

The exact sales route was not always the same. Frequently, I chose to sell in predominantly white neighborhoods. There I was always treated with the utmost cordiality, with several of my customers becoming regulars and engaging me in conversation about whether I was in school and where, and did I plan to attend college. Many of them complimented my entrepreneurship, an embarrassing contrast to the attitude quite frequently displayed by a significant percentage of those from my own racial group.

During part of the summer, and since I was taking early summer school classes, I went to school in my all-white uniform. After class, I rushed down to the wholesaler located in Chinatown at Sixth and H Streets, N.W., purchased my ice cream and dry ice, packed my cart, and then hurried back to First and N Streets, N.W., the site of Dunbar, ready to greet the students who were leaving at about 12:00 noon. My sales route walked me back towards home. On most nights my older brother, Joseph, whom we called by his middle name, "Pearson," would carry the cart back down to Sixth and H Streets for night storage, where I had arranged with the wholesaler to keep it for my use in the morning. Otherwise, I would have been forced to take it to Dunbar empty each morning before class.

Selling ice cream to my own classmates proved to be one of the most unnerving experiences that I have ever endured. While most of the classmates were cordial, and some actually friendly, a few took this as an opportunity to heap abuse and scorn upon me. To several of them, it seemed that if I was college bound, then I needed to be engaged in something more intellectual than selling ice cream on the sidewalk in front of the school. The first few times this attitude was displayed towards me, I was really hurt and dismayed, and repeatedly asked myself, "Why? Why? Why?"

But other students were consolers, and I quickly came to realize and appreciate that this was a real problem that plagued us as young, educated, up and coming Negroes in that time. We were the first generation that had a chance to receive a first class education, something universally unheard of for blacks in America, except for a few small pockets of society, including here in Washington, D.C.

Virtually all of these people certainly knew better, being themselves the upper class in black Washington, D.C., society. But the children generally fell into their parents' own footsteps and attitudes, and where the parents were hurtful and showed their ignorance and own prejudices, all too often the children did, too. On some days I did not start my sales route at Dunbar, electing to start closer to home.

One incident in particular stands out above all others. I was pushing my cart up Fifteenth Street at about S Street, N.W., when an older man, someone who was closely related to Dr. Wilder, came out onto the sidewalk, cursed me, and called me horrible names including a "damn foreigner" and a "dirty West Indian." He then proceeded to order me off the public street, as if the street belonged to him. What was so hurtful about his hate and ignorance was the fact that he was spreading it to his own young grandchildren, who at his urging, joined in the excoriation, likewise calling me disparaging names and laughing at my distress.

He had no idea who I was, or that my own Quander family's history and 17th century documented presence in these United States most likely predated his own. Further, he was unaware that I knew his daughter who was a teacher at Dunbar, or his relative, Dr. Wilder, who was my own doctor. And here he was, a fellow African-American, electing to attack me for my entrepreneurship rather than lauding me as a young, enterprising young man, someone who was on his way somewhere and who was going to be somebody someday. Further, based upon how well the ice cream business was doing at the time, and considering the daily and weekly wage of even the professional worker in 1934 and 1935, I would wager that, despite my youth, I had perhaps as much money in the bank as he at that time.

This same incident is an example of the split in opinion between intellectuals like W.E.B. DuBois and Booker T. Washington. DuBois was more intellectually focused upon the uplifting of the race via more opportunities for formal education. Out of this effort and focus grew Dunbar. Conversely, Washington felt that more emphasis needed to be placed upon the manual trades, because if the African-Americans learned how to take care of themselves through the trades, economic stability would follow as the key to future successes. Out of this effort and focus grew Armstrong.

While both views are worthy of consideration, on the date he interfered and ordered me off the public street, in certain circles Dubois's point of view had prevailed to the point where there was little room at the upper reaches of the Talented Tenth society for any other thought. How sad that one of the type men that both

DuBois and Washington most certainly had in mind took the matter to one extreme and hurt all of us, including himself, in the process.

Rather than appreciate that I was an independent, young businessman seeking to earn his way and save a few dollars for college in the process, this man and his two little grandchildren chose to ridicule what they perceived as manual labor, something that was beneath them. I was already toughened by negative experiences I sustained at the hands of several of my classmates; and his nasty, unkind words just bounced off me as if I were wearing a suit of armor. What had simply been my uniform then became a badge of pride and honor.

Today, in a matter of fashion, this same negative attitude and scenario continues to play in African-American communities. We are underscored more as consumers, very little as entrepreneurs, and almost not at all as producers, savers, or innovators. Unfortunately, the current generation has lost sight of the struggle that their ancestors endured to create the lifestyle that the younger people now take for granted. And in the process, our entire race suffers from the negative attributes of expecting instant gratification, unwillingness to sacrifice or do without, and refusal to engage in tasks, including work, which we consider to be beneath us.

I was never too far from my love of the theater, and in high school, I continued my theater work with great gusto. Having been bitten by the theater bug in junior high school when I played a member of Robin Hood's band and sang a duet with William "Dubb" Bullock, high school presented an entirely new and expanded opportunity. Only this time, it was significantly more professional.

Due to the Great Depression era-created Work Progress Administration (WPA), the directors, producers, and drama teachers were compensated for their artistic efforts by the federal government under an artistic grant program established under the WPA. While most people have heard of the Writers Project, which paid people to interview several thousand freed slaves and capture them on reel-to-reel tape before they died, far fewer realized that there was also a theater component to this artistic effort.

With the Great Depression in high gear and the federal government committed to get people back to work as quickly as possible, little theater presented our trainers a stellar opportunity to work and teach what they enjoyed, and for us to learn more about theater and the performing arts.

Initially starting in junior high, I remained with little theater throughout high school and would even continue with it in college. We did mostly cabaret-type activities, creating smoky nightclub scenes. We took our plays around town and appeared wherever we could find an audience. Vaudeville and variety shows were all the rage. We most often practiced in the Dunbar high school auditorium, but since my little theater group was not directly connected to the school, we were not limited to the event having a direct school connection. When we were searching for a name for our troupe, we decided to call it "Little Theater," and that is what it was.

Florita Jordan Roy was our director, an accomplished musician and tap and ballroom dancer. She was extremely good and capable at putting Broadway type shows together. During the day she taught math at Robert H. Terrell Junior High School, and she did little theater in the evening. One of our favorite places to appear was the Lincoln Colonnade, singing and dancing up a storm, entertaining as if we had not a care in the world. I am a tenor and can still sing pretty well. In those days I was routinely assigned to sing solos.

I sang *Paper Moon* all around town and still remember the words. Another popular tune of the day was *Sweet and Lovely*. Another song that I sang was *These Foolish Things Remind Me Of You*.

Not being the least bit Afro centric, we modeled ourselves after Caucasian people who were popular singers and dancers at the time. Both Joan Crawford and Ginger Rogers were becoming known dancers then, and William Powell was a singer of show tunes. We, as young people, emulated their dance and show tune routines.

I was not a part of every production because I had other activities, especially schoolwork and my paper routes. But I appeared in at least four productions, as well as many dance contests. Although I could dance very well, and was recognized as a gifted dancer, Mrs. Roy wanted to divide up the talent and always gave me singing parts. While I was never assigned a dance routine for upcoming productions, she regularly pressed me into service to coach the dancers how to do certain routines. In a real sense, I was a choreographer and taught the Buck and Wing, steps in tap dancing, Black Bottom, and other popular dance steps and routines.

# Chapter 8

# In Pursuit of Academic Excellence

No purpose would be served to dwell too long upon what happened that day at 15th and S Streets where I was selling ice cream. Although several of my Dunbar classmates did not understand what I was doing, in later years many of them remarked that they appreciated my straightforwardness and the fact that Jim Quander did not put on any "airs" about who he was or where he came from. I had no "reputation" to protect, nor was I too "cool" to sell ice cream from a pushcart.

The most beneficial aspect of the entire ice cream experience was the great exercise that I got. Walking several miles a day, even though I was moving relatively slowly, proved to be the best medical therapy. I burned off all the excess sugar that I might have otherwise accumulated, and the fresh air in my lungs assured a good rest every night. Whenever I kept my regular medical checkups with Dr. Simmons, he remarked at what good shape I was in. Although my diabetes was never under full calm and control, as a juvenile diabetic's condition seldom was in those days, I had learned to master the condition. Checking my blood sugar at least twice a day, and determining my insulin and food intakes based upon my condition, my body components were operating in harmony.

Having earned ice cream sales money in the summers of 1934 and 1935, I concentrated upon my schoolwork and school-based activities during the academic year while still maintaining an on-and-off paper route. Dancing continued to be one of my favorite activities. I danced both solo and with partners, especially with Annette Ewell, my dance partner and girlfriend. Only this time, I was dancing at the Lincoln Colonnade located in the 1300 block of V Street, N.W., behind the Lincoln Theater. When we were coming along in high school, dance couples would demonstrate popular and incoming dances. It was like the popular American Bandstand, except that there was no television.

As we exhibited our talents, crowds gathered on the dance floor, often cheering us on. These were not necessarily competitions but rather participatory actions, great exercise, and sugar burners as far as I was concerned. I cannot recall ever getting sick during one of these stress-inducing events because my sugar level was apparently routinely reduced to within ranges of normalcy whenever I was performing in one of these activities. Because our society at large was significantly white-focused, we demonstrated primarily ballroom dancing like waltzes and fox trots, plus a dose of African-inspired tap. Both Annette and I were quite good at tap dancing. We also demonstrated a lot of swing-type dancing, a precursor to the also Afro centric inspired jitterbug era that swept the nation shortly thereafter.

Still, on several occasions, almost without much warning, health complications would occur. While I had no diabetic-related hospitalizations during my high school period, I had at least three or four periods where I was ill enough to miss several days of school at a time. One particular incident occurred in late 1935 or early 1936. It came over the police short-wave radio that James W. Quander was gravely ill, in a coma, and might not survive the weekend. While the report was greatly exaggerated, and to this day I still do not know the source of their information, when I returned to school on Monday, everyone wanted to know why I was not dead, or at least in a hospital.

Not only was I not in a coma, all that occurred was a severe insulin reaction and the summoning of an ambulance to the house to transport me to the hospital. I came out of the shock, regained my consciousness, recovered, and took the rest of the weekend easy. I did not need the ambulance, but by the time I got back to school on Monday, several of my classmates had me in the morgue, or close to it.

Incidents like this one occurred at least three other times while I was in high school, although this incident was undoubtedly the most serious. Mama and Papa were always concerned about my health, especially since my brother, Edward, had died of tuberculosis in 1924, at age 15, when I was six years old. I did not fully appreciate their concerns about me until I was a young adult. Not only were they fearful of losing another son, they fully expected that I could die at any time. When I was six years old and the diabetic condition that had already been present for a few years was officially confirmed, they were likewise aware that, given the severity and uncontrollability of my condition, I would most likely not live to be ten years of age.

They closely monitored my activities as best they could, often to the point that, at least subconsciously, I felt stifled. Many people have told me in my later years that as a young person, I was always so fatalistic and frequently negative, despite my continuous efforts to move forward, to achieve something. I never realized it at the time, but these characteristics were the result of what I had always come to believe, i.e., that I would die very soon, very soon indeed. But now, at 86 years of age, and looking back upon my life, I can see how I was treated, "favored" if you will, to the point that my next older sister, Ruth Elvira, became very jealous of me and remained so for all of her life, until her 1998 death at 85 years.

My parents' concerns were manifested and translated into monitoring both my male and female associates. They were very particular about whom I associated with and what kind of families my young friends came from. If they did not already know the other parents, it was not uncommon for discreet inquiries to be made to see who these people were and what type of values they had. The structure of Washington, D.C.'s racially segregated community of the 1920s and 1930s lent itself to knowing who people were. Most often they lived in the immediate neighborhood, since several of my friends and associates were often also our neighbors. As well, the school districts were geographically based, so there were not many people around about whom nothing was known.

I was unaware of it at the time, but my parents were already looking for a suitable future wife for me. Not a particular person, but a particular type of person. Knowing my health condition, they scrutinized all of my male and female company, the latter group with a special eye towards their personal qualities, how they expressed themselves, and in the backs of their minds, asking themselves, "Is she someone who would willingly and lovingly take over the role that we have played, and see Jim through life, especially after we are dead and gone?"

This parental protectiveness, which they manifested actively in my earlier years, was maintained for the rest of their lives. Eventually I found her for myself, and when I took her to meet my parents on that cold Sunday afternoon in March 1942, after knowing her for only an hour, Papa said, "Jim, this is really the one for you." I do not want to get too far ahead of the story at this time, because at this point in my life story, I am still in high school.

At the risk of repeating myself too often, I again underscore that the primary key to living successfully as a diabetic, juvenile or otherwise, is DISCIPLINE in all you do. With discipline, a diabetic will meet with success, and learn much along the way. As I completed my high school years and got involved in academics, extracurricular activities, and entrepreneurial pursuits, it was the sense of discipline that I had developed earlier that saw me through, and this same discipline has sustained me to this day.

I participated in both the debate club and the yearbook and gained a reputation as a "Modern Thinker," a moniker based in part upon my debating and in part upon the name of a then popular magazine which looked towards a brighter day to come. So I was cast as "the Modern Thinker" and debated subjects such as new careers for women, family-related issues, and the need for teachers to be professional in their work, which included effective teaching methods. While some of this effort bordered on public speaking, a related topic, it was under the umbrella of the debate club. Students took opposing viewpoints, and we all worked to develop our differing attitudes and ideas to see how well we could handle diverse topics.

I remember the day that I argued that the Breed method for teaching French was better than any other. My favorite teacher,

Mrs. Hundley, who used this method, helped me to prepare. This method was all-inclusive and was designed to use the natural human senses in learning a foreign language, particularly the sense of sight (to see the words), the sense of hearing (to hear the words spoken), and the sense of touch (to write the words down), thus creating a mastery of the subject. It worked very well for me and is the reason why I still have significant French proficiency today, well more than 60 years beyond my last class of high school French.

One of the hot topics of the day was racial segregation, a recurring topic that the debate club argued about each year. During my turn, I was selected to argue against the injustice of racial segregation. I freely stirred Adolph Hitler and his Aryan race superiority concepts into my debunking the racial inferiority of people of African descent. I often wonder how I would have functioned on the other side of this issue, as the opposing students had the unenviable task of defending segregation, arguing that people of color were inferior to whites, yet approaching their subject in a reasoned, calm manner.

In many ways I admired their efforts greatly because it made us all realize that people have differing viewpoints, and that sometimes we are called upon to defend an unpopular side of an issue, even if we do not personally agree with the principles being extolled.

As noted above, when Drs. Wilder and Simmons refused to allow me to have fuller high school participation, particularly in ROTC and swimming for health reasons, I determined that I would not be as denied as they would have it. I decided to make up for my inability to do military and to swim with a stellar academic performance. I set my sights on the National Honor Society, an achievement that I knew was within my grasp. While some of the guys looked good in their uniforms, and others caught the girls' attention with their talents in the swimming pool, I decided that Jim Quander was going to get his share by letting it be known to all that he was a really good, focused, and determined student.

I told my children on several occasions that I received only one "C" grade in high school, the rest being all "As" and "Bs," and I proved it to them in 1999 as we were researching for this book. How I got that one high school "C" grade is a story unto itself. It was September 1934, and I had just been enrolled in Gladys Toliver's College Algebra class. Miss Toliver was a respected math teacher, but it was believed that she also gave favor and greater attention to those students whose parents she either knew or who were particularly prominent in the local community. On this particular day, she asked Highwarden Just, my friend, a math question. He did not seem to know the answer. After some prompting, she said to him, "Highwarden, I know that you must know the answer to this question, because your father is a professor at Howard University." His father was Ernest E. Just (1883-1941), an internationally renowned multidisciplinary scientist (cytologist, zoologist, biologist), who had taught biology to many of the colored doctors during their undergraduate studies at Howard University. As well, in 1911, also at Howard, he was one of the four original founders of the Omega Psi Phi Fraternity, Inc., of which I am a proud, sustaining member.

Incensed at such overt pandering and favoritism, I blurted out, "Miss Toliver, his dad is not in this class. Why should Highwarden know? And, you don't know whether his dad even knows the answer. You have to grade him (Highwarden), not his dad." She gave me such a look, that if looks could kill, I would have been dead on the floor in front of everyone. And to this day, classmates still recall that fateful day in September 1934, when James Quander and Gladys Toliver tied up. We were hardly equals. I was a 16-year-old outspoken student, and she was in charge of the National Honor Society. While I did not realize it that day, that incident put an end to my opportunity to be selected for induction into the society. Further, I never anticipated that this incident would still be a subject of conversation almost 70 years later.

A few minutes later, during that same class, I asked a math question and was very curtly and sarcastically told by Miss Toliver, "We'll get to that issue next semester." She refused to answer my question. Everybody in the class knew that I was in for a rough ride. Seemingly, as if by Divine Providence, Mr. Smith, our principal, entered the class within a moment or two thereafter and advised that there were too many people enrolled in the class. He wanted volunteers to leave this class and to enroll in the same course being offered during this academic period by Mr. Ulysses Bassett, an older teacher.

Already anticipating that I was in for a very rough time with Miss Toliver, my hand was the first one to go up. Unwittingly, I jumped out of the frying pan and into the fire. Mr. Bassett, although a Yale University graduate and the son of a former United States Ambassador to Haiti, was concluding a long teaching career, and he no longer seemed to grasp the subject matter the way that I thought he should have.

Maybe he was distracted by something, but at any rate, the class had a terrible time getting through, with his handing out several "D" and "F" grades, and sending these prominent Negroes' children to summer school. With the exception of one or two "B" grades and maybe two or three "C" grades, all the rest were below that. I got one of the "C" grades and was glad for it. Essentially, I taught myself the course, and his poor communication of the subject matter only added great confusion to my effort to understand the material.

That one "C" grade alone should not have kept me from National Honor Society membership. Members were inducted twice per year. There were at least four induction ceremonies held during my junior and senior high years. Yet not once was I approached for membership or even given any consideration of which I am aware. Each semester, as the students' names were called in the awards assemblies, I kept waiting for them to say, "James Quander, please come forward and be inducted into the National Honor Society." But it never happened. Never!

I wanted to demonstrate that despite my health limitations, despite my diabetic condition, that Jim Quander could still do. But I was never accorded the chance to register my accomplishment with my peer group and am psychologically damaged by that denial to this day. I can only conclude that I was the victim of outright discrimination inflicted by a vengeful teacher who decided to have the last word.

My fellow students routinely asked me each and every semester, "Jim, why haven't you been inducted with us? We know that you are one of the top students in the class and always on the honor roll. You should be inducted, too." My close friends and other associates, including Eleanor Felton, Anna King, Almira Perry, Highwarden Just, Joseph Dwyer were all inducted, and my grades were on par or better than theirs. But I was left back.

Why no other faculty member or administrator successfully countered her with regard to my membership remains a mystery to me, but I do believe that in certain people's minds, the idea that I had health problems, the nature of which they did not necessarily know the details of, made me a less-likely candidate for membership. By today's standards, in which we emphasize full citizen participation, and leaving no one behind, it would be ludicrous and discriminatory on its face to exclude a qualified person with physical limitations from the National Honor Society just because he did not participate in a mandatory ROTC or swimming program for documented health reasons.

Yet in 1935 and 1936, it was exactly this type of discrimination to which I was exposed and victimized by. Remember, women had only been voting since 1920, and African-Americans were very much second-class citizens. Being victimized by my own racial group was not that unusual, given that I was not one of the favored.

Had my parents been prominent Negroes in town—professionally, economically, and socially connected—things probably would have been different, as they often were when the son or daughter of someone "important" had academic or other difficulties. But my parents, loving as they were, and concerned as they were for my health and well-being, were very docile; and they allowed the teachers to prevail with all of their children. I guess in a way they felt that the teachers knew best, and perhaps they simply did not feel competent to question the system, Miss Toliver, or why I was not inducted.

The subject came up again in 1999 at the Dunbar High School Class of 1936, 63rd Annual Reunion luncheon, when Eleanor Felton, a dear classmate and lifelong friend, noted that she always knew that it was wrong that I was not inducted, and that I should have been given recognition for my academic achievements. I competed head-to-head against several students who eventually went to Harvard, Yale, Smith, Howard University, and other top colleges and universities.

Had there been organizations similar to those that have germinated from the passage of the Americans With Disabilities Act, the overt ignoring of my qualifications for the National Honor Society would have been a "cause célébre," a primary case for highlighting acts of discrimination.

While I had the academics in place, my parents had sustained economic losses and had no money, my father having lost his produce business during the Great Depression. Therefore, while I prepared to graduate from Dunbar High School, my academic future was anything but certain. I was determined to continue my education and to go to college somewhere. Considering my diabetic condition, it is doubtful that I would have been allowed to go away to any college or university. Still, it would have been nice to know that I had been recruited and accepted by at least one.

To some extent, a number of the Dunbar graduates were pre-selected for the Ivy League schools by the faculty, the application for admission apparently being only part of the process. But I had no connections to be a part of that group, not being a part of the "insider's club" or my family being socially prominent.

Graduation was in mid-June in 1936, and although I marched in the commencement exercises with my class, I still had to complete one more class before they would give me my diploma. This was a leftover from my Scarlet Fever days when I decided to make up the lost semester by going to summer school every year so that I could graduate on time—with the class of 1936.

I took an English class that summer and earned my final high school grade, another "A." Pending completion of my high school requirements, I had been provisionally accepted for admission to the recently created Miner Teachers College, whose predecessor institutions had been operating since 1879 as the public normal school for Negro students. Most of the students enrolled there were pursuing professions in teaching.

One day in late 1935, as graduation day drew closer, my dad called me into his room and told me that he wanted to talk to me. I knew from the look on his face, tone of voice, and overall demeanor that we were about to have a serious conversation. What started out as a father-son talk degenerated into an emotional breakdown as my dad started to cry when he told me that he had been able to provide a college education for Joseph Pearson, my older brother, and to send Cora, my older sister, to nursing school in New York. But now he was flat broke, due to the Great Depression, and he had not a cent to send me to college.

He felt like a failure, as his honor-roll son, who had worked hard and distinguished himself academically, and as a young entrepreneur, was now faced with not being able to continue with his education. But at that moment, the tables turned. He was upset and crying about what he could not do for me. Yet I was calm and collected, comfortable with my entrepreneurial abilities, and the fact that I knew how to make money. At that moment I realized that if I was going to college, and indeed I was going, I would have to pay for it myself. Subsequently I was able to do just that. Not only did I pay for my own college, I also paid for my younger sister, Catherine's, initial tuition, too.

Because of my newspaper routes and my various jobs, I always had money squirreled away, and it was enough to give me confidence that I could assemble whatever additional I needed. By today's standards, the tuition costs were low; but in 1936, when more than 25% of the nation's work force was unemployed, and the ratio was much higher among African-Americans, getting tuition together was difficult.

As school was ending and the Class of 1936 planned activities incidental to graduation, there were a number of picnics and parties. This was a particularly emotional time for many of us, the end of our personal eras of having been together for several years— from elementary through high school in some cases. Many of the more socially prominent classmates were holding elegant affairs, to which several others of us were not invited. Somehow, I was invited to a number of these graduation-related events, but I elected not to attend in most cases.

I never developed much of a liking for picnics: it always seemed that the food was not ready whenever it was my scheduled time to eat, or they did not serve things that were on my diet. So rather than be put into a situation where I would decline to eat when the food was served, on the basis of having eaten before I went to the event, I simply elected to express my regrets and to not attend.

Although I had no graduation party of my own, I took a modest advantage of a few activities and attended the celebrations of a few of my closest friends and acquaintances. Out of precaution, I always ate before I went, having learned as a young child that I could not rely upon what someone who was unaware of my dietary needs might serve, and when. If the fun got to be good, the food might well be delayed in being set out; and when it was set out, it might be pork ribs, or greens, or something spicy that was not on my diabetic diet.

By having eaten before, I always knew that I was pretty much under control; and when the food finally did get set out, I could pick and choose, and choose nothing, if that was how I felt. It got to be somewhat universal as parents and some of my contemporaries would say to me, "Jim, come on and eat," or "Jim, you need to have some more. No wonder you are so small." Usually they had no clue that I had already eaten and felt uncertain about how I would be affected by what they were offering.

As previously mentioned with my selling ice cream, I was focused and disciplined in my eating and not tempted to succumb to their kind-hearted inducements. I learned early to simply say "No!" when the situation warranted, and I have stuck to "No!" ever since, where necessary. Because I needed to monitor my sugar intake so carefully, I could not be too concerned about hurting other people's feelings by declining to eat their food. It was my health and safety, not their egos, which were at stake.

In my planning, I often elected to partake in the desserts, and "saved" myself for them. By having carefully monitored myself earlier, when dessert was served, I usually took the smallest piece of cake or pie. When fruit or some item that had the lowest sugar content was offered, that was the first thing I reached for.

I was 18 years old, making my own food-related decisions. My personal attitude and presence at these type of activities lent an atmosphere to the overall event, demonstrating that Jim Quander was still a regular guy, even if he did not eat the ribs and greens. Yet I still partook in the reason for the celebration, and having a piece of cake, for example, was a typical example of this.

My summer job for 1936 was elevator operator at the Windermere apartment building, 1825 New Hampshire Avenue,

N.W., just a block from our home. My dad knew the custodian there, and when an opening came for the position, he advocated me before the management. Those were deemed to be "colored jobs" in those days, as the continued level of racism and discrimination in the job market, even in the federal government, limited what a young person of African extraction could expect in the labor market. Because of racial restrictions, whenever I entered the building, I had to go around to the back and enter through the "colored entrance." The only reason why I was tolerated and present was because of a service being rendered to the white-only residents.

Still, the operating policies for this building were not as severe as the policies for the Albermarle, located just across the street at 1830 17th Street. There the elevator was segregated into two separate cages. The white cage, which was elegant and nicely appointed was on the top, while the cage on the bottom looked more like someplace where animals would be held temporarily, just before they were slaughtered. The elevator could stop twice on each floor. This was intentionally done to keep the colored help "in its place," and out of sight, which meant that the white residents would never have to share an elevator with a person of color, other than the one person who was in direct and immediate service operating the elevator.

All day long, ring, ring, ring. Up and down! Up and down! If ever I had not intended to go to college before, running that elevator and attempting to cater to diverse white people made me more certain than ever that continuing my education was absolutely necessary. While certain of the residents of this all-white building probably thought that I had little or no common sense or a mind of my own, there was also a significant number who demonstrated otherwise.

They befriended me and asked me questions about my future and myself. Observing that I was doing my English summer school homework or always had a book in my hand between rings, this group was an inspiration, some telling me that they too operated elevators and did valet service when they were in college. They urged me on to continue with my education. Running that elevator was a great experience: it addressed several components of where I was in my life.

I was just completing high school and was exposed to my first full time job, which could have been my career if I had not been so steadfastly focused otherwise. For the first time in my life, I was having close and personal contact with Caucasians, many of whom were middle class, even though my entering their apartments was primarily to deliver groceries from the elevator or to provide some modest valet-related services.

Yet those brief contacts and the diverse attitudes that many of them displayed were enough for me to understand and appreciate the differences within their own respective racial group. Some were better off in all ways—education, employment, and culture—while others, even though residing in the same building, were far less well off and sometimes showed their lower levels of exposure and ignorance with negative attitudes, either stated or implied, towards me and the other persons of color on staff.

I took my English class at Dunbar as early as possible, then made a dash to work, went home for lunch each day, and finished that job with a renewed attitude and determination to do very well and succeed in my next great adventure—college.

# Chapter 9

# On to College and Other Challenges

As previously mentioned, Miner Teachers College was created by an Act of the U.S. Congress in 1929, having been germinated in former institutions created to educate Negro students. As a newly accredited college for the purpose of training students to be teachers, Miner graduated its first class in 1933.

Its namesake, Myrtilla Miner, a Caucasian woman from Brookfield, New York, had come to Washington, D.C., after teaching plantation owners' daughters in Mississippi. Upset that the Mississippi slave children and their parents were being denied the book knowledge they thirsted for, she agitated for permission to at least teach the young black children but was told by her employers in the most derisively racial terms that if she wanted to teach niggers, she should go North. She did just that and migrated to Washington, D.C., in about 1851. Upon arrival in Washington, Miner was outraged at the virtually nonexistent opportunities available for the education of young Negro children.

With only $100.00 and three students, she opened her school "for free girls of the Negro race," as noted in Geneva C. Turner's history of Miner Teachers College. Quickly the school grew, and Harriet Beecher Stowe, the author of *Uncle Tom's Cabin*, donated $1,000.00 from the proceeds of the book for building a place to house the school. Miner was outspoken about the abhorrent educational conditions and lobbied hard for public education for all youth—black and white—to be sponsored by the local government. Falling largely upon deaf ears, except for those who heard her pleas and responded with threats to do bodily harm to her for her decision to teach black females, Miner's efforts were not widely embraced within the white community, but with a few exceptions. To the black population, however, she was a champion. They embraced her dedication and determination without reservation and supported her efforts to educate their people. Before her early death in 1860, Congress recognized her school as an integral part of the educational program of the District of Columbia and incorporated it into the regular public school system, although naturally segregated by race. It was more than fitting that the college created later should also be named in her memory: her legacy and her contribution lives on in me and my generation, and generations now to come.

Integration came to the D.C. public school system as a result of the May 17, 1954, Supreme Court decision in *Brown vs. the Board of Education of Topeka, Kansas*, and its D.C. companion case, *Bolling vs. Sharpe*. In 1955 Miner became a part of the merged Miner (black) and Wilson (white) Teachers Colleges. Renamed the District of Columbia Teachers College, it is now an integral part of the University of the District of Columbia. The Miner building, located directly across the street from Howard University, is owned by the university and soon will become a national cultural and historical center for African-American history, culture, and archives, an expansion of the current Moorland Spingarn Research Center already located at the university.

But when I, as a new student in September 1936, first climbed the mountain of steps up to the Miner building, located at Georgia Avenue and Euclid Street, N.W., integration of the races in education was still just a thought, a hope, and a dream. It was something that I always knew within my heart was the right thing to have happen, but I was personally powerless to do anything about it. Or so I thought. College days would be a new awakening for me, an opportunity to not only explore new academic ideas and goals, but a chance to intellectually interact with a limited number of white people, many of whom were college students at the nearby all-white Wilson Teachers College located at Eleventh and Harvard Streets, N.W.

My father cried on that afternoon in late 1935 when he called me into the bedroom and told me that he had lost all of his money due to the failure of his fresh produce business. I remember saying to him, "Papa, you gave me a good home life as a child. You were a good father. And what you gave to me, no one can take from me. Ambition! That's the gift you gave me, Papa. And you don't have to apologize to me. I'm going to make it. I will make it." I told him not to worry, and that Kitty and I would both be fine.

I was perfectly satisfied with the challenge. I was not yet 18 years of age, but the entrepreneur in me, who was never far below the surface, was still very much activated. I realized that if I were going to attend college, I would have to pay for it myself, and with money saved from my ice cream and paper routes, I was further determined to not spend any of my savings unnecessarily. College was my goal, and the money needed to pay the expense was mine alone to provide. At Dunbar I was in an academic atmosphere where virtually everyone was college bound, and if you were not, then you were considered to be the oddball.

Academically, college was more demanding than high school, but I was up to the challenge and did well. I liked math and took classes in statistics and economics; and during much of my professional career, I would be known as a both a statistician and an economist.

In terms of diabetes, the summer of 1936 was one of the calmest periods in my diabetic life. I was fully regimented to my eating habits, got plenty of exercise playing softball and basketball, worked my job operating the elevator in a racially-segregated apartment house, and managed to get an "A" in my summer school English class, plus process all of the final paperwork to begin college. Working full time, I temporarily let my paper delivery route go but returned to it later. It still amazes me to recall how busy I was getting ready for college, yet my health seemed to be in a good balance. Believe me, it would not last.

As noted earlier, Dunbar was unique: not only nurturing but also rigorously academic. Yearly graduates went to places like Harvard, Yale, Radcliff, Smith, Sarah Lawrence, other Ivy League schools, plus Howard University. I had the smarts to go to those institutions, too; but coming from a background where my parents had no clue about how to access those places, I was left to my own devices. Fortunately, the "device," Miner, was a good alternative resource for me. But think about it. The year 1936 was the height of the Great Depression, yet Dunbar graduates were focused upon getting into college, to become the new generation of young Negro leaders—the doctors, lawyers, teachers, ministers, government workers, and other positions—despite the economic hard times.

While I had no desire to become a teacher, I was focused upon earning a college degree; and the economic hard times were merely an obstacle to overcome, not an absolute barrier to my determination. Miner was the means to a Bachelor of Science degree from an accredited college. I took the opportunity and ran with it.

Despite the Great Depression, the overwhelming majority of my Dunbar classmates also graduated from college and went on to become major leaders in their own respective professions, including one United States senator, Edward W. Brooke, III, a Washington, D.C., native and a Republican. He represented Massachusetts, and in 1966, he was elected as the first African-American to sit in the U.S. Senate since the Reconstruction era ended. He served two terms, until 1979.

Upon arriving at Miner and already knowing several of my fellow students, I dropped into a comfort level not dissimilar to what I had experienced at Dunbar. I also learned of the work-study opportunities offered through the National Youth Administration (NYA), co-founded by Dr. Mary McLeod Bethune, to benefit all American youth, without regard to race. She also headed the Negro Division of the program on the national level. I worked in the book room as an NYA youth at Dunbar, and at Miner I was immediately eligible to work in the cafeteria and kept that job throughout my entire four years.

Entering college was a major adjustment. First, the teachers addressed the students as "Mister" or "Miss"—far more formal than at Dunbar. Several of the teachers had cultivated reputations that mandated that the students were on their own—not babies or children any longer, but adults who had to work independent of the supervision that we had become accustomed to over the prior kindergarten to 12th grade school years.

As well, some teachers basked in their reputations of "to be feared," which inflicted emotional distress upon many of us young freshmen. And that same emotional distress was the primary thing that my doctors told me I must avoid at all costs. I had learned the hard way, and frequently, that emotional distress can inflict significant adverse effects upon a diabetic's condition. To be figuratively thrown into such a situation almost without warning was an emotional challenge that I had to address.

From time to time when I hear young African-Americans say, "It's a Black thing!"—referring to some item as culturally inherent in African-American culture—I am immediately thrown back to those Miner days, September 1936 to June 1940, and later comparisons with my graduate school professors, the majority of whom were Caucasian. I noticed a very discernible difference in attitude between the African-American professors and their few white counterparts. The main difference was an air of accomplishment and arrival that the black professors had—the "I've got mine, but you've got yours to get" attitude—which their white counterparts simply did not possess.

I concluded early on that this attitude was inherent in the black culture, since few of us had earned college degrees prior to my generation. Even in my generation, the overall number of college graduates was still quite small. Therefore, it seemed that to those who possessed a degree, even if only a bachelor's degree, this was a basis for a self-imposed sense of superiority, even if it was falsely based. And here they were, perhaps only one or two generations away from slavery in some cases, and already we had become so important. While not all of the Negro professors possessed and exuded this air of having "arrived," this self-importance about themselves, enough of them did possess this characteristic as to be rather universal.

Conversely, the white professors were very unassuming, perhaps because higher education was considered more a matter of right routine and less a privilege possessed by a relative few. In that totally different atmosphere, they saw no need to pretend or convey a sense of exclusivity that their Negro counterparts relished. What

I observed at Miner, and later to some extent also at Howard University, was so different in this regard from my other academic pursuits at Lake Forest University, the University of Chicago, and the Hudson Shore Labor School, New York, this group of schools being white institutions.

But my focus now was not to be spooked by emotional distress, but to learn to roll with the academic punches. I learned quickly, unlike some of my classmates who were immediately afflicted with emotional blockage that made freshman year a greater challenge than it otherwise would normally be.

Although I never planned to become a teacher, it was hard to tell anybody that fact: they would want to know why I was there if I did not intend to teach. Many of us had no teaching intent, but we did not have the money to attend Howard University. As well, there were few scholarships for young African-Americans to go anywhere else. Although I flirted with the idea of becoming a math teacher, that hope got dashed early when it was noted that the opening for math teachers was quite limited in the Colored Division of the D.C. Public School system, and that the critical need now was for young Negro men in the elementary school level.

I targeted my Bachelor of Science degree curriculum towards elementary education, and my academic career at Miner was turned in that direction to prepare me to teach the fourth, fifth, and sixth grades. One of my first teachers was Irene Miller Reid, the only person who taught me in junior high school (math), and then again in college (Elementary Mathematical Analysis). Because I also had an interest in statistics, I took courses in that subject and would later use those credits as an entree into a career in the federal government.

While this was one of the most stable periods of my diabetic history, history also repeated itself in Mrs. Reid's class. In junior high school, while attempting to take a math test, I went into a diabetic shock, and my entire math recollection went completely blank. I told her that I could not function and that something was wrong. Without interrogating me that day in the early 1930s at Garnett-Patterson, she sent me home and told me to come back and take the test the next day.

But now, six or so years later, I had another diabetic reaction at the blackboard in her math class and went into some type of a trance and could not function. The class knew that there was something wrong with me, but they did not know what it was. Mrs. Reid immediately recognized that I was ill, led me away from the blackboard, and sent me to the infirmary to see the school nurse, Mrs. Helen Jackson, who in later years would become a personal friend.

But Miner was a small place, and the last thing I wanted to have happen would be for the school community to learn that I was a diabetic. Rather than go to the infirmary and tell Mrs. Jackson what had occurred, I found solace in the hallway, took some hard candy, which I always kept with me, and came around to my full senses within a short time. I was in a cold, cold sweat, and emotionally drained by the experience, but my "secret" was safe. I always suspected that Mrs. Reid had figured out that I was a diabetic, but since she never asked, I never told her at that time.

As I mentioned earlier, years later when I saw her socially and mentioned my ailment to her, although she never verbalized a response, she had an "I thought so!" look on her face. What she probably had suspected all along was now confirmed. Both of those incidents underscored how important it was for people to know that you have a particular ailment, because had I deteriorated and emergency medical personnel had been summoned, they would not have known what was wrong, or how to treat me. At a time when a few precious moments could mean the difference between life and death, I easily could have lost that battle and died.

If I had any doubts about whether I wanted to teach elementary school, they were clearly removed when it came time to practice teach. I was assigned to practice teach a sixth grade class at the President James Monroe school, located on Irving Street at Georgia Avenue, N.W., just above the Miner building. I considered the experience to be six weeks of hell.

While the children seemed bright, cooperative and energetic, my supervising teacher, Miss Lillian Duckett, proved to be the problem. A dyed-in-the-wool professional, she was so critical and demanding of any student assigned to her, that virtually all of us, including me, reassessed our attitudes towards teaching, based

upon her approach to it. It was my senior year, and I was focused
upon graduating, taking the teacher's and other pre-employment
examinations, and finding a job. In her critique of my approach to
teaching, she complimented me several times, telling me that she
could see that I was really showing that I could teach, but on a
much higher level. She urged me to continue pursing a higher level
of education and to consider becoming a college-level teacher.

Still, during this six-week practice teaching stint, she wanted
me to focus on writing original stories for the children and making
up new examinations from scratch. When I queried why it was
necessary to do that, considering that there were already
professionals who wrote those stories and prepared those tests
according to grade levels, her reply was that every teacher needed
to know how to do it from his or her own initiative. She was
unrelenting in her insistence. Since I already had a full plate, and
this six-week practice-teaching assignment was a graduation
requirement, I had neither the desire nor an interest in writing
stories or creating sixth-grade-level examinations, and was
immediately turned off from both her and a teaching career.

Washington, D.C., is a government town; and jobs for African-
Americans in government in the late 1930s/early 1940s were
largely restricted to the postal service, the Government Printing
Office, messengers, or as elevator operators. The best entry-level
job was considered to be the post office. I decided during my senior
year to take the postal employee's examination, and when I was
eventually called, I gladly accepted.

My college days at Miner were not all books—far from it. I had
already been involved with theater since junior high school, and
Miner presented ever more opportunities for theater and other
extracurricular activities. I immediately got involved with show
business and was involved in several musical productions during
my four years there.

Miner had a yearly big carnival of dance, song, and drama, and
each year I was a key part of it. I had already established myself as
a singer, and upon arrival at Miner, several of my Dunbar
classmates who were a year or two ahead of me, already knew of
my singing and dancing abilities. I was asked to help choreograph
tap dance routines, including teaching the popular sisters,

Jacquelyn and Arlyn Gordon of Chicago, how to do the *buck and wing* and the *over the top* steps in tap. They were great dancers and well received in our theatrical productions. They came to Washington in the mid 1930s when their mother secured a federal appointment at the Bureau of Printing and Engraving through Oscar DePriest, the first African-American U.S. Congressman elected after Reconstruction ended.

I auditioned for and was selected to sing several solos during that era, including *Don't Worry About Me*. It went like this:

> *Don't worry about me*
> *I'll get along*
> *Forget about me*
> *Be happy my love*
>
> *And so the story goes*
> *Let's call it a day*
> *The sensible way*
> *And still be friends*
>
> *Look out for yourself*
> *Should be the rule*
> *Give your heart and love*
> *To whomever you love*
> *Oh don't be a fool*
>
> *Darling, why should you cling*
> *To some faded thing*
> *That used to be*
> *If you can forget*
> *Don't worry about me*

I sang that during my sophomore year, 1937-38. Those productions were diversified, too. Sometimes we had concerts that were more classically focused in the music. But during this era, I also sang *Gina Nina Mia, The Desert Song, One Alone, I'm So Wild About Harry*, plus others. More than 60 years later, I can still sing those tunes, and most often still remember all of the words. Now that is remarkable, since sometimes I can't remember what happened yesterday, but I can recall events and details of events that occurred that many years ago.

One person who was particularly consistent in both his music and his presence was Dr. Billy Taylor, the great pianist, who at 80 years of age is still going strong as both an interview host on *CBS Sunday* and a major luminary at the Kennedy Center here in Washington, D.C. In high school, and then continuing on through college, Billy was an invited guest to all of the parties, and he played in many of the theatrical productions at Dunbar. Because of his vast knowledge, talent, and versatility, he was much in demand and well appreciated.

He always seemed to be attached to a piano, and in those days when the amount of prerecorded music was much less than it is today, it was common and popular for Billy to either play while we danced, or to accompany the records and give us a lot extra as we danced the night away.

My point is that despite being a juvenile diabetic and living with the realization that anything can go wrong at any minute, I lived a full college-era life; and nothing that was offered was refused because of my health. When I did not feel well or up to a particular activity, I simply declined and skipped the event. But that did not occur too often, and never on the night of a big production. On those occasions, my mind prevailed over my body to keep me calm. In college I was still dedicated to keeping the "secret," i.e., that Jim Quander was a diabetic. The last thing I needed was to have a stress-induced insulin reaction on the stage with all of the excitement that was inherent when a stage production was actively ongoing.

Maybe I should have shared my situation with Helen Jackson, the school nurse, who in later life, along with her daughter, Lucy Neal, became a good friend. But Miner was small, and she was very social, so I did not wish to confide in her or anyone else. In retrospect, it was dangerous for me not to have shared this information. If anything of a truly serious or emergency nature related to diabetes had occurred, no one would have immediately suspected the condition, or known what to do about it. But the very private Jim Quander did not wish to be potentially ostracized if someone broke his confidence, and the recipients of the information elected to use this newfound knowledge about my health against me. Based upon the few instances when someone found out, and this did not occur often, the negative attitude expressed about diabetics was not unlike the experience that AIDS patients frequently face now.

In later years when Mrs. Jackson learned of my condition, she chastised me, saying, "Quander, why didn't you tell me?" I thought to myself, "If I had shared that information, would you have kept your counsel?" That was a chance I was not willing to take. As well, I did not trust the security of the medical records that were kept in the office. Who had access to those records? I elected to say nothing about diabetes and to take my chances that nothing would happen for which my family and I would be sorry later. Fortunately, nothing of such an emergency nature occurred during my college days.

During my entire Miner years, I had a work-study assignment in the cafeteria. Usually working as a team with my classmate and friend, Jeff Lane, we washed dishes after lunch and dinner, since many students maintained long hours in the building to study. I earned $21.00 a month through the National Youth Administration (NYA), wrapping up my daily work about 8:00 p.m. nightly. This experience also carried through as a summer job in the U.S. Department of Commerce cafeteria.

In both places, staff generally tried to get me to eat my dinners there while working. However, because of my strict diet and my discipline to adhere to my own regimen, I rarely ate in either cafeteria. Both locations cooked with an institutional approach to food preparation, often using fat meat for seasoning. Rather than take a chance and get sick, I usually declined and waited until I got home to eat dinner. Mama had always prepared food for me, and it was waiting when I got home each night.

Between these two jobs, plus occasional newspaper routes and other odd jobs, I earned enough money to meet all of my college tuition expenses, with enough money left over for my kid sister Kitty's tuition, also at Miner in 1939 and 1940. Living at home, I had no other expenses and continued to enjoy basic support from my parents. I belonged to a co-ed social club, the "Sporty Ques," and the members studied together and went to basketball games at Murray's Casino, located on U Street between Vermont Avenue and Ninth Street, N.W. We also planned our social activities together and went to dances as a group.

In 1937, I even joined the Rho Delta Rho Fraternity at Miner, a one-chapter-only organization that was so full of zip that our basketball team, of which I was not a member, managed to defeat all of the national-level fraternity teams for the championship, including the Omega Psi Phi Fraternity team. After college days, I too would join Omega Psi Phi, a prestigious fraternity of African-American professionals, which is still an integral part of my life. Joining Omega was a lifelong commitment that I share with over 100,000 African-American men who have likewise committed themselves to its cardinal principles of Manhood, Scholarship, Perseverance, and Uplift.

As I entered my senior year at Miner in September 1939, the war clouds, which had been gathering in Europe, finally precipitated into the Second World War. Already several members of the class were excited about the prospects of war, and later many of my male classmates would be called to war. Some would even die in the conflict. But in September 1939, the war was not on my mind. I was focused upon graduating, getting a job, and being prepared for the unknown that lay ahead.

Miner being a teachers college, we routinely signed up to take the teacher's qualification and certification examination, a necessary precondition to being hired in the District of Columbia. Annually there were always new vacancies, and likewise a scramble for the limited number of positions in the Colored Division.

# Chapter 10

# A Juvenile Diabetic in Pursuit of a Career

As I noted before, I had no desire to become an elementary school teacher, and despite Lillian Duckett's urging that I pursue teaching on the college level, I rejected that as well. But we were the new crop of graduates, and our professors at Miner urged us to consider new career opportunities, opportunities that still hardly existed for African-Americans. Despite the official racial segregation that was our daily lot, there was an increasing dissatisfaction, even among many of the whites in the community, about the enforced racial separation that relegated black men and women to the lower rungs of the ladder.

There was no loud shrill or crescendo from the white community urging that the Negro be given a real opportunity to prove that we as a race could perform just as well as the majority, if only given equal access to education, followed by like access to jobs and economic opportunities. But there were isolated pockets in the community where a few influential people were beginning to make definite movements to accommodate qualified black citizens and give us consideration for professional career opportunities in the federal government.

It was towards those few opportunities that several of our Miner professors steered us. Unknown to us, our professors were quietly evaluating who they felt would be the best candidates to pursue the few federal government positions that were beginning to open up. I had already made it known among certain people that I had no interest in teaching, so I was one of those persons they sought to target elsewhere.

One of my professors, Dr. Teresa Brown, who taught Reading Techniques, became a mentor as well and encouraged me to pursue a placement in the federal government as an economist or statistician, since I had shown a love and facility for those areas. I followed her advice. In the fall of 1939 I took and passed the junior professional assistant, civil service and the Federal Bureau of Investigation (FBI) examinations. Sixty-five years later, I am still waiting to hear from the FBI, which did not hire Negro professionals at that time. I then made applications through the U.S. Civil Service Commission that resulted in a series of job placement interviews.

My family was upset about the prospects of my seeking federal employment outside of the realm of designated "colored jobs." Although Mama and Papa were kind and loving parents, dedicated to my happiness in every way, they did not understand what was happening. Their concern was primarily that my health must be protected; and for me to venture into the unknown would surely be stressful, and perhaps even dangerous, not only due to diabetes, but also because of the racial climate.

They both urged me to not pursue this new path but rather to stick with the safe tried-and-true path that so many of my fellow Negro college graduates had been fulfilling for the last several years. To me, Papa's recommendation was out of character, as he had always been such an upbeat person, urging people to try something new. But this time he was different, more defensive. My older brother, Joseph Pearson, echoed the same sentiments.

His wife, Algetha, felt differently and urged me to follow my dreams and to place my trust in both God and what the professors at Miner were attempting to do. She vocalized that our race would never get ahead if we did not challenge the white man who was still holding us back, and that one of the best ways to get ahead was to prove that we were just as qualified. First, we needed to graduate from college, and then sign up for all qualifying examinations, interviews, and jobs that we could get. She said, "Go ahead, James. Do it! I'm supporting you on this one."

Not just a few eyebrows were raised when I showed up at the Civil Service Commission for my first job interview, appropriately dressed and quite knowledgeable about the role of a statistician and how statistics played integrally into the economy. But despite everything, including the sincere best wishes of some of my interviewers, at the end of that interview I was told in blunt terms that no agency was hiring Negroes as mathematicians, statisticians, or as economists. One interviewer advised me that they were taking the liberty of referring my job application to the U.S. Post Office for consideration.

Another of the interviewers told me, "Young man, you are ahead of your time, and perhaps *some day* things will change, and Negroes will be hired for these positions. But in the meantime, we are referring your application to the local post office." I did not go to college and earn a bachelor of science degree to become a mailman, but the reality of the situation was that diversity in job opportunity for the colored citizens in 1940 was very limited.

If you did not become a doctor, lawyer, minister, or teacher, then you virtually had no access to becoming a professional, as the federal government's positions for colored were generally limited.

But still the message of the process that a select few of my classmates and I went through in 1940 was laid out clearly. We were the new crop of young, bright, and academically prepared Negro students, fresh out of college and eager to learn and be of service. The day was soon coming when the white majority could no longer openly discriminate against us because of our race and not have to face the consequences of their actions.

By continuing to train, by continuing to apply, and by being available, we were carrying the banner for our race and were the conscience of the white minority who sided with us. Soon we would be in better positions to assure that at last the Class of 1940, and the other classes of African-American students that followed, would be readily accepted into career fields for which we had prepared ourselves. Eventually World War II and the sudden demands for qualified personnel would change the complexion of several offices in the federal government, but that action was still a little ways in the near future.

I got a call from the U. S. Post Office in March 1940 to begin working immediately, but they agreed to defer until after graduation. The effect was that I had been hired for my first post-college job, while most of my classmates, who were hoping to teach and also awaiting the results from the teacher placement examination, were still searching for a placement.

And so on July 1, 1940, James William Quander reported to the U.S. Post Office as a substitute mail carrier and was assigned to the 15th and U Streets station, just two blocks from my house at 17th, between "T" and "U" streets. The rate of pay and long-term benefits were pretty good for 1940 as the nation was finally emerging from the Great Depression. It was a job that allowed for a lot of overtime, and I took full advantage of that option, too; and in all likelihood I was instantly one of the better-paid members of my graduating class.

I had been an early riser for years, given that I delivered the *Washington Post* in the morning seven days a week, and the *Sunday Star*, also in the wee hours. During that entire one-year post office employment, I arose between 3:30 a.m. and 4:00 a.m. My usual daily routine in 1940 consisted of testing my blood sugar and preparing a full breakfast, which by today's diabetic eating standards might be considered as out of date—two soft boiled eggs, three to four slices of bacon, oatmeal sweetened with Saccharin, milk on the cereal plus a glass of milk, orange juice, black coffee, and gluten bread. My mother generally fixed my lunch the night before, which was usually a full meal of leftovers from the dinner of the night before, carefully separated and wrapped in brown paper, and intended to be eaten at room temperature. I carried it with me. I then headed off to work and reported in by 5:30 a.m.

Being so close to home when I started working at the post office was a blessing. My work site was closer to home than at any time during my entire school career. As a substitute, I was given different mail assignments every day, including carrying door-to-door mail on various routes for absent employees, stacking mail in the station for delivery, and delivering as a backup on certain routes when there was an extra heavy delivery. In the process, I often delivered mail to my own house and to the homes of my friends' parents. At the time I did not fully appreciate that this amount of exercise and walking was a continuation of my careful health regimen, which helped to keep my diabetes within functional range.

The only real concern was for my feet, since circulation is always a concern for diabetics. I was on my feet all day and began to experience some dry skin and breaking out on my feet, which the doctors partially attributed to the dye in the socks and foot perspiration. I was directed to wear only white cotton socks against my skin and to get shoes that would allow ventilation to my feet. This was similar to my directions when I was pushing the ice cream cart while in high school. Carrying a heavy mailbag was always a challenge given my small stature and weighing only about 120 pounds. To relieve myself of some of the weight, I found it beneficial to work as expeditiously as possible.

After only a few months, I was transferred from 15th and U Street up to the Brightwood post office station, located on Georgia and Missouri Avenues. I had to get up by 3:30 a.m. each morning in order to follow my health-mandated diabetic regimen, catch the streetcar at 17th and U Streets to Georgia Avenue, and still arrive by 5:30 a.m.

Working from the Brightwood station was a sobering experience, one that quickly rocked me back to the realities of the world of racial segregation. While the neighborhood at 15th and U Streets was integrated, although the buildings themselves were separated by race due to legal restrictive racial covenants, everything in the Brightwood area was white only; and many of the residents were Italians or Jews who had local businesses in the neighborhood or downtown.

Yet the mail carriers were almost all black, except for the white supervisors. My own supervisor, Mr. Wise, was a fine, fine man. Despite our racial difference—he was a Caucasian Jew—he was like a father to me, then a 22-year-old recent college graduate. He shepherded me through the many trials and tribulations that I was exposed to while serving an all white, and occasionally hostile citizenry.

My first lasting negative experience came when I had to use the restroom. While I could understand some apprehension about allowing me into a private home to use the restroom, it was incredible to me that several of the apparent buildings' managers declined to allow me to use the restroom in the janitors' quarters, attempting to restrict my presence in the building to the lobby where the mailboxes were.

I complained more than once to the management of these buildings that I, as an agent of the U.S. Government delivering mail in my official government uniform, should be allowed to use at least the janitor's bathroom, if needed. While a few of them did relent on occasion, there was a clear pattern of denial of access, which despite my filing a written complaint with my employer, did not change.

But the most heart-wrenching experience I had while delivering mail was in Crestwood, that section of 16th Street that begins at Shepard Street, N.W. It was quite a nice neighborhood on the street that is commonly called the "Avenue of the President," since the White House is located at the base of 16th Street and can be seen for miles as you approach it.

One day, as I was delivering mail at the Crestwood Apartments, my first time on that route, I was shocked and devastated to arrive upon a large black sign on the lawn, which stated in bold gold letters, "This is a restricted building. No Jews, no dogs, and no niggers." I was absolutely dumbfounded that in the Nation's Capital city, on the Street of the President, that someone could be so bold as to erect a public sign and prominently display it on the lawn of one of the better apartment buildings.

There are still a number of people in my generation who recall that offensive sign, and we marvel about how times have changed. Still, that they would be so bold and outspoken in Washington, D.C., in 1940-41 explains how the Ku Klux Klan was so self-empowered in 1925 as to march 25,000 members of their organization, fully hooded in white sheets and adorned with pointed cone head coverings, down Pennsylvania Avenue to the White House.

I never once mentioned my diabetic condition in filling out the application forms for the teacher's exam, the Civil Service Commission, or the FBI, as the attitude of the era would have rendered me essentially not hirable. I had learned long before that some of your so-called friends could also be a source of trouble because of their ignorance or perceptions about diabetes, what it was and how one contracted it.

So for certain, I was not about to list this ailment on any job applications, which would have reduced to writing a perceived permanent disability. It became a life of concealment, of hiding something in the shadows, but which would occasionally rear its head in a threatening manner.

When I decided to make application to the U.S. Government Printing Office (the GPO) in late 1941, I was confronted with this question, "Do you have or have you had tuberculosis, a nervous breakdown, epilepsy, or are you a diabetic, and if so, explain your answer?" I consciously left that inquiry about my health blank, hoping that no one would notice the unmarked space, and that no questions would be asked.

By signing the application, I was certifying that its contents were correct, and I did not want to lie on the application. I discussed the issue with both my doctor and my priest, and they each said the same thing—leave the space blank, and hopefully no one will ask anything about the blank space. That is exactly what I did, and nothing adverse occurred. And throughout my entire federal career, which spanned from 1940 until 1973, no one ever commented that I had left that question unanswered each time that I applied for a new position.

In retrospect, while some might argue that my inaction amounted to a cover-up of the truth, in reality had I answered that question with a "Yes," being a black man who was striving to break the color line, not only for myself but for my entire race, and in an era when there were no civil rights laws to protect me, and no Americans with Disabilities Act protections to ward off discrimination, I would have literally been left with nothing. That was more than I should have been asked to bear.

I tired quickly of the postal service. Besides the heavy mailbag, I did not care for the all-weather requirements of the job. When it was a nice spring day, and the bag was light, it was great to be alive and outside. But when it was cold and raining, or even snowing, I hated it. I was called to work by the GPO but assigned to work with the printing presses on the midnight to 8:00 a.m. shift. The pay was comparable, or a little better, because of the night differential, and the work was all inside. But I never really adjusted to this schedule, and with my health considerations, I was always concerned that I would get off my diet and have a hard time getting my regular blood sugar analysis and food routine back in line.

Because there is always a danger for a diabetic to operate any equipment while under the influence of an insulin reaction, it was necessary to monitor myself carefully. This was especially true when I worked at the GPO, but was likewise the case later in my life when it came time to learn how to operate a motor vehicle. To at least make certain that my diabetes was being monitored medically, it was always necessary for me to obtain a letter to that effect from my physician whenever I renewed my driver's license.

While I was always conscientious about not driving while under the influence of an insulin reaction, looking back I have concluded that there were some occasions when I was not at my best, and that I was at least on the fringe of having a reaction. Since obtaining my first driver's license in 1951, I was careful to keep peppermint hard candy in my glove compartment, and if necessary, I would take several pieces of it before attempting to drive. Never once do I feel that I drove unsafely. I was consistently conscientiousness in waiting until "I felt like myself" before getting behind the wheel. This was a responsibility that I never knowingly shirked.

My job title at the GPO, "skilled laborer," was a high-class term for working with the printing presses. This was the official federal agency that did all of the U.S. Government's printing and operated 24 hours a day. Operating the printing presses was hands-on, but dirty, dirty work—loading, unloading, cleaning, inking, and pulling out paper that got caught, and noisy too, sometimes to the point that all you heard was a constant roar. The job was hardly befitting my college degree. But due to racially related imposed limitations, I could not do better at that time.

I sustained paper cuts routinely, and with ink on my hands, sometime all over my hands, it is amazing that none of my cuts got infected. Had they done so, I surely would have had a hard time healing, as cuts and abrasions can be very dangerous for diabetics. Occasionally an employee would lose a finger, or even a hand, due to problems related to the machinery. I never suffered any problems with low blood sugar while I was there. I always remained on guard given the inherent danger that was associated with this dirty work.

My first order of business was keeping my diabetes under control, which focused upon getting exercise, monitoring my insulin intake, and my diet. My mother was dedicated to my diet, and me, always adjusting her cooking to accommodate my needs. Assigned to the graveyard shift, I plotted my eating and sleep time, but I stuck to my regular food-intake program. I reversed my routine and ate a full dinner when I arrived home in the morning, generally around 9:00 a.m., slept between 2:00 p.m. and 9:00 p.m., and then had a full breakfast at about 10:30 p.m. before I caught the streetcar down to work.

I stayed with the GPO until 1944. In the last several months before leaving the GPO, management noted my abilities; and upon application I was selected for a sales clerk position in the bookstore. There I directly served the general public and also filled book orders placed from other sources. It was a much cleaner environment. While I would not consider it to be intellectually challenging, the position did carry an aura of professionalism. I was shifted to daytime hours, wore a tie to work, and was working directly with books.

The World War II effort had been in full swing for quite some time, and in 1944 the Office of Price Administration (the OPA) was looking for more qualified people to work in that effort to monitor and control the prices of goods and services. Notice I said "people," as the war effort strained the available manpower resources of white males to the near-breaking point. With so many of the young white males out of the United States engaged in the active military component of the war effort, the U.S. Government turned in many other directions for replacements—white women, black men and women, and older workers returning to the labor market. The war, despite all of its negativity, loss of life, and root causes, was also a golden opportunity for people of color, as we were called upon to prove ourselves; and we did so with distinction and have never looked back since.

I had been called for military service and given three physical examinations. They knew that I was diabetic and really could not realistically serve in the military, but it seems that somehow the medical examiners did not get it. I was examined the first time and listed as "4F," due to health reasons, but it was as if the second and third round of medical examiners did not believe the prior documentation. But after the third call and physical examination, including a review of my medical records and diabetic history, they finally figured out that I was for real, and I was finally declared "4F" and not summoned further.

I was hired at OPA as a statistical clerk and given various assignments tracking statistical data related to setting and adjusting prices for goods and services. The government wanted to know what items were being manufactured, in what quantities, and what the companies were charging for them. Given that this was the era of rationing of many products, the federal government was particularly concerned about how goods and services were being distributed, and what wages were being paid to various sectors of the economy's workers. It was an era of federally imposed wage and price controls, temporarily mandated by the needs of the war effort.

Into this equation I stepped, still in my 20s, not long out of college, and presented with an opportunity to utilize the statistics and economics courses that I had taken at Miner. I stayed in that clerical position for only three months when my supervisors promoted me to Statistician, a professional category that included the opportunity to analyze the data, forecast trends, and make recommendations. This was a major break for me and moved me from the clerical status as a Grade Four, to P1, the first rung of the professional grade levels. The salary differential was significant as well.

Left: James W. Quander, Easter Sunday, 1930, age 12, in front of family home, 1913 17<sup>th</sup> St., N.W.   Right: James, a college graduate, ~ 1940.

James, a Ph. D. Candidate, Hudson Shore Labor School, 1947.

Left:  James married beautiful Joherra Amin on December 6, 1942.
Right: James with first-born son, Rohulamin and daughter, Joherra, 1949.

Left: Rohulamin was 4½ when Joherra was born.
Right:  James & Joherra, 1949.

James studying to be a Deacon, ~ 1968. (Photo by Carl Balcerak)

Rev. Mr. James W. Quander, far right front row,
at Diaconate Ordination in first United States ordained group,
standing with Patrick Cardinal O'Boyle and Rev. Joseph Marino,
at St. Matthews Cathedral, September 11, 1971.

James and Joherra Quander
celebrate their 50<sup>th</sup> wedding anniversary December 6, 1992.

Deacon James W. Quander gave an invocation
at his granddaughter Fatima's high school graduation, 1997.

| MAJOR SUBJECTS | MARKS | MAJOR SUBJECTS | MARKS | MAJOR SUBJECTS | MARKS | MAJOR SUBJECTS | MARKS | MAJOR SUBJECTS | MARKS | MAJOR SUBJECTS | MARKS | MAJOR SUBJECTS | MARKS | MAJOR SUBJECTS | MARKS |
|---|---|---|---|---|---|---|---|---|---|---|---|---|---|---|---|
| Eng. | A | Eng. | B | Eng. | A | Eng. | B | Eng. | B | Eng. | A | Eng. | A | Eng. | A |
| Hist. | B | Hist. | A | Hist. | | Hist. | | Hist. | A | Hist. | B | Hist. | A | Hist. | A |
| Math. | A | Math. | A | Math. | B | Math. | C | Math. | A | Math. | | Math. | | Math. | |
| Fr. | | Fr. | | Fr. | | Fr. | | Fr. | B | Fr. | A | Fr. | B | Fr. | B |
| Ger. | | Ger. | | Ger. | | Ger. | | Ger. | | Ger. | | Ger. | | Ger. | |
| Lat. | B | Lat. | B | Lat. | A | Lat. | B | Lat. | | Lat. | | Lat. | | Lat. | |
| Span. | | Span. | | Span. | | Span. | | Span. | | Span. | | Span. | | Span. | |
| Biol. | | Biol. | | Biol. | A | Biol. | A | Biol. | | Biol. | | Biol. | | Biol. | |
| Chem. | | Chem. | | Chem. | | Chem. | | Chem. | | Chem. | | Chem. | | Chem. | |
| Phys. | | Phys. | | Phys. | | Phys. | | Phys. | | Phys. | | Phys. | | Phys. | |

| MINORS | | MINORS | | MINORS | | MINORS | | MINORS | | MINORS | | MINORS | | MINORS | |
|---|---|---|---|---|---|---|---|---|---|---|---|---|---|---|---|
| Draw. | A | Draw. | A | Draw. | | Draw. | | Draw. | | Draw. | | Draw. | | Draw. | |
| Mus. | B | Mus. | B | Mus. | | Mus. | | Mus. | | Mus. | | Mus. | | Mus. | |
| Ph. Tr. | B | Ph. Tr. | | Ph. Tr. | A | Ph. Tr. | A | Ph. Tr. | A | Ph. Tr. | A | Ph. Tr. | B | Ph. Tr. | C |
| Mil. Tr. | | Mil. Tr. | | Mil. Tr. | | Mil. Tr. | | Mil. Tr. | | Mil. Tr. | | Mil. Tr. | | Mil. Tr. | |

| ATTENDANCE | | ATTENDANCE | | ATTENDANCE | | ATTENDANCE | | ATTENDANCE | | ATTENDANCE | | ATTENDANCE | | ATTENDANCE | |
|---|---|---|---|---|---|---|---|---|---|---|---|---|---|---|---|
| Days present | | Days present | | Days present | 37 | Days present | 86 | Days present | 85 | Days present | 88 | Days present | 84 | Days present | |
| Days ab., ex. | | Days ab., ex. | | Days ab., ex. | 29 | Days ab., ex. | 5 | Days ab., ex. | 6 | Days ab., ex. | 6 | Days ab., ex. | | Days ab., ex. | |
| Days ab., unex. | | Days ab., unex. | | Days ab., unex. | | Days ab., unex. | | Days ab., unex. | | Days ab., unex. | | Days ab., unex. | | Days ab., unex. | |
| Times tardy | | Times tardy | | Times tardy | | Times tardy | | Times tardy | 2 | Times tardy | 1 | Times tardy | | Times tardy | |
| Department | | Department | | Department | | Department | | Department | | Department | | Department | | Department | |

## High School Transcript for James W. Quander

He believed he was the victim of disability discrimination and kept out of the National Honor Society, since he did not do ROTC or swimming. He had only one "C" throughout high school. After earning his Bachelor's Degree, he earned several graduate credits towards a Doctorate in Economics, but he chose not to endure the rigors of completing a dissertation while working full time and raising a family, thereby testing his physical health to a dangerous extreme.

Left: On the verandah at George Washington's Mount Vernon Plantation, Rohulamin Quander reads the annual Enslaved Remembrance Program, 2001. Several Quander ancestors were in service to the first president.
Right: Rohulamin with his wife Carmen Torruella-Quander, 2005.

The extended family poses for photo at Virginia Beach, 1977.

James Quander surrounded by his four children,
from left, John, Ricardo, Rohulamin, and daughter Joherra (seated),
with tribute to Joherra (mother), Christmas, 2002.

Left: James Quander with grandson, Alexander James, Duck, North Carolina, 1996. Right: James with great grandson, John Dimitri Quander, 2004; and granddaughter Iliana holding Egypt Amparo Quander-Crenshaw, his great granddaughter born January 2005, three months after he died.

Christmas, 1994, grandchildren of James W. and Joherra Quander: Iliana A., Alexander J., Fatima DLS, Ricardo V., II, Julian B., Christopher G., J. Dominic, Joherra D., Matthew J., and Rohulamin D.   All are Quander surnamed except Joherra D. Harris, daughter of Joherra Quander Harris. Given the prognosis to die before the age of 10, it was really a very special privilege to live to be 86 and have not only 4 wonderful healthy successful children, but also 10 grandchildren and 2 great grandchildren. What is even more wonderful, none of them have diabetes, another statistic that makes James Quander's story remarkable.

Left: John Edward and Maude Pearson Quander, James' parents, in front of family home, Easter Sunday, 1930. Right: James with grandmother, Hannah Fraser Pearson, and little friend, Ione Corbett, at 662 Acker Street, N.E., ~ 1922.

James Quander (in center in wheel chair) receives award for the Quander Family at Black Family Reunion, September, 2001. The Quander Family is one of the oldest recorded black families in the U.S., dating back to at least 1684.

# Chapter 11

# The Gifts of Marriage

On December 6, 1992, my four children gave my wife and me the most beautiful 50-year anniversary celebration at one of the local salons. What made the celebration even more rewarding is that I, as a juvenile diabetic, was not expected to live to see my tenth birthday.

And now, more than ten years beyond the 50th anniversary celebration, I am blessed with not only four wonderful, responsible, and loving adult children, but also ten grandchildren who are of a similar mind, and my first great grandchild, John Dimitri Quander.

I met my wife in January 1942 when one of my coworkers at the Government Printing Office (GPO), Saxton Howard, told me about this new girl who had just come to town from New York and was his neighbor living in Ivy City, a section of colored Washington. He said she was pretty and had kind of a "funny, foreign name." He had just met her casually a few days before, adding that while he could see himself with her, he was already involved in a serious relationship. He also considered her to be a little young for him.

I was on the rebound, having broken up with my girlfriend of many years whom I had expected to marry. I was hurting. Papa, always the wise counsel, said, "Jim, don't worry about that. Life is too short, and there are many more where that one came from. And besides, she wasn't Catholic and that relationship was headed for nothing but trouble. Your mother and I could see it for a long time, but you were so in love that you didn't. Forget about her and move on."

So by the end of 1941, I was fully "available," 23 years old and looking for a wife. But not necessarily too actively looking, although I had my eyes and mind both open, waiting to see who might come along. I had essentially known only one type of woman, Washingtonians; and most of them lived in my part of town, had graduated from the all academic curriculum Dunbar High School, and then attended either Miner Teachers College or Howard University.

The idea of meeting someone truly exotic never crossed my somewhat narrowed mind. But when Saxton mentioned that she was foreign, and pretty, I decided that that was surely enough to get started. He got her telephone number and permission for me to call her. Although I am somewhat retiring in my personality, I was never really that shy, once I got started initially. So on that Sunday, in early January 1942, I telephoned, introduced myself, and asked if I could come to see her that afternoon. She said, "Why, certainly!" The hour of rendezvous was set

The United States had only become actively involved with World War II the prior month, December 7, 1941. She had come to Washington from New York City just a few days before Christmas 1941 to take a clerical job with the federal government, as the U.S. geared up to meet the German and Japanese enemies. She did not know a single soul in Washington before she arrived, and she was lodged in the home of Mrs. Eva Richardson in Ivy City by a placement service that found suitable accommodations for women who moved to Washington to work in the federal government.

As she would later relate to me, that was the loneliest Christmas she ever had. During all previous Christmases, she was surrounded by family and friends and celebrated a spiritual Christmas, as was the tradition in her native homeland, Barbados, which was then a part of the British West Indies. Raised in a Catholic home, she had certain standard expectations for Christmas that were not realized on December 25, 1941.

When I reflect how and when we met, I realize that had she been in Washington a little longer than two weeks, and had she met more people during that short time, perhaps I might not have been so fortunate to have her become my girlfriend, and later my wife. But time, fate, the right place at the right time, and a little good luck were all on my side that day.

Our early relationship was a Sunday kind of love—I would catch the street car to Ivy City and visit, and we would take long walks in the neighborhood, especially around the campus area of Gallaudet College (now University), the nation's only university created expressly for the hearing and speech impaired. It was and still is a truly beautiful campus, and walking through that general neighborhood in early 1942 was a great personal pleasure. We would later rent our first apartment just two blocks from the campus after we got married and continue with those long walks.

As Valentine's Day 1942 drew close, Joherra invited me to a party being given by the out-of-town girls at the Phyllis Wheatley YWCA, located at 9th Street and Rhode Island Avenue, N.W. But because of my diet, the 12:00 a.m. to 8:00 a.m. shift at the GPO, and the need to eat my full breakfast before reporting to work, I stopped by the party for only a short while—empty-handed. Earlier, and because I never expected to get there at all, I asked my older brother, Joseph, to deliver a box of heart-shaped chocolates to her at the Y.

During the party, when someone mentioned my name and that I was absent from the celebration, she commented that actually she did not particularly like me, but despite her feelings at the moment, she just might have met her future husband—me. She left New York engaged to a Jamaican guy who was part of her West Indian cultural scene. But as our relationship grew, she returned the engagement ring.

After a fairly short period of friendship, which quickly gave way to courtship, all between late January to mid-June, 1942, I proposed to Joherra while taking one of our long late Sunday evening walks, once again near Gallaudet College. It was mid-June and the daylight was at its longest. The weather was not unduly hot for that time of year in usually humid Washington, D.C., but I was sweating bullets, brought on by my extreme nervousness associated with what I was about to ask. I had written and rehearsed the words that I wanted to use in my proposal speech; but in trying to get up the nerve to pop the question, everything got fouled up and forgotten, and I sort of just blurted it out.

Finally, I asked the straightforward question, "Joherra, will you marry me?" Having asked that question to someone else once before, and being accepted and then later rejected as being "too slow," my heart was pounding. It seemed a lifetime before she said, "Yes, why of course." In reality, though, it was only a few seconds before she replied in the affirmative as we strolled arm in arm past the Florida Avenue main entrance to the college.

Only moments before I had revealed to her that I was a diabetic. I did not want to continue this relationship or prepare for marriage under false pretenses. I had never specifically told her what my medical ailment was, although she thought my eating habits a bit strange. We had never discussed it up to that point. After explaining to her what diabetes was, in the best and most direct manner, I quickly realized that she still did not have the slightest idea of what I was talking about.

She had never heard of diabetes, let alone the debilitating effects that it can inflict upon some of its victims. She told me, "What difference does that make, if you love someone?" And to this day, Joherra did not have a real clue what she was getting into when she said "Yes!" on that early evening in mid-June of 1942 when she agreed to marry someone who would continue to suffer the effects of this ailment for the rest of his life. Only in more recent years have we learned that her own father, Mohammed Abdul Rohualamin, who migrated to Barbados from Calcutta, India, in 1913, suffered gravely from the effects of diabetes: he even sustained the loss of both legs below the knee when he was in his late 50s. He had neither the blessings nor the benefits that I have. My mother-in-law, Oquindo Amin, and he were divorced; and she and most all of her children migrated to the United States, leaving Mohammed alone and in relative poverty with no family in the Barbados. He eventually went to live in a poor house. Without good medical attention, easy access to insulin or balanced nutrition, he could not take the best care of himself and properly attend to his diabetic condition. Later, in about 1943/44, at the age of approximately 56 years, he died from diabetic complications.

We were married at 6:00 p.m. on Sunday, December 6, 1942, at Saint Augustine's Roman Catholic Church, then located on 15th Street, between L and M Streets, N.W., Washington, D.C. St. Augustine's is the oldest black Catholic Church in Washington, D.C., founded in 1858 by free people of color and former slaves, some employees at the White House. They raised needed construction funds with teas and other social events held at the White House, some hosted by President and Mrs. Lincoln, who each made monetary contributions towards the founding of the church and school.

Our wedding did not occur without local controversy over whom I was marrying. Not a few people expressed concern that I was marrying a foreigner. A few even chided me that apparently no American girls were good enough for me. Others whispered behind my back, and some said to my face, that I should be extra careful in marrying this East Indian, West Indian, Afro-Caribbean girl, about whom I knew little or nothing.

I was warned that all sorts of things might happen, including that she might boss me about or chase me out of my own home with a knife. Initially, I thought that the persons saying those unkind things were both few and isolated, but as the wedding day drew closer, much of this barrage of dissenting comments came from the mothers of the local Washington, D.C., girls, many of whom I knew in high school.

One mother confronted me and said, "Huh, my daughter wasn't good enough for you, I see!"

I shot right back, "Look, I couldn't select my parents, brothers and sisters, but I'll be damned if I am not going to select whom I marry!"

I was 24 years old, still young enough to have respect for my elders, but appalled at the attitudes that I was facing from some of the family members of my peer group. The men really did not seem to mind. I guess it was a bit of exotica that appealed to them. But the women clearly felt threatened by the prospect of someone different coming into their environment, and taking one of "their" men, a potentially lost husband opportunity for their daughters.

The wedding itself was a great success, a new start in life for me. My cousin, Eunice Quander Taylor, a well-known and talented soprano singer, sang the most beautiful songs, including *Ave Maria*, which is frequently sung at Catholic weddings.

Sunday, December 6, 1942, was wartime; and the entire country was focused on that effort, geared to a war economy, prioritizing the country's needs related to beating the Germans, Japanese, and Italians. In that atmosphere, we planned our wedding realizing that many of my best friends, buddies that I had been with most of my life, would not be present. They were overseas in the theaters of operation.

If ever any wedding day was fraught with mishaps and complications, ours certainly was. I look back at all of the things that went wrong that day and consider them as a blessing in disguise.

My mother-in-law to be, Oquindo Amin Florant, and her best friend, Edna Bagowee, decided to make Joherra's wedding dress and all of the bridesmaid's dresses in New York where they both lived and worked as seamstresses in a factory. Even though the bridesmaids' dresses were made and timely mailed to Washington, D.C., they did not arrive in time. They were both excellent seamstresses and remade all of the dresses again the night before the wedding.

Joherra's dress was the last to be completed, and not wanting to take a chance on the mail, her dress was brought with them on the train in a garment bag.

Other wedding day mishaps—the organ broke down on the morning of the wedding, and as a result, we got married to violin music played by Howard University professor Louis Von Jones; several inches of snow fell on the morning of the wedding; the black cake, a traditional West Indian fruit cake, arrived in the mail broken into many pieces, which Oquindo and Edna "glued" back together with a delicious almond paste icing; and Joherra cut her finger and got blood on her wedding dress just a short time before the ceremony. Halfway through this bizarre scenario, my kid sister, Kitty, broke down and cried, "This wedding is jinxed. Everything has gone wrong. This wedding is jinxed."

There were more mishaps: an old girlfriend called on the day of the wedding and begged me to not marry that foreigner, that "'Amen' girl, or whatever her name is," so that she and I could try again; we overslept in the train to Baltimore where we spent our honeymoon and almost missed our stop; arrived at the hotel where colored patrons were accommodated and discovered that the furnace had exploded, there was no heat, and each of us consequently caught terrible colds.

My wedding day was the first and only time that I ever saw my father drunk. He was so happy that he cried—tears of joy. His baby son, Jimsen Weed, the juvenile diabetic, had not only lived well beyond the ten years that the medical professionals had predicted, but he had also graduated from college and had now taken unto himself a wife, a pretty, exotic wife at that.

Both Mama and Papa were so unbelievably happy, but it was Papa who made the lasting impression upon me that evening. Before the night's reception festivities were over, I actually had to put him to bed.

The reception was at the house, which was quite small, but we scrubbed and polished the house from top to bottom to accommodate our guests who wandered among all three floors. We had the latest records, including Ella Fitzgerald's song, *Stairway to the Stars*, which was popular at that moment, along with the Duke Ellington, Count Basie, Jimmy Lundsford, and Lucky Millender bands, all playing great swing tunes which made you want to get up and dance the night away.

Another reception remembrance is Cousin Mary Diggs Brown, my father's favorite first cousin. I can still picture her stationed at the punch and cake distribution table, wearing a long deep-red velvet dress, a single string of white pearls with matching earrings, and a huge wide-brim black hat. She was the same relative who in 1926, when I was eight years old, witnessed me injecting myself with insulin and exclaimed that she would rather be dead than to inject herself daily with insulin. Papa was so angry with her for making such a statement in my presence that he ordered her out of his house.

They loved each other too much for either of them to stay angry very long. Within a day or two, Cousin Mary was back in Papa's good graces, having begged his pardon for letting her mouth get away from her. Papa immediately accepted, and they embraced. The incident was long forgotten, but on this joyous occasion, her words of long ago, which pierced me like a dagger as a young child, returned to my mind. I thought to myself, "See, once again, I have proved them wrong."

Here she was, almost two full decades later, at my wedding and enjoying all of the festivities. For years she was the housekeeper for Mr. Justice McReynolds, an associate member of the U.S. Supreme Court, whose reputation was well known for being a social conservative and holding racist views about colored people.

Several of the good things of life were not supposed to happen to me, since I was a juvenile diabetic and predictably would not be on this earthly plane for too long. But here I was, 24 years old, with a college degree, a career which was quite promising, considering that not until about this time had Negroes been given any meaningful access to career opportunities in the federal government. And now I was a married man, with an exotic, beautiful, and interesting wife from another country, Barbados. She was someone whose ethnic background was entirely different from my own.

Marriage opened up an entirely new vista that I had only dreamed about. Throughout my adult life, I have tried not to unduly focus on many disappointments, intentional exclusions, and personal heartaches that I felt as a juvenile diabetic child and in growing up. Because of my precarious health situation, many insults were directly visited upon me, and several behind-the-back whisperings also got back to me. Yet, like negatives directed at me because of my racial identification, the only thing that I could do was to prove them wrong, to excel, and demonstrate that Jim Quander was focused and not going to let his perceived deficiencies hold him back.

But as I have gotten older, I frequently revisit those earlier days. Born in 1918, and now confronting a slowly-advancing case of prostate cancer, I have become more reflective than at any prior time in my life, sometimes breaking into bouts of crying over my frustrations of the hand that life has dealt me.

But it does not last long. My wife, children, and grandchildren all remind me to always look on the bright side; and that my tears, of which there are sometimes many, should be tears of joy, not sadness, a celebration of what Jim Quander did achieve, despite the odds. They urge me to never feel sorry for myself and not to wallow in reflections about what might have otherwise been. I try desperately to do just that. For the most part, this advice works.

After marriage my life moved in new directions. For the first few months we lived with my parents on 17th Street. In the spring of 1943, with our first child on the way, we moved to our own one-bedroom apartment at 1631 Montello Avenue, N.E. At $35.00 a month, the rent was affordable, especially with both of us working.

My first son, Rohul Amin was born on December 4, 1943, a first anniversary gift from my wife, and was named for his maternal grandfather, Mohammed Abdul Rohualamin. He was born in the colored maternity ward at Garfield Hospital in Washington, D.C., where non-Caucasian appearing women and their newborns were housed during their hospital stay. Being of East Indian, Irish, Scottish, and some Afro-Caribbean background, they certainly would not have placed her in the white ward. Further, had she erroneously been placed in the white ward, they surely would have moved her out as soon as I appeared on the scene. Although Joherra spent our first anniversary in the hospital, we both rejoiced and thanked God for our gift of love—a healthy first-born son.

Shortly afterwards, in February 1944, I started graduate school in economics at Howard University, Washington, D.C., the tuition being a Christmas gift from my wife. It was from that point that I began developing specific academic credentials to buttress the work that I was doing on a daily basis. Although I had been accorded professional status in the federal government, that status was based primarily upon my being a college graduate, but it was not reinforced by academic credits earned in economics and statistics.

As a black man in the early 1940s, if you were running an elevator, working in the post office, or working as a laborer at the government printing office, there was little to no perceived connection between the job that you were doing and the worth of earning a graduate degree in a specialized field. Times were slowly changing, but we still had very far to go.

Howard University had a small but impressive number of Caucasian professors on its graduate school faculty. My assigned advisor was Dr. Wasserman, a kind and knowledgeable Jewish man. Because of the extreme shortage of Negroes in certain fields, including economists, in the federal government and professors teaching in universities, he urged me to bypass the masters degree and directly pursue a Ph.D. in economics. In discussions with me early in my academic program, he said, "Quander, I don't want you to stop at the masters; I want you to go directly to the doctorate. We need young Negro professionals in the field." Several other professors concurred.

Following their advice, I elected that academic path with a secondary emphasis upon statistics. The graduate program in economics at Howard University was small, and I was promised a lot of individual attention there. As well, enrollment at Howard would also segue into opportunities to study at other northern and midwestern universities outside of the District of Columbia.

Although I did not realize it then, the smallness of the Howard program proved to be disadvantageous. Several of the courses that I had hoped to complete at an earlier time within my program were either postponed to a later date due to the lack of sufficient enrollment or not scheduled frequently enough. That circumstance contributed to my not being able to complete my own course work in a timely manner; and likewise, I suffered adversely due to other intervening factors.

Initially, I had been hired in 1944 at OPA, Rent Control Division, as a GS-4 Statistical Clerk, a good "colored job" at the time. Shortly after hire, I was upgraded to a P1, "Economist." When I advised my supervisors that I wanted to pursue a graduate degree in economics at Howard University, they were amenable to adjusting my work schedule to attend class. This was a totally new experience. Most of my racial peers had no idea that several days a week we could leave a full time job early, sometimes working less than a full day, and go to a university to pursue higher education. I was on focus.

This amenity was just now opening up to us, something that white professionals had been doing for years. But the black employees, most all of whom were still held down in menial positions, were totally unaware of these opportunities and the relevancy that earning an advanced degree would be to the type of work they were doing.

I met Patricia Roberts Harris, then an undergraduate student, in one of my first economics classes at Howard. She was brilliant and showed every indication that she was destined for greatness. Before her early death at age 59, she completed several firsts, including Ambassador from the United States to Luxembourg, Secretary of Housing and Urban Development, Secretary of Health and Human Services, and Dean of Howard University School of Law. Further, she was a major national officer in the Democratic Party and served on the corporate boards of several Fortune 500 companies. We remained friendly throughout our lives.

Things were going very well indeed. My diabetes, while never really permanently under control, seemed to react well to my self-imposed discipline: early to rise, a full breakfast, and then off to work. On school days, I would complete a full workday, have lunch at 11:30 a.m. and leave work about 3:00 p.m.

To assure that I would not have a problem, I would eat a small dinner before my 4:00 p.m. class and a full dinner afterwards. If I stayed on campus for after-class research, then I ate either in the cafeteria or at a nearby restaurant. Otherwise, I waited until I got home to have my full dinner, which was often well after 9:00 p.m. Naturally when I planned to stay later on the campus, I carried my insulin with me and found some private place to quietly administer the dosage.

Unable to test my blood sugar, because the convenient technology for doing so did not then exist, I estimated how much insulin to take based upon personal experience. I had always been a well-disciplined diabetic, and this tight regimen seemed to agree with me, not dissimilar to when I was in college while servicing two newspaper routes, seven days a week, and also doing work study in the cafeteria.

The quiet before the forthcoming storm lulled me into a false sense of security and place. One beautiful morning in 1946 when the world was finally at peace, three white men in suits came charging into my office demanding to know where Jim Quander was. Not knowing who they were or what their business was, I feared nothing and readily identified myself. Ordered to go with them, they refused to answer my questions as to who they were and what they wanted with me. They escorted me to a vacant room somewhere close by in the building.

With the door firmly shut behind them, and me with no notion of what my rights were, they accusatorily interrogated me in a most gruff manner for what seemed like an eternity. I protested vigorously, and demanded to know what this was all about, to which they repeatedly replied, "You know! You know! You know what you did and exactly why we're here." Again and again, I protested that I had no clue. And again they scoffed at me derisively. Seeing that they were making no progress, they finally told me the story and then demanded that I "confess." Confess? Confess to what?

As it turned out, a white employee from Mississippi had reported that while she was sitting on the toilet in the ladies room the day before, a colored man had gotten down on his knees and looked into the stall where she was seated. Terrified, she screamed and reported the incident to internal affairs, and the office sent a team right to my desk the following morning. As I later learned, they were not initially looking for me by name. However, the early facet of their investigation focused upon me since I was the Negro male employee who sat closest to her, although not in the same room.

The interrogation was much longer than it needed to be, especially since they at first declined to tell me what the whole thing was about. Finally when they shared the incident's details with me, and I asked them when this incident allegedly occurred, I immediately realized that I was in class at Howard University after 5:00 p.m. on the date and was nowhere near the ladies room peering into any toilet.

By now it was well past my appointed lunch hour, and with the stress related to these false accusations apparently causing my blood sugar to drop precipitously, I started going into a diabetic shock and rapidly began to lose my ability to effectively communicate with them. They realized that something was wrong since I was no longer conversant, and one of them asked me if I was a diabetic.

For one of the very few times in my entire 33 years with the federal government, I answered that question in the affirmative. Suddenly they got frightened and abruptly ended the interrogation, admonishing me in a very loud and gruff voice, "Don't tell anybody about the incident or this interrogation." One of them helped me to the cafeteria and guided me in getting my lunch, and then he too left.

I later learned that they checked with Howard University and verified through class attendance records that indeed I was in my economics class by 4:00 p.m., and obviously nowhere near the ladies room at OPA on that fateful late afternoon. I never heard from them again, not even an apology or admission of having committed a colossal error in making the false accusation. To this day it remains unclear whether they were from some internal affairs office or the Federal Bureau of Investigation (FBI).

When I returned to my office after lunch, and just coming around to feeling like myself again, I learned that the whole building was buzzing about three white men wearing suits visibly removing me from my office. But none of my coworkers, white or colored, yet had any clue about why I was removed. But their curiosity got the best of them, and they pestered me with questions.

Having been sternly admonished to tell no one about why I was removed from the office and to say nothing whatsoever about the incident itself, I elected to do the exact opposite. I told everybody that would listen about the incident, and every detail of what they alleged had occurred. The audience, black and white, was not small. With the assistance of the many young African-American females who worked in the building, for the first time I learned who the accuser was. I did not know her and had only seen her in the hallways. But my fellow female coworkers were quick to identify her, and she soon became isolated as someone who made a terrible false accusation for which she should be punished. Nothing ever happened to her, however, but for me it was both a sobering and humiliating experience.

Within days I was summoned to meet with Chester Bowles, the director of OPA, who would later become Under Secretary of State, Governor of Connecticut, and Ambassador to India and Nepal, and was also touted as a possible Democratic nominee for President of the U.S. He assured me that I had done nothing wrong. He expressed outrage at what had occurred—an inquisition, confronting and accusing me of such a heinous act, without first gathering sufficient evidence upon which to make a proper determination of who most likely committed the act. All they heard was that a man of color did it, and off they were—straight to Jim Quander's office, and accused him of the act.

I had so many ideas, so many things that I wanted to do with my career. Despite the racial limitations that were placed upon African-Americans at that time and my diabetic health limitations, I was determined to press onwards and upward. The wartime economy was boom time for virtually everyone in the federal government. But I encountered a profound shift after the war ended.

With many GIs back home from the war effort, all of them receiving five and ten point veterans' preferences on federal job applications, they had the inside track on being selected for many of the better jobs, and in many cases, even for the menial jobs. I left OPA in 1946 for career advancement and went to the Office of the Housing Expediter (OHE) to help prepare the country for the postwar housing shortage that we all knew was coming.

OHE was the forerunner agency to what later became the Department of Housing and Urban Development (HUD). With a severe housing shortage predicted for the post-World War II period, price gouging in certain parts of the country was sure to follow. The federal government wanted to assess the nation's available housing stock and to place appropriate rent controls and other restrictions to lessen the likelihood of the returning GIs being subjected to unscrupulous housing vendors.

What started as a promising opportunity soon became a bust. The postwar recession, caused by the massive conversion from the wartime to a peacetime economy, necessitated a major reorganization within the federal government. I was there only a short time, and with no 5- or 10-point veteran's preference, I got laid off. My fallback was that my wife was working full time in the War Department (now called the Department of Defense).

I was still enrolled at Howard University, and through a combination of favorable circumstances, I was able to remain enrolled, although our budget was tightened severely. My wife was always a great saver, and we had already starting setting aside a down payment to buy our first and only home. Fortunately, because of our joint determination and by working together, we were not forced to invade those funds to meet our daily living expenses.

Since I had been working with economics and statistics at both OPA and OHE and studying the same at Howard University, I decided to pursue a worthwhile project—examining the labor-related activities of Negroes in the AFL-CIO, with a narrowed focus upon worker education. In my evaluation of much of the material that had come to me over the few years of my working with statistics, I was appalled at the lack of education among the members of the American work force, and even more particularly among those of the African-American persuasion.

There was simply too much talent being wasted as workers continued to do the same thing in the least productive way. I believed that even simple office skills and decorum would make a significant difference in terms of output, morale, and even safety in the workplace. Most of my concentration was on workers in the federal government, and while safety there was not the critical issue that it was in factory work around heavy equipment, safety and efficiency in the workplace was still of paramount concern to me.

I applied for a summer 1946 AFL-CIO study and research fellowship. My focus was upon the activities of African-Americans in the workplace, especially those within the ranks of the AFL-CIO membership. Based upon research that I had already undertaken on my own, my plan was to teach office skills, office decorum, and techniques related to the better utilization of office time and space to create an overall greater efficiency in the workplace.

My planned local research and case study sample was to be selected members of the Holy Redeemer Catholic Church parish, a local parish just a few short blocks north of the U.S. Capitol building. Quander relatives founded the parish in the early 1920s when the Archdiocese of Baltimore (of which we were then a part) decided to create more colored Catholic parishes in response to protests about rigidly enforced segregation in the church. The cross-section of membership in the parish would be a good microcosm of the larger Negro community, and being within the shadow of the U.S. Capitol, the symbolism of the case study's results would have been useful.

Prior to this time, with the exception of St. Augustine's Church, founded in 1858, and St. Cyprian's Church, founded in 1893, both of which were founded as all-Negro parishes, except for the

Caucasian clergy, colored Catholics were included as a part of the larger white parishes. However, we were rigidly segregated by race within the church community—we had to sit either in the back of the church or the balcony during Mass. Further, we were also restricted or denied participation in the usual schedule of church activities such as May Day celebrations, first communion for the children, and Christmas pageants. We were directed to conduct our own separate activities, which were often at less convenient times than made available to our white counterparts.

Although the worker education research project never got funded, there was a significant silver lining. My knowledge, talents, and enthusiasm as a young Negro college graduate trying to get ahead caught the attention of several influential people. I was urged to apply for AFL-CIO funding for a different purpose, i.e., to underwrite further Ph.D.-related studies at universities other than Howard.

Certain people in the labor movement focused upon me as an individual. I was urged to apply for an AFL-CIO fellowship to pursue economics and statistics-related studies in the field of worker education. They suggested that I expand my horizon and refocus and would then be better able to accomplish my worker safety and production goals in the context of improved worker education once I completed my Ph.D. Upon application buttressed by my efforts, credentials, and enthusiasm, I was selected for a 1946 AFL-CIO summer fellowship and reselected to continue with the academic program in the summer of 1947.

During my first summer, I studied at the Hudson Shore Labor School in the Hyde Park area of New York near the Roosevelt family estate. The following summer, I took courses in Illinois, initially at Lake Forest University, complemented with seminars at the University of Chicago. In addition to economics and statistics courses, these classes included labor law, the history of the labor movement, money and banking, and evaluation of business cycles, with an emphasis upon how the work force played a role in each aspect of the labor movement.

Several of my professors were distinguished, including Colston Warren, a member of the Council of Economic Advisors to President Truman; James Warburg, an advisor to President

Roosevelt; and Ethel DuPont, of the Delaware DuPonts—all teaching at either Lake Forest or University of Chicago.

While there were people from all over the world studying labor-related subjects at all three of these distinguished schools, I was the only African-American man in any of them. I was not really surprised at that situation: many of my fellow Negro brothers simply were unaware of the opportunities that were available to them. Even for those who were aware, in most instances they were not economically able to participate given their family responsibilities and the monetary sacrifices required, despite the availability of some scholarship money to help with the overall costs.

I had learned earlier that my white counterparts routinely took leave from their jobs to pursue higher education. I was economical during the year with the use of my accumulated annual leave and generally tried to save it for out-of-town academic study, all of which locations were at significant distances away from home. Being still a relatively new federal employee, I had not accumulated that much leave; so much of my time away from the job was leave-without-pay. However, by proving myself to be a good worker and being in pursuit of higher education, my scheduled absences did not create a problem.

Despite the academic rigors of these two summers, I managed my diabetes surprisingly well. My self-discipline of many years paid off handsomely. And the food menu seemed to have been made to order for me—a lot of salads, fresh vegetables, Jell-O desserts, dairy products, and lean meats. Many of the students were from wealthy families, and I learned for the first time that the dietary habits of wealthy whites were significantly different from that of African-Americans, many of whom were both less well-educated and had been exposed to entirely different type foods.

With most of my Ph.D. academic course work completed, I needed quality and dedicated time to devote to my worker education-related thesis, the last step before earning the degree. In the fall of 1947, I was encouraged to apply for the 1948 and final Julius Rosenwald Fellowship, an academic fellowship established earlier in the century by Julius Rosenwald, a Sears and Roebuck magnate, to help African-Americans earn graduate degrees in a number of academic disciplines.

I traded upon my recent contacts and solicited excellent letters of reference from Chester Bowles, director of OPA, and Ethel DuPont, my former professor. While each of them was enthusiastic in their recommendations, I still recall Miss DuPont saying, "Now James, I am only too happy to write this letter on your behalf, and I do hope that you get the fellowship. But I do have to tell you that a letter from me, a Delaware DuPont, can have a negative effect, too. They may think that because you know a DuPont, you don't need the money for the fellowship." But I assured her that I still wanted her to write the letter on my behalf.

My Rosenwald application proposal, still related to my earlier worker education project, was a forerunner to what later became organized manpower programs in the federal government and included a number of components that 25 years later would be incorporated into the War on Poverty. In that respect, I was a man well before my time. Although I did not get the 1948 fellowship, I was the first runner-up to Pearl Primas, the famous dancer.

She was awarded the fellowship to study the cultural significance of Afro-Cuban dance. Primas was a very fitting selection for an important subject. The fund source was exhausted, and it was known in advance that the one fellowship of 1948 would be the last in a series of annual academic awards.

Suddenly things were pretty rough. In addition to not getting the Rosenwald, my recent work history included two consecutive job layoffs, one each from OHE and the Census Bureau. The nation was still adjusting to a postwar economy that favored the returning veterans for jobs. Individuals like myself, who had been exempted from military service for health-related reasons, repeatedly lost out.

I was forced to temporarily take a much lower-paying job as a messenger and relocated to Buzzard's Point in Southwest Washington, D.C. But it seemed to be of little significance. I was still greatly inspired by the contents of the workers education proposal that I had previously submitted to Rosenwald and was likewise still convinced that the program would work, once I had the opportunity to implement it.

Despite all of these temporary setbacks, I still had a great wife, a young son, and was in graduate school. My diabetes seemed to be under control, not in the least due to my strict schedule and self-discipline that had carried me forth since I was a little boy. I pressed on, stayed in school, and anticipated that this setback in career was to be only temporary.

Having been the object of considerable health-related derision as a child, I ignored those who chided me about taking a job as a messenger at the GS 2 grade level after I had earned a college degree and already entered the professional ranks in the federal government, a position from which the Negro was still widely excluded. Several of my former colleagues said to me, "Jim, aren't you ashamed to work as a clerk? You're a college graduate." And I looked at them and scoffed. I said, "Ashamed? Ashamed of what? Ashamed of surviving? No, I'm not ashamed. This is just a bump in the road, and I'll be back up soon."

How quickly we forget. Several of these critics had immediate family members, often their own parents, who had earned college degrees, yet were relegated to "Negro jobs" in the government. While relatively few members of that group were ever elevated to the professional level, it seemed odd to me that most of my critics, my age contemporaries who were likewise the first wave of professionals of color in the federal government, had quickly forgotten where they came from, or the circumstances that Negro federal workers faced less than a full generation ago.

I had only worked as a messenger for a couple of months in the fall of 1947 when I learned that my wife was pregnant again. With the good news came a job offer from the U.S. Department of Commerce. I was called back to the U.S. Census Bureau in Suitland, Maryland, my sixth job since graduating from Miner Teachers College. This was the opportunity that I had been waiting for—a chance to use both my statistical and economics experience in forecasting trends and keeping records of various components of the U.S. and world economy. My job title was "Economist," and I was assigned work in the foreign trade section to assess U.S. trade and trends in the international trade arena, working with data and reports relative to types of goods being shipped, annual tonnage, and where goods were being sent and received.

Starting at the GS 7, I was the first African-American professional to go there and rapidly rose to the rank of GS 11 before being reduced in force once again during the recession of 1953.

I enjoyed immensely working at the Census Bureau. The work was both interesting and challenging. I had a strong sense of accomplishment and could see the direct fruits of my labor. Some of my reports found their way to the databases upon which international trends and forecasts were based. Some of my statistical calculations and economics-related observations were picked up and used by my superiors as they plotted where both the U.S. economy and the economies of a number of foreign countries were headed.

With the birth of Joherra, my daughter and second child, in June 1948, coupled with my not being selected for the Rosenwald Fellowship earlier that year, I put my Ph.D. pursuit on hold—"temporarily." For the next years, I entertained myself with the belief that "next semester," I would actively return to pursuing the degree, especially since my course work was just one academic semester short of being completed. However, with increased family obligations and expanded job-related duties, I never returned to pursuing the degree, perhaps undone by the thought of the amount of research required before I completed my dissertation.

Whether the efforts required for the final research and dissertation components of the degree would have adversely impacted upon my diabetes is anybody's guess. But in retrospect, I certainly could not have ignored the fact that stress related to the effort required to finally earn the Ph.D. degree would assuredly have been significant. While my diabetes seemed to be relatively under control during that period, from experience I learned all too well that "control" is a word that is often inapplicable to juvenile diabetics, no matter how careful they have been.

Had I obtained the Ph.D. degree in economics in about 1950, I would have been one of the very few Negro men in the United States with an earned doctorate in that discipline. While I have some regrets at not seeing the degree through to completion, in retrospect I have received so many other bountiful blessings in other areas, both personal and job related, for which I remain eternally grateful.

One of these great honors and highlights was offered to me circa 1948-49, after my statistical work was evaluated. I was offered the position of Primary Coordinator and asked to accompany a team from the U.S. Census Bureau to Ethiopia to conduct that country's first census in modern times. I would have gladly accepted the offer, but for the fact that I was a juvenile diabetic and the conditions in this extremely poor African country would most assuredly have been adverse to my health. Given the overall conditions of the country at that time, I did not feel that I could handle any diabetes-related problems that might suddenly arise in Ethiopia. So I turned down the offer, and someone else was selected for that responsibility.

# Chapter 12

# Hitting My Stride,
# Coming Into My Own

With the election of Dwight D. Eisenhower as the 34th President of the United States, followed by a recession and readjustment in the U.S. economy, I was once again laid off from my second job at the U.S. Census Bureau. This time I had worked there since 1947. It was 1953, and I was now the father of three children—Rohulamin, Joherra, and John.

As noted earlier, my eldest son, Rohulamin, was named for his maternal grandfather, Mohammed Abdul Rohualamin, who migrated to Barbados from India in 1913. My daughter, Joherra, who was born in 1948, was named for her mother. When my second son came along in February 1951, we named him John Edward III, after my father, who died in August 1950, and my elder brother John Edward II, who died of tuberculosis in 1924. I promised Papa at the time of his death from pneumonia, after a fall on the job, my good and faithful Papa, that if my next child was a boy, I was going to name him for him. And I did.

But suddenly with no job for the first time since graduating from college in 1940, I turned to teaching. I knew key people in the D.C. public school system and signed up as a substitute teacher. I had long ago rejected the notion of teaching school; but here I was, out of economic necessity, teaching the third grade at Richardson Elementary School in Washington, D.C.

What initially started out as an on-call substitute quickly turned into almost a full year of teaching when one of the teachers, whom I knew from college days, went out on maternity leave. I was asked to complete the school year to assure stability in the classroom. I took the assignment, and frankly, it was a welcome change from what I had been doing since July 1, 1940, when I started working in the U.S. postal service.

I retreated back to some of my former eating habits. Since there was no cafeteria in the school, I was unable to buy a balanced meal. I took particular care to bring a nutritious meal from home each day. My selections were varied, but similar to my room temperature meals from childhood—full portions carefully wrapped, often something left over from last night's dinner.

There were no microwaves in those days, although the school had a warming stove. In addition to a meat and two vegetables, I also ate salads almost every day, with the tomatoes wrapped separate from the lettuce to prevent sogginess; fresh fruit; small containers of bread, rice, or tapioca pudding made with Saccharin; a thermos containing ice tea or hot coffee; plus occasional homemade soup that my wife or I had made the night before. Naturally my luncheon meals attracted quite a bit of attention, but I never let on why I elected to eat such "elaborate meals," as one of my fellow teachers used to call them. A sandwich alone, without significantly more, was too risky given my insulin requirements, although at that time I was not taking midday injections.

In the fall of 1954, after having been out of the federal system for an entire year, I was hired by the Department of Defense as a GS-7 and assigned to the U.S. Army Signal Corps located at Fort Myer, Virginia. It had been a demanding year teaching third grade, and I was looking forward to getting back into the federal government. My teaching assignment had ended in June, and I resisted the urgings of my former Miner and Dunbar classmates to sign on with the D.C. public schools and pursue classroom teaching as a career. Some of them also encouraged me to enter the field of educational administration, noting that perhaps I would work better as a principal or a school administrator, but that was not what I wanted to do.

Because my wife knew someone who was able to intercede on my behalf, I was selected for this job from a field of other likewise qualified applicants. I had broken the color line several times before, and I thought that maybe the military, which had been integrated in 1949 by an executive order from President Truman, might be ready to have a Negro man as their instructor. This was partly because so many black men and women had served in the armed forces during both of the two recent wars.

I had enjoyed working as a statistician and economist at the Census Bureau, and had risen to the GS-11 grade level at the time of being laid off. I was the first professional in my area and had risen up through the ranks and garnered personal satisfaction and recognition from the other Negro employees as someone who was on the move. To suddenly lose that when the layoff came was a personal disappointment.

Fortunately, I had not only the constant encouragement of my lovely wife to keep my mind focused on getting back into the federal system but also the strong memories of my father, my soul mate in my youth, who has always been with me in spirit, even today in 2004, 54 years after his death.

I carry him in my heart and talk to him daily as if he were still here with me in the flesh. He was such wise counsel, seemed to have answers to many things; and he had a calming influence on everyone, especially if he did not have a ready answer for them. We need to have more people in the world like him. His strength was not so much formal book knowledge—he only completed the second grade—but he possessed what the elders used to call "good horse sense." That was Papa.

I had the strangest job title: "Organization of Methods Examiner." I did not know it at the time, but with this job, I was preparing myself for what would eventually be the legacy of my professional career with the federal government. I was about to become a teacher.

For the prior several years, the federal government had been conducting a comprehensive self-examination about methods and how to improve the efficiency of its own work force. The self-assessment confirmed that there were too many workers doing duplicative work. Many of them were far too slow, and other employees had no clue about what they were doing or what was reasonably expected of them in the workplace.

Clearly, production had to be significantly improved, and comprehensive training on work habits and methods was an integral part of improved production. Initially, I was assigned to visit local work sites, observe people working both alone and in groups, and determine and document who among the group was a "poor" or "slow" worker, according to some previously established criteria. Today we call this assessment and adjustment "industrial engineering."

Conversely, when I observed good workers, I was to document what it was about those workers that made them better. This eventually led to the creation of methods to simplify yet enhance worker output. It continues to amaze me that in the federal government, as late as 1954, they were still struggling with the basic question about how to improve production. It seemed odd at the time, but the efforts I exerted in the 1945-1948 period related to workplace safety and conditions and worker education was, belatedly, going to get its play after all.

With little to no resources, I created materials to guide me, work simplification procedures that encompassed everything from placing the furniture in more efficient locations, to reducing the distance and amount of time spent commuting from location "A" to location "B," to placing most frequently-needed items right beside the worker eliminating the need to go searching for them. The goal was to create objective standards for measuring performance output.

As a college-trained man, I assembled information and developed a complete set of work procedures to enhance their functionality in the workplace. Falling back upon my skills as a writer and securing materials to aid my students in improving their own writing abilities, I set up a comprehensive course and settled into being a classroom teacher. Instead of children, I was working with adults. After writing the manual, I then taught the class, sometimes writing just a day or two ahead of the teaching schedule.

Suggesting the need to place things closer together could have been construed as elementary and as an insult to the men who had recently won World War II and now were engaged in the Korean Conflict. Yet these simple things seemed to elude those who were spending billions of dollars of taxpayers' money on war and weaponry.

Until that time, I had never worked with the military. My only prior exposure was high school ROTC, which was under the supervision and guidance of active military men, people whom I saw but did not necessarily come into contact with. Now at the U.S. Army Signal Corps, I was exposed to both military and civilian personnel, all working for this military operation. I never developed a taste for it, and what little exposure I did have, I consider as overall negative.

In my then 36 years, I had never met people like this. With a couple of exceptions, the students were all white, generally from the lower economic backgrounds, and not well educated. Many of them had dropped out of school, some even before reaching high school; and now I was expected to teach them better working habits, how to follow instructions, and to monitor their writing skills.

Compared to my own Dunbar and Miner experiences, primarily with smaller groups of well-educated and informed members of the black middle class, the tables were turned on me. These were the rudest, crudest, most uninformed people I had ever come in contact with. Their vulgar language, clearly lower-class values, method of speaking, and attitudes combined to show me a side of white America that I did not know.

While a significant number of them had difficulty accepting as beneficial anything that a black man told them, even those who seemed not too troubled by this arrangement still demonstrated their ignorance. They perpetuated and verified the widely-held belief that most of the enlisted men, and a few women, had enrolled in the military simply because they had nothing else to do.

Most of the people I was assigned to work with and teach came from the Southern states, and Mississippi seemed to be the state of choice. As well, the first person that I came in contact with on a sustained basis was my supervisor, William Farrell, who was also from Mississippi. He made it very clear from the outset that he never would have hired me, or any other man of color, but that I was imposed upon him by his higher-ups. This was a great way to start off a new job after having been out of the federal service for over a year.

He never had a Negro professional in his office before. Most of the men of color that he came in contact with were military men from a lower socioeconomic and educational background. Farrell really did not know what to expect, and neither did the other members of the office. The idea of having a black man watch and monitor their work habits, make suggestions to them, and then even teach them how to improve those habits in a structured classroom setting was not only alien to all of them, but also an opportunity for some of them to resist everything that I was trying to impart.

Although this was a stressful experience, it was a great learning opportunity for everyone as well. I drew upon all that was within me for inner strength to find a way to work with these people; I had to reach them before I could teach them and make them want to benefit from what I had to offer. The students were routinely rotated into my class; and after several sessions and organizational projects, they were sent back to their job assignments to implement what they had learned.

I was up to my elbows in lesson plans, module creations, and planning skits to demonstrate how they could improve their skills. Before I realized it fully, I had reinvented myself as an "expert" and created a whole new sense of marketability for myself. It was the very early stage of the computer era; and while I did not yet realize it, my skills were notable elsewhere, even beyond the Department of Defense. Eventually I was picked up by the U.S. Labor Department and trained as one of their early computer programmers. But that story is still some time in the future.

What I was doing at the U.S. Army Signal Corps was a long way from my practice teaching days at Miner, although I organized the mission and functions the same way with lesson plans focused on purpose, desired outcomes, objectives, and procedures. I had done this for elementary school children, and they seemed to understand and grasp what was going on. Sorry I cannot say the same for a significant portion of my former Signal Corps students. Many of them never did seem to get it no matter what I did.

The stress factors of my two-year stint with the Signal Corps caused my diabetic condition to flare up on several occasions. I found myself taking sick leave at a higher level than I would have expected and even had more than one insulin reaction on the job. On one particular occasion I had to be revived by an ambulance crew, although I declined to be hospitalized afterwards. Because I was still in the "diabetic closet," no one at work knew what was wrong with me, and not being particularly savvy about it, I still doubt that they ever figured it out.

One day I had a severe insulin reaction before lunch. I was supposed to meet my wife for lunch and managed to get to the pickup area where she was driving over from the Pentagon. Somehow I deteriorated into what would appear to be a drunken stupor—unable to speak, unable to ask anyone for help, and seemingly lost in time. I have no real recollection of the incident and might well have lapsed into a coma had it not been for a coworker, James Texeira, who happened by and seeing me realized that something was drastically wrong.

As he would later relate to me, he came over and started asking me if there was something wrong. I looked at him with a blank stare, but no words came out of my mouth. Then he asked me, "Jim, are you a diabetic?"

I nodded "Yes!"

"And on insulin, too?"

Again I nodded in the affirmative at which point he immediately took me by the arm and led me to the infirmary where he told the nurse that I was a diabetic and was experiencing a low blood sugar attack.

She gave me some orange juice with a dose of stirred sugar added and let me cool my heels there for a while. By then, Joherra arrived at the infirmary; someone had told her when she drove up that I had gotten ill. That incident, plus the day the ambulance crew revived me, were the worst of the stress-induced diabetic experiences that I had while working there.

But there were other days when I could feel something coming on. On those occasions, I was always able to offset those possible reactions with hard peppermint candy that I always kept on my person to raise my blood sugar level. Noting the deterioration in my health, my doctors urged me to work my way out of that job since the atmosphere was not conducive to my medical condition.

I vowed to get out of that place as soon as humanly possible, but the terrible experience that I had next came before I could get away. One day a white female coworker climbed onto a swivel chair with wheels to adjust the Venetian blinds. As she reached even higher to adjust the blinds, the chair suddenly rolled away, throwing her bottom first onto the floor.

She screamed and fell backwards, landing hard onto the tile floor. As a reflective action, and being both a gentleman and the person located closest to her, I instantly jumped up and ran to her aid, intending to comfort her and help her up. Instead of accepting my act of kindness for what it was, and despite the obvious shooting pain that she was experiencing, she still mustered up enough strength and hatred to utter, "Don't you put your goddamn black hands on me!"

I was so shocked at what she said and how she reacted that I recoiled in disbelief. As others in the office came running to her aid, she raised her voice; and they all heard her shrill repeat of what she had initially said, "Don't you put your goddamn black hands on me!"

I temporarily became blind with hurt and rage and then extreme embarrassment, unable to see anything or anybody around me. I found my way to the men's room where I broke out into a cold sweat, and then I cried like a baby. I was a grown man, 37 years old, and some low-class white woman had insulted me in the office when all I did was try to be a decent human being to aid her in a moment of her great physical pain.

But the matter was not yet finished. When I came out of the men's room, perhaps as long as an hour later, to re-present myself in the office, I then learned that she had lied about me: she said that I had tried to get fresh with her, she had resisted me, and this resulted in her falling on the floor. There was no mention of her having fallen off the chair while engaging in an act of stupidity. Who in her right mind would stand on a wheeled swivel chair and then reach even higher to adjust some Venetian blinds? That act underscored that she was not very bright, to say the least.

Fortunately, several of the other white women in the office came to my rescue and told Farrell, my boss, that she was lying and trying to manufacture an excuse for her own inappropriate office behavior on that and other prior occasions. However, I was never able to bring satisfactory closure to the incident. Farrell called me in after the in-office investigation, and instead of apologizing to me on her behalf, he said, "You know, some people just don't like 'ya,' and never will like 'ya.' And don't say anything to them unless they say something to you first. Don't you offer to assist them in any way unless they ask for assistance."

After that chastisement, all I could do was wonder. Did I do something wrong? She told the big lie, and now I was the one being punished, admonished if you will, and told to stay out of certain people's way. Hey, listen up William Farrell—I was not the perpetrator of this incident, so why am I being treated this way? I vowed once again, and this time with even greater determination, to get out of both the Department of Defense and the U.S. Army Signal Corps.

But the daily stress of that job, later exacerbated by this horrible experience, caused my diabetes to spring out of control. For the first time in many years, I found myself reverting back to some of my old methods, methods that I had not had to use for several years, to combat the wildly fluctuating blood sugar levels.

Based upon my prior experience with this same situation in the past, the first item was to adjust my insulin intake. On those days when I was plagued with high blood sugar, often the result of stress, I increased my insulin intake. Conversely, on those days when my blood sugar was lower than "normal," I concomitantly reduced the insulin. During much of this era I was taking U-80 insulin twice per day, and occasionally three times per day, plus NPH, a slower acting but more evenly distributed insulin.

Although I have always maintained a strict diet, it consistently included a relatively high carbohydrate and starch intake, usually potatoes every day. This diet was somewhat contrary to what some diabetic nutritionists have recommended. However, my body chemistry always seemed to accommodate this diet without adverse effects. But in the context of the above-noted stress situation, I sharply reduced those intakes temporarily to quickly force my blood sugar back into acceptable limits, even though it never consistently stayed "normal." Still, my objective was to establish a more usual pattern of blood sugar level; and from that pattern I could determine whether things had reverted back to a more normal level, given my overall physiology.

And of course I fell back into my old pattern of getting more exercise. As an adult I never belonged to a gym or engaged in any specific pattern of exercise, but when this stress-induced condition recurred, long walks and more overall physical activity were always a part of the remedy. When going to the supermarket or a Cub Scout or community meeting in the area, I often walked the 10 to 12 blocks to the event. Sometimes my wife would drive there and meet me when I had heavy packages to bring home or when I was returning late in the evening. It was a workable solution, and I am convinced that it contributed to my longevity as a juvenile diabetic.

On another day, shortly before I left this job, Farrell and I were engaging in one of our always-strained conversations when he volunteered to me, "I didn't make the rules, but I'm going to abide by them. But you know, people of color have to be twice as smart, do twice the work, and stay on their toes at all times, to get half the recognition." If that was supposed to be a compliment, or if in his convoluted way he was trying to say that this overall condition was unfair, it evaded me completely. And I told him as much.

He never seemed to understand just how offensive his attitude towards Negroes was. He was frequently devoted to agitating me to say or do something that could result in my being written up for insubordination, but I was not that stupid. I bit my tongue and bided my time. This was an approach that Jim Quander was not necessarily known to follow, but under these circumstances, I had little choice.

My fourth child, Ricardo, was due in December 1954, and my wife would soon be going out on maternity leave. One of us had to keep getting out in the morning, and that responsibility fell squarely on my shoulders.

It seems somewhat ironic now to look back on my strained relationship with William Farrell. He was an Irish Catholic from Mississippi, seemingly very religious and always running to Mass. And I am a native Washingtonian whose family has been here for generations, also a born Catholic, raised in a strict religious environment in which all of the holy days and religious traditions were observed. Yet he and I were so different, the result of our vastly divergent life experiences, not the least of which was the racial legacies of Mississippi and the Nation's Capital City.

Looking back on these early days of racial integration, I have mellowed somewhat, although I am not ready to concede that

Farrell was really trying to reach out and be friendly towards me. I guess that he wanted to get to understand African-Americans better, but he did not have the personal rapport tools at his disposal to indicate such. Rather than extend a hand of friendship I had no interest in, he would extend himself towards me by asking such questions as the following: "How does the Negro feel about whether schools should be integrated?" "What does the Negro want anyway?" "How do the colored people feel about this issue?"

I had to tell him more than once that I was a trained economist and statistician, had come to the Signal Corps to teach workers how to be more efficient in their jobs, and that there was no "Negro position" on any single subject or issue. After he asked the same question several times in the context of some current event, I told him in the most direct way that I could that if he wanted that information, he should contact the Urban League or the NAACP and ask them. They had resources, studied issues, and took and defended selected positions. Recoiling from that suggestion, he called both of those organizations "fascist" and never raised the issue with me again.

My writing and training experience at the Signal Corps was the base upon which I built my opportunity to transfer out of that organization. It was early in the computer era, and names like UNIVAC, International Business Machines (IBM), and Remington were the coming things in the new computer age. Hardly anyone knew what computers were, and the term "computer" was synonymous with the term "calculator" in many people's minds. That an entirely new field of knowledge and approach to gaining knowledge was on the threshold of being developed was within the purview of a relatively small group of people.

But for those people who were aware, including the military, as we pursued the Cold War against the Communist bloc countries, there was a coming use for computers. The Army Signal Corps was at the forefront of developing and adapting computers for military use. It was widely recognized that the future belonged to the most highly technically organized society; and in the face of daily threats from Russia and an emerging China, the United States needed to be number one in this field and application.

I was deemed to be one of those ripe for prime time. I had heard on the periphery that a military application for computers was the coming field, and by 1955-56, the first generation of the computer era was upon us. The computers then were nothing in comparison to today's supercomputers that can pinpoint an interplanetary landing to within a few yards. Initially, these were large, bulky, first-generation tube-operated computers of the late 1940s. They soon gave way to transistors making the successful operation of the computer faster, more efficient, and smaller. Of course by today's standard, those 1950s era computers were dinosaurs.

Farrell, who had never wanted to hire a Negro professional in the first place, and said as much shortly after I was imposed upon him, soon found out that his non-favored employee was now in great demand to become a computer programmer. I was identified as someone who could learn the system and then teach it to the same basic group of people who had recently been exposed to work simplification procedures.

Despite the potential and the opportunities that were on the horizon, I disliked the military intensely and decided not to pursue the computer-related employment options there. Just as the military had computer operations, the civilian community realized the same potential for application to all aspects of the civilian population and society.

Upon application in 1956, I was selected for a position as a computer programmer at the U.S. Department of Labor in the Bureau of Labor Statistics (BLS). Working for the Labor Department was the longest assignment I had in my 33 years of federal service: it was the agency from which I eventually retired in 1973. With my background in statistics and economics, coupled with my teaching and writing experience at the Signal Corps, I was rated highly and recommended to be one of the first computer programmers at BLS.

Upon being hired, I was enrolled in comprehensive computer programming training classes that were designed to teach me how the different computers worked, their potential applications, the various computer languages of the day, how to relate those applications to the everyday workplace, and how to train other employees on computer uses and application. It was a great challenge...and something that I eventually grew to dislike. I wanted to work directly with people. Contrarily, my entire early career as a computer programmer was spent in small settings, working with only a few people, and spending an enormous amount of time working alone, focused upon how to use these new machines for the desired benefit.

Despite the high stress levels associated with learning the technicalities of computer operations, my diabetes stayed reasonably in check. When I went to Labor, I was 38 years old. My diabetic condition had "matured" somewhat. This is not to say that it was under control; it never has been. But I was still adhering to my strict routine that included classes at a certain time, a balanced lunch diet at a certain time, and keeping hard peppermint candy handy to use as needed, especially in the afternoons when my blood sugar would sometimes drop precipitously with little or no warning. Following my standard procedure, I had never indicated on any job applications that I was a diabetic; and if anyone knew about my condition, they apparently never reported it to personnel. I was still in the "diabetic closet" and elected to remain there,

Eventually, after I had spent a considerable amount of time devoted to computers, I had an opportunity in 1968 to transfer from BLS to the Office of Manpower Development (OMD) with the job title of Program Analyst—in essence a return to my first love, workers education. The federal government was concerned about the state of youth in the private sector job market and the need for all levels of employment to attract and train the younger people to the work force.

Through federal legislation, the government was sponsoring programs, incentives, and training to help the private sector reach out to these younger people, including monitoring what steps to take to retain them in the work force. America was still suffering from the effects of a poorly trained work force and had come to realize the necessity of training younger workers, to get them to understand the concept of the work ethic, including the somewhat still-not-yet-appreciated component of the need for the worker to be happy and satisfied in the job.

My role in the manpower development program was to coordinate statistical data that had been assembled concerning the manpower development effort, interpret it, and reduce it to written reports on various aspects of the sustained effort. This time I was not putting the worker educational programs together, but rather I was interpreting the results of others' efforts to monitor whether worker education programs were successfully reaching their intended targets.

I had always been a self-motivator, and my years at Labor were no different. Whether attending computer class, developing a statistical report on the younger worker training efforts for Manpower Development, completing a special assignment, or interacting with my coworkers, I always did strive to do my best. And in pursuit of "the best," on at least two occasions I got so involved in what I was doing that I overlooked getting my lunch on schedule. When we got wrapped up in a project and faced a deadline, it was not unusual for staff to put lunch off for a while since no one in the office realized that I was diabetic.

Daily I was taking two types of insulin before breakfast. First I took several units of U-80, but the dosage level depended upon my blood-sugar level immediately prior to that meal. Almost immediately this insulin took effect in my blood stream reducing that level of blood sugar fairly quickly. I also injected several units of NPH at the same time, but not mixed in the same syringe. NPH is much slower acting, spreading the infusion of insulin over a period of several hours, and thus maintaining a certain level of some insulin in my system at all times.

For that reason, it was critically important that I eat a balanced lunch on time each day. But on two separate occasions, spread some years apart, my calculations went askew, and I had severe reactions. During each of these incidents I became extremely sweaty, could not speak clearly or communicate that I was having a problem, and then passed out, including falling out of my chair and hitting the floor. On both occasions, I ended up in the emergency room at the George Washington University Hospital.

In each instance, I was totally unconscious when the ambulance arrived. No one at the office knew what was wrong with me, and I later learned that they thought I was having a heart attack each time. In retrospect, had they known of my diabetic condition, brief diabetic-related hospitalizations probably would not have been necessary.

Further, only in later years did I come to appreciate that each time I had a diabetic-related health problem at work, I placed myself in potentially mortal danger: valuable time was lost on each occasion for the medical personnel to figure out exactly what was wrong with me and to treat the condition. A direct infusion of glucose into my blood system would have increased my blood sugar quickly and dramatically.

However, in addition to periodic racial discrimination, the stings of health-related discrimination had also burned me; and I was fearful of trusting anyone. As a member of a minority group— college educated, black male in a new field—I was breaking the ice and under a lot of pressure to do well for my race. Many would argue that I was not the water carrier for the race, but I strongly disagreed then and still disagree now.

Daily the newspapers reported crimes and transgressions that the black man was involved in committing; and following their long-standing racist policies, they always identified the alleged criminal as "colored" or "Negro" where applicable, yet they said nothing equivalent about race if the perpetrator was white.

Likewise, the continuing stings of illegitimate births, low-educational levels, grinding poverty and female-headed households, all exacerbated the black man's burden. While I was none of that, I still felt very strongly that it was my burden and responsibility to carry my share, and the share of those still to come, in demonstrating that I was but one of many African-American males who did not fit the imposed negative stereotype.

My precarious health situation, therefore, was something that I deliberately chose not to divulge. In my estimation, it was still important to keep my diabetes a secret. I saw no reason to give any potential enemies ammunition to use against me, especially since I had accumulated about 20 years of federal service and had never revealed my health condition on any job applications. Nowhere in my personnel file was it reflected that I was a juvenile diabetic and had been formally diagnosed with such in 1924.

By far, not all white people were the enemy. But my personal concern, as I continued to break the ice for the next generation of young blacks, was that any one individual who did not like me personally, or resented the ascendancy of the African-American worker into the professional realm of the federal government, could undermine me. Anyone with an agenda could report that I had concealed a long-standing health condition and had falsified my personnel records.

As I noted earlier, whenever I applied for a new job and completed the application form, invariably the question was asked, "Have you had a nervous breakdown, tuberculosis, cancer, a heart condition, or diabetes?" I continued to leave this item blank and never checked off "Yes" or "No," having discussed this question with both my priest and doctor, each of whom suggested that I just leave the item blank, so that no one could say that I actively lied on the federal job application form. For the entire time of my professional career, I am pleased to say that no one ever said to me, "Hey, Jim, you forgot to answer one of the health questions."

My continuing position on this subject is reinforced by the aftermath of a severe diabetic reaction that I had at the Census Bureau, which I mentioned earlier. One of my supervisors there, upon learning that I had had a diabetic reaction on the job, told me that he was going to have me fired because I was a diabetic. He came to me that day and said, "You didn't tell me that you were a diabetic. If I had known, I never would have hired you." He concluded his chastisement with, "I'm going to get rid of you!"

And that is why years later at the Labor Department, Charlotte Johnson, my good friend and coworker, and later herself an adult-onset diabetic, elected not to reveal to anyone what she knew was wrong with me the second time that I passed out at work. After losing consciousness and while being transported to the George Washington University Hospital by ambulance, I woke up in a cold sweat, soaking wet, as she repeatedly but gently slapped my face, calling, "James, James, can you hear me?" As I came to, I asked her what had happened and where was I. Telling me that I had passed out at work, she also advised that she had not told anyone what she thought had occurred. My secret was safe with her.

That particular experience was enlightening. I was now well past 40 years old, and my body chemistry had long ago "matured" and adjusted to the chemical components of my diabetic condition. Yet as I recovered from that particularly critical attack, I noticed some changes. I was not able to spring back from the low-blood-sugar insulin-related reaction as quickly as I had in the past. With the tremendous drop in my blood glucose level to 22, my energy level was completely drained and did not immediately restore upon the infusion of glucose into my system. This was a sign of aging. I further realized that these severe diabetic reactions imposed a tremendous toll upon my entire body systems—in particular, my heart, brain, eyes, and kidneys.

When I joined the U.S. Labor Department in 1956, I did not yet realize that I would complete my federal career from that agency. By then, I had rendered diversified federal service that included the U.S. Post Office, the Government Printing Office, the Office of Price Administration, the Office of the Housing Expediter, the U.S. Department of Commerce (the Census Bureau), the Department of Defense (U.S. Army Signal Corps), intermittent assignments in lower federal paying positions (messenger) during layoff periods, and almost a full academic year teaching in the D.C. public schools.

But with the Kennedy and Johnson Administrations came an officially changed attitude, one that specifically reached out to attract and place qualified minority race and female employees throughout the government. I interpreted this publicly stated position as a good sign, one that potentially could give me the break that I had always hoped for but still had not gotten. When John F. Kennedy was inaugurated on January 20, 1961, I was 42 years old and primed for anything that came my way.

At the time I was still at the GS-9 grade level, trying to get a GS-11, working with the civilian applications of computer programming to the general work force. Beyond the requirements of my job description, I voluntarily wrote another manual on work simplification in a computer-assisted office operation that had far-reaching application well beyond BLS.

The manual was well received and used throughout the agency. Rudolph Mendelson, my division chief, recommended that the book be published and that I be given a monetary incentive award for my effort, neither one of which recommendations ever occurred. But the effort increased my visibility significantly, and eventually I was promoted to the GS-11 grade.

Armed with this incentive, I felt that just maybe, after more than 20 years of federal service, I might finally get the big break that I had always hoped for in the federal system. I contacted Assistant Secretary of Labor Reynolds and requested an appointment to discuss my career in the context of President Kennedy's early 1963 initiative to increase minority presence in decision-making positions in the federal government.

The appointment was granted, and I prepared and presented carefully crafted remarks to Secretary Reynolds. Noting that I had read in the *Washington Post* that the new administration was undertaking a diversified effort to attract and place qualified minorities, particularly those of Negro descent, into decision-making leadership positions, I presented myself to him. I was a member of the prime class that should be considered—the worker with diversified background and experience who still had many good years of dedicated service to provide. I stated that I was interested in being better utilized.

I asked to be considered for a position at Labor as an integral part of the President's recently stated effort. I concluded our brief but cordial meeting by providing him with a copy of a Form 57 personnel application that also included a reference to the extra work that I had done for years in work simplification techniques.

Despite his seeming cordiality, I left the meeting with a sense of unease about how I was received. Had he really listened to what I said? Would he give me the leadership opportunity that I had longed for yet never received? Although I did not particularly care for the depersonalization associated with working with computers, my coworkers readily recognized that I had a good grasp of the subject area and was talented in helping them and others simplify their work efforts to the benefit of not only BLS but throughout other offices in the Labor Department. It was this talent that I was seeking to share with a more widely-based work force at the Department.

What occurred next had a long-standing negative effect upon the balance of my entire career, an effect from which I never recovered. Instead of being considered for a new appointment, Reynolds wrote a statement that he sent to my supervisor stating, "While Jim Quander did not actually say that he has been discriminated against, I think that he thinks that he has been."

And like a bad dream that repeats itself, this statement spread widely throughout the upper levels of the agency; and pretty soon the alleged statement got back to me in a distorted form. It was initially reported that I had said I had been discriminated against because of my race. Further, it was also reported that I had filed a discrimination complaint against both my immediate and secondary level supervisors and the agency. Yet none of this attribution was true. Not one word of it. I was most careful to pre-select my words before I met with Reynolds and just as careful to adhere to what I planned to say.

My words were horribly contorted, and what I actually did say was turned against me, perhaps to the point of a self-fulfilling prophecy. For while I never claimed discrimination, and likewise never filed a discrimination complaint, the white power structure seemed determined to seek retribution against me for what they believed I thought. And from that day forward, until I eventually retired, I always felt that many of my supervisors looked upon me with a jaundiced eye and a great deal of suspicion about what I was going to do next.

In retrospect it seems hypocritical that the federal government would put new regulations in place to aid people who were generationally and historically the victims of racial discrimination, yet at the same time expose some of its best employees to the personal retributions of supervisors who exercised their whim of possible retaliation against that same class of employees.

For the next three years I went literally nowhere career-wise. Many of my coworkers urged me to file formal charges of discrimination; but I resisted knowing that if I did so, I would probably be even more isolated than I already was, and that none of them would be joining me in my lonely and costly pursuit of proving discrimination. I elected to bide my time and look for an opportunity to escape from BLS and the computer field at the earliest opportunity.

When I transferred into the manpower development program at OMD in 1966 as a Manpower Development Specialist, I was awarded a GS-12 grade level. The joys of having finally escaped BLS and computer programming, plus the promotion itself, were only short-lived. Carrying the false mantle of what he had heard, my new supervisor, James Decou, introduced himself to me for the first time by saying, "So you're Jim Quander, the one who brought charges of discrimination. The big chief will take care of your black ass."

When I denied the accusation and immediately told him that I had never filed such charges, he said to me, "Are you calling me a liar?"

I immediately got up to leave, and he shouted at me, "I have not dismissed you!"

I retorted, "No, you have not dismissed me, but I have dismissed you!" And I walked out of his office. This is how you start off in a new job? I hardly think so.

Fully realizing that this matter had gone much too far and that lies had been told and then perpetuated at the highest level of the agency, I finally went to my union representatives, filed a formal complaint with them, and asked them to investigate. Still, this was not a racial discrimination complaint, a civil rights matter that can be long, detailed, and difficult to prove. This complaint was more in the nature of a grievance, to ask for a full investigation as to why this lie was being so widely perpetuated when there was not a word of truth to it.

It was only after the union took on the project and interacted with the top officials of the agency that it was realized that I had never filed a discrimination complaint, and that the false assertion to that effect grew out of the Under Secretary's own opinions about what I was allegedly thinking.

During one of the follow-up meetings between government staff and my union representative, with me also present, it was accidentally disclosed that the agency had created what best can be described as a "secret file" on me. It was a file that contained a dossier of adverse information compiled by various supervisory persons in the BLS, OMD, and others. Upon a threat of filing a suit and making everything public by going to the press, we demanded to see and review the file.

Quite reluctantly it was shared with us. It contained the written thoughts of various persons who had essentially capitalized upon what they had heard, but little to none of it was based upon actual fact. Primarily, several of the comments focused upon the writers' reactions to my having filed a discrimination complaint, except for one main problem. I had never filed a discrimination complaint and had specifically elected not to do so. The file itself was libelous, full of lies, misimpressions, and statements based upon what various white men thought that I was thinking, or what they perceived to be my objectives. Since I had long weighed what the long-term effect and financial costs of filing a complaint would be and decided not to undertake that route, it still interests me greatly to ponder why they went in that direction and developed it to that point.

Of course the file was destroyed, and the agreement was that nothing in the file was to be disclosed. They relied upon the excuse that they created a separate "investigatory file" that was not a part of my regular personnel file so that they could focus upon what my work-related problems were and hopefully resolve them without causing any adverse information to be placed into and become a permanent part of my personnel file. The problem with that statement, however, was that no one ever interviewed me or discussed the file's contents in my presence prior to its accidental discovery. The context of the file's contents seemed more focused upon building a wall of isolation around me, to paint me as a pariah, someone who was to be isolated, left alone, and encouraged to retire.

Once again, the thoughts of a white man were being attributed to, and in this case used against a black man to the latter's detriment. In the final report of investigation that the union issued, it was noted that Jim Quander had been the victim of hidden and false accusations, which report also concluded that I had truly and unknowingly been the victim of discrimination. I was advised, and indeed encouraged, by those few coworkers who knew what had occurred, to file a civil suit. But once again, I elected not to do so. My diabetes was acting up, and I fully appreciated the extent of effort that would still be required. I did not have a stomach for that. I let it go and satisfied myself with the vindication that eventually became a part of the record.

After the true scope of what had happened was fully uncovered and appreciated, in 1968 I received one more promotion, to the position of Program Analyst, GS-13, before I retired. Whereas my immediate prior job was to assemble labor data that was provided on youth employment, analyze it, and reduce it to written reports, my job now encompassed much of the same effort but factored in editing and often rewriting the initial reports, initially prepared by other employees, some of whom had less-than-acceptable writing skills.

After discussions with my wife, Joherra, I decided to seriously consider retiring when I reached 55 years of age (April 19, 1973). By then I would also be completing 33 years of service (from July 1, 1940), despite periods of temporary layoffs due to two reductions in service (1947 and 1953). I figured that by then it would be time to hang it up, to leave the daily regimen of getting up early and out to work. But the end of my career did not come as I had expected it. But then again, things frequently occur in life in a manner much different from what had been anticipated.

One day in November 1973, I told Charles Carter, a fellow African-American coworker over whom I had some editing responsibility, although I was not his supervisor, that a certain standard operating procedures report that he had completed was not up to the office's standard. The document that he was attempting to put forth was simply incomprehensible. As an organization and methods person, who by then had had many years of experience in the federal government preparing different kinds of reports, I pointed out to him why I believed that the report was poorly written. In addition to some grammatical errors, the content and the style were just not right. The content did not flow, and the procedural steps explained in the report also contained factual and process errors that would mislead the reader and not achieve the desired result in the end.

How can you present a report that purports to be a manual on operating procedures, and the procedures themselves are fouled up? Rather than receiving the constructive criticism that I tendered, and I tried to be as diplomatic as possible when I directed him to reorganize the report to include certain particulars, he grew extremely hostile and combative. All sense of civility was lost as he questioned who I thought I was to be telling him to do a report over. By the time this heated conversation ended, I had referred to his operating procedures report as "garbage," and he maintained his hostility towards me and refused to receive any of the pointers I offered on how he could improve the document.

Our last conversation was by telephone. I left the report on the corner of my desk, telling him where it was, and directing him to retrieve and rewrite it. Scheduled to take a week of use-or-lose annual leave, I expected that he would collect the report and make a decent effort to comply. Upon my return, imagine my surprise to learn that the report, errors and all, had been issued. He had gone over my head to James Ring, my immediate supervisor, and Aaron Browning, section chief, and gotten their approvals. The report went forward and somewhere in the chain of command, the upper level supervisors were apparently told that I had approved the document before I went on leave.

Despite my personal signature never appearing on the approval buck slip, the report quickly fell into the administrative chain of command, complemented with a verbal indication that I had approved the operating procedures report. Eventually someone higher-up read the document and found it strange that something of this poor quality would be in the system for distribution. That the report was "garbage" came to the attention of the Secretary of Labor himself; and to his queries of who was responsible for this grossly inferior document, Ring and Browning proceeded to hang me out to dry by asserting that I had approved it and perhaps had "forgotten" to sign off before I went on leave. I was the scapegoat, and the matter percolated for several days with me totally unaware of what I was about to face.

Upon my return to work, Ring called me into his office, directing me to close the door behind me. Then he said, "You no longer have a job here because of that very bad report." When I inquired what he was talking about, only then did I learn that the report had been issued. By then both he and Carter were in deep denial of everything, having suddenly developed symptoms of amnesia regarding my prior refusal to pass the document on as initially written. I had been stuck with the full responsibility for everything that occurred and reminded him that before I went on leave, I personally told him why I could not approve the report as presented to me and what I expected to be done to correct it.

Neither Ring nor Browning apparently expected such a wide-reaching fallout. Now with the heat on, they threw me to the wolves to save their own skins. I did some investigating on my own and discovered that Browning apparently authorized Carter to take the report off of my desk and forward it, despite my prior rejection. In the end and because of their cover-up, I was the only one who suffered any repercussions. And they were long and lasting.

Previously, in 1972 and again in early 1973, Browning invited me into his office under the guise of wanting to discuss some aspect of the job. Closing the door, and after engaging in some strained small talk, he drifted into telling me that as of April 19, 1973, I would be 55 years old, with more than 30 years of federal service. Next he told me that I should consider retiring, perhaps to make way for some younger workers. Without even waiting for me to respond, he slid directly into a question, "When are you going to retire?" This event was repeated two to three more times.

After trying to initially hedge on my answer, I eventually told him, "I'm going to retire when I'm good and damn ready!" With this harassment, I dug my heels in and hung on, determined to stay a bit longer. I wanted to leave when I was ready, not when Aaron Browning, through his harassments and illegal conversations, decided that I should go. During the next several months, life at the job was nothing, if not miserable.

Carter's sustained resentment made the environment most inhospitable. Ring refused to look me directly in the eye. He knew what he had become a party to when he allowed the standard operating procedures report to go forward, with its negative impact upon me at the end of my 33-year career. Of course Browning knew that each mention of retirement was both harassment and illegal. But as these conversations only took place between us, in his office with the door closed, he always had a cover of deniability.

The next morning after Ring had told me that I no longer had a job, I initiated a visit to Browning's office. As I neared his office, I saw him in the hallway. He shrank as he saw me approaching. Not waiting for a word of greeting, I immediately asked him two quick questions. First, why was the report issued in my absence when everyone knew why I refused to approve it? And before he could answer, I asked him very directly why Ring was telling me that I no longer had a job? I got no reply to either inquiry—only a Judas laugh as he stood there, seemingly dumbfounded at having been confronted and cornered in the hallway, uncertain what to say or how to reply to me.

I spoke up again and told him that he should be ashamed of himself and how he had acted throughout this entire mess, and especially now, since he knew the full story and had every opportunity to correct it. Yet he let the matter unfold, reinforced by the great lie that had been told at all levels, and was quite comfortable in letting the truth remain hidden. Next I told him that, if nothing else, he should be man enough to admit that he made a grave error, but there was still an opportunity to set the record straight. He was zombie-like, just standing there, a piece of stone, saying nothing, not even cracking that cynical smile that he had shown just a few seconds prior.

I was so angry that I could hardly see straight. Further, my anger grew as my frustration level increased at not being able to get him to open his mouth. This was the last straw. I was carrying several documents in my right hand, which I rolled tightly, and bopped him squarely on his head. Yes, I guess you could call it assault and battery. But at that point I simply did not care anymore. Turning on my heels, I marched myself to personnel and immediately put in my retirement papers. It was November 19, 1973. I listed December 31, 1973, as the effective date of my retirement, but as of November 19th, my 33 years of federal service came to an abrupt end.

Just as the word spread in certain circles that Jim Quander had allegedly approved a standard operating procedures report that was grossly erroneous and ungrammatical, and which could have potentially caused the agency great embarrassment, it likewise became equally known that such was clearly not what actually occurred. I had to protect myself and let it be universally known exactly what happened. Who believed me and who did not is of no significance. There were two stories abounding, and I knew which one was the truth. Several of my coworkers came to me saying the same thing, "Jim, you were set up. You can bet this. This is clear discrimination against the older worker, and your credibility is on the line here. You can fight and win this one." I agreed with them then, and in retrospect, I still agree with them.

A grave injustice was done, and it really needed to be addressed and corrected. But I had to ask myself, "At what cost? Should I stay and fight, not retire, and try to prove my point? Should I resist with all my being their efforts to get rid of me for whatever reason? Or should I simply let it go, chalk it up to experience, and move on?" As you read this book, you appreciate that I have fought many a battle. Most of them I won, and some I did not. But the key here is that Jim Quander was never afraid to claim his place in the sun, no matter what other people thought. But I asked myself this time, and Joherra agreed with me, do I really need to take this on at the same time that I already said that I was going to retire?

What would be the toll taken, not just in terms of money to pursue the claim, although I would retrieve that as a part of the victory? I mean the physical and emotional tolls upon my family and me. Already, my diabetes had been reminding me that I was under great stress. The blood sugar levels were fluctuating wildly, usually quite elevated in the morning and by about 4:00 p.m., dangerously low. Because I was taking my proper dosages of insulin and eating correctly, there was only one cause for this wide divergence—job-related stress. As long as I was under this great strain, I did not see getting my physical condition under control.

I believe that I would have won that battle, but in the long term, I might just as well have lost the war. So Jim Quander, who had fought the good fight for 33 years, starting as a mail carrier with the U.S. Postal Service in July 1940, and been the first or one of the first Negroes or African-Americans in the professional ranks in many of the federal offices or positions that he had held, beginning with the Office of Price Administration on January 3, 1944, had now decided to hang it up. My life and family were much more important to me than this job. I quit! Still, it was a shame that my career ended on such a bittersweet note, as the last incident is often the one that stays with you the longest. I never wanted a negative incident and experience to be the prompt for my immediate departure from the federal government.

But I left and never looked back. I already had my long-term plan in place—to serve my God, church, and community in my newfound career as a permanent deacon in the Catholic Church. Having been ordained in 1971, there was some overlap, but not a conflict, since my church work was primarily on the weekends.

But before I was able to leave the government and pursue my second career, there had to be one more glitch, an event in which certain forces tried for the last time to humiliate and harass me on the job. My decision to retire and the events leading up to my actual departure happened quickly. When I submitted my retirement papers, several of my coworkers, mostly women that I worked with, came to me and expressed their feelings about what had happened.

Charlotte Johnson, a good friend, with whom Joherra and I had also worked in the Cub Scout movement and the Northwest Boundary Civic Association, said, "Jim, you've been on the forefront for a long time, a role model to all of us, leading the way in the fight against discrimination. We know that you've suffered and been mistreated, often by our own people. Unfortunately, many of them just don't understand how difficult it was for our race to make meaningful progress in the job market, even in the federal government. We know you're retiring now, and we heard about what happened. But we've discussed among ourselves and decided that we cannot let you just leave us without giving you a decent send-off. So we're planning a retirement party for you on the last day of your being here."

Charlotte, who was herself a Type II diabetic, took the lead in putting the party together, and several of the women worked with her to reserve the use of the conference room and to assure that there were plenty of diabetic-friendly foods served. They set up the tables and chairs, put up some decorations, and made the occasion festive and colorful. They also planned a program centered on the theme of the then television program, "This is Your Life." Joherra and my children attended, as did my favorite teacher, Mrs. Mary Hundley, who taught me French at the Dunbar High School and likewise became my lifelong and dear friend. Several of my Omega fraternity brothers also came by to wish me well.

An open invitation was extended to the office and many of my coworkers stopped by to wish me well and give me a send-off. I was particularly gratified that several of my guests were white, a positive measure, since too much emphasis had always been placed on race as a dividing factor. All of us worked together in an effort to achieve the agency's common goals, so it was good to have them there with me. My federal career, community service, and personal and religious lives were highlighted, some speakers stirring in my new and budding career as a Catholic permanent deacon. This latter touch also helped the entire program to take the high road and to have a positive spin, although many guests were fully aware of what prompted my immediate decision to retire.

The December 19, 1973, celebration started at about 1:30 p.m. The room had been reserved until 4:00 p.m. to accommodate everyone and to clean up afterwards. Right in the middle of the celebration, Browning, who had been the actual prompt for my sudden departure, pranced into the room. The mere sight of him at this occasion was foreboding of what was to come, and those who were aware of what had recently transpired between us, knew it all too well. Approaching me, he abruptly announced, "You people have to get out of this room now, because 'the big chief' wants to use the room for a meeting that he's calling in a few minutes." And just as abruptly, I retorted, "This room has been reserved in advance until 4:00 p.m., and we're not going anywhere before then."

Looking daggers at me, he elected to remain in my presence, an intimidation, implying that at any moment he might make a public announcement ordering my guests to clear out. I was ready for him if he did, but I could not help but see that he was nothing but a patsy, sent to my party to inflict one more wound, something to remember them by. Up until that point, only a couple of people in attendance knew why Browning was there and what he had said to me.

Shortly, he repeated his demand, but this time it was clear to everyone that he was interrupting, even though most of them could not hear what he was saying. I did not loud talk him when I responded to his "Clear the room!" order. But I spoke louder than he, and those within my earshot all got the message. "We're not leaving, and that's that. These people whom you claim want to use this room mean nothing to me anymore, and they can wait or go somewhere else. Besides, these ladies have worked hard to prepare this food and program. This is my day, my last day here, and we're going to enjoy it until the end, and that's that. You can go back to wherever you came from, and tell them that I said so. You and they have already hurt me enough, and that day is over now."

Several of my guests and the planning committee members related that they were glad that I stood my ground with Browning.

Further, several coworkers also related that they had always felt that Browning believed that he could intimidate both women and African-Americans, that he needed to be checked, and that I was just the person to do it, even though my departure was imminent.

Finally, it was my turn to speak, I reflected upon those many years since July 1, 1940, and recalled some of my work experiences, mostly positive. I did not unduly harp upon the difficulties related to race that I had encountered. Still, it was impossible to leave it out completely since racial discrimination and incidents related to race were a major component of the difficulties that my generation and I faced, the first generation of African-American professionals, fighting to break down the barriers which denied us access to all the professional levels in the federal service.

I thanked everyone for their many kindnesses that had made my life and career path easier, noting that some had cleared the path for me and that others had worked with me as a battering ram, collectively pushing the gates open and clearing the way for the current group that was now following in our footsteps. Thanks again for the efforts of my generation's ancestors, people like my own beloved father, John Edward Quander, who had never been given access to the professional ranks but still served in lower-level positions, demonstrating in their own various ways that they were intelligent and capable but needed only be given an opportunity. Now officially retired, and unlike some of my former coworkers who made it a point to personally stop by the old office to see how their former coworkers are doing, I never darkened the doorstep of the Department of Labor again.

# Chapter 13

# A Spiritual Renewal

If I have learned nothing else in more than 80 years of life, everything that happens to you happens for a reason. Yet too often we do not understand what is occurring, or we neglect to heed the experience and turn it to good. That nearly happened to me in this circa 1968 period, and I came close to missing what in retrospect was the opportunity of a lifetime.

The situation on the job was not at all good. I had been lied on, and the lie about my allegedly having filed a discrimination complaint simply would not go away. It made me bitter and caused lasting personal animosity between some of my white supervisors and myself, which spread to some of my coworkers, both black and white.

Generally the whites were of the opinion that, despite the labor union having conclusively proven that I had never filed a discrimination complaint, I had in fact made a formal claim to being the victim of racial discrimination, and further that I was angry about my "complaint" not having gone anywhere. There were whispers in that community, many of which false rumors and accusations perpetuated the belief that I thought that I was better than most all of them, and that I felt that I should be promoted and given a big break simply because I was black. Several of them apparently resented me for what they perceived to be my personal belief on that issue, and the perpetuation of the false rumor only served to validate their preconceived notions about Jim Quander.

On the other hand, among my African-American coworkers, a number of them likewise approached me with skepticism. I was one of the older professional employees at the agency, having achieved a GS-12 and later the GS-13 grade levels, coupled with then close to 30 years of federal service. Despite the Kennedy and later the Johnson Administrations official ban on discrimination based on race—which resulted in the creation of affirmative actions plans to bring more minorities into positions of leadership—many of my younger African-American coworkers also formed the opinion that because I was actively trying to push ahead that I was a troublemaker.

Throughout my entire life I have always considered it to be my responsibility to lay the groundwork for those who are to follow me. Not just within my own family was this applicable, but for the entire African-American race. Being a juvenile diabetic, born with a seemingly insurmountable health curse, I learned early, and the hard way, that if Jim Quander was going to make it, I would have to do much of it on my own and not depend upon others to lay the groundwork or paint the yellow brick road for me.

It reminded me of my Signal Corps days as a civilian employee with the U.S. Army when my prior supervisor, William Farrell from Mississippi, said that the Negro, in order to get anywhere, would have to be twice as smart and do twice as much work to get half as much as a white man.

While several others did help me in significant ways, including my doctors, parents, wife, family, and certain close friends, the tone was set by me alone. I undertook my mission, drawing upon the long-standing internal fortitude that I had honed and utilized on many prior occasions when facing adversity, and had a heart-to-heart talk with my dead father, John Edward, asking him to help me, to come to me in my hour of need, and be a firm guiding hand on my shoulder as I faced the uncertainty.

I focused upon whom I was and what I had to do to survive. That this eventually came across as "Jim Quander is a troublemaker," or even worse, was the side effect of people not understanding how my personality and psyche were formed. Without that knowledge, or an appreciation of how I got to be who I was, they reached their own conclusions; and too often those conclusions were wrong and misapplied to me.

My deep regret then is that my own African-American brothers and sisters had no clue about the life history of what I had been through, what I was then going through on the job, and likewise no comprehension of why I came to be the seemingly assertive person that I was in this circa 1968 period.

I was 50 years old, getting to the latter part in my career, and perceived by many as just an angry middle-aged black man. Regretfully, some people in my own racial group were among those who formed this opinion and maintained this one-faceted perception of me throughout the brief time that they knew me. I was totally frustrated and essentially gave up trying to get my message across of how I had struggled, yet survived. In the eyes of many, "the great lie" was in fact the truth.

It was in this atmosphere that the silver lining of my personal and spiritual renewal came. A born Catholic, I had been active with several parishes over the years. But there, too, the experiences were mixed: the adverse racial atmosphere in the Roman Catholic Church is well documented. Only in the black parishes of St. Augustine and St. Benedict the Moor, both of which were a part of my religious life, had I escaped the tinge of racism in the church.

While I always remained a faithful, practicing Catholic, my focus was upon God and the faith and belief in salvation that was the Church's message. I learned early, and had my belief reconfirmed often, that men disappoint. They bring their own personal prejudices and shortcomings to the table in all of their interactions, as was consistently demonstrated to me in several of my work environments, particularly at the Census Bureau, Signal Corp., and the Labor Department.

So many of my supervisors and coworkers were also lifelong Catholics, primarily of Irish descent, some even daily Mass attendees, yet they demonstrated both in words and deeds, overt and covert, negative racial attitudes. What was particularly galling was that many of them seemingly had no clue as to what they were doing and how their actions and messages were being both perceived and conveyed.

Cast into this long-standing adverse office atmosphere and overall environment beyond the workplace, I was frustrated with the attitude of my own fellow Catholics and contemplated my options. I asked myself, "Should I leave the only church that I have ever known and look elsewhere for spiritual fulfillment? If I remain in the church, what approaches should I take to resolve within myself that the shortcomings of human nature should not be allowed to cause me to lose my personal focus of what the Roman Catholic Church meant to me?"

I discussed this issue frequently and at great length with Dale Harger, my coworker and friend, who had himself been in the seminary studying for the priesthood before electing to leave and return to secular life. Despite having elected not to become a priest, Dale was still very much a staunch Catholic and became a source of strength for me, someone who I learned to lean on and depend upon in this time of great personal turmoil in my life.

Strongly counseling me against making a hasty decision and leaving the church, he told me about a new program that the church was instituting, i.e., the reinstitution of the Permanent Diaconate in the Roman Catholic Church, the revival of a religious status that the church allowed to lapse some 800 years prior. He referred to the program as one to create Ministers of Service.

The Permanent Diaconate, what's that? Of course we both knew that the sub-deacon and the deacon were two intermediate steps towards being permanently ordained as a priest in the church, but the creation of a "permanent deacon" was something that neither of us had previously ever heard of. It was no secret that the church was facing an increasingly acute shortage of priests, and young men were simply not electing to study for that vocation.

Dale read an article in the *Catholic Standard* newspaper that the shortage of priests was particularly acute in the United States, and it was hoped that one major solution would be to revive another level of clergy that could share in discharge of several of the traditional religious duties that had been exclusively assigned to the priests.

He gathered the information on the revival of the permanent diaconate, brought it to work, dropped it on my desk, and said, "Here, this is for you. Now do something with it." The idea of me as an ordained Catholic clergyman seemed alien at the least, and crazy at most. "How is this possible?" I asked myself. I envisioned the new deacons as parading around the altar with their newfound status, much like several of the priests that I already knew, at least a few of whom seemed to be so full of themselves at times.

But here was a new opportunity presenting itself, which, if I was selected for the program, could be an answer to a lifelong journey towards spiritual fulfillment. The information Dale provided that day explained that historically the deacons were the original elders of the church in the first century when there was no officially ordained priesthood, and that their duties were diverse and encompassed virtually everything.

Their tasks included preparing for the religious services, leading the prayers, and tending to the daily spiritual and temporal needs of the small, but growing Christian community. Tasks encompassed providing food for widows and children, visiting the sick, burying the dead, and providing shelter for the homeless. They were truly ministers of service, just as the title implied. Seemingly not a single task was accomplished within the growing Christian community that did not also include a role for the deacons to play, especially since the early church still lacked the later-adopted hierarchical structure, and there was no official priesthood yet created. At that early time, the deacons functioned in an atmosphere that was most hostile. From ancient Rome's perspective, the church was much considered to be a rogue outfit, and its members subject to many persecutions for their faith. One of the best known of this early group of martyrs was St. Stephen Martyr, who is officially credited with being the church's first deacon, and after whom the role of the original deacons and now the permanent diaconate is structured.

The deacons actually became so powerful that when the formal priesthood was later created, it was soon realized that steps had to be taken to define, and in some cases to confine, the role of the deacons, to "keep them in their place," although many of them would also elect to became priests.

Often the influence of the deacons, who knew the people and worked with them on a daily basis, exceeded that of the priests, who were often ivory-tower fellows who intentionally separated and exalted themselves from the people. As God's spiritual representatives on earth, it was fairly easy for the early Christian church's priests to create and perpetrate this exacted hierarchy and image of themselves. But this stellar placement also removed the priests from serving other than the spiritual needs of the Christian population. Eventually the deacons acquired so much popular support among the faithful that they rivaled, and in many cases surpassed, the respect and influence that the priests had, a position in the church hierarchy that the priests were not willing to share.

As a result, the deacons' powers were trimmed as the priests attempted to extend themselves more into the community, to attend to more than the spiritual needs of the faithful. Over time, the priests got the upper hand, and they eased the diaconate out of existence. After perhaps 800 years, the church, recognizing that there is both an increasing shortage of priests and an ever-increasing need for men to serve, has revived the program; but they established it at a level where they can keep a close eye on the reins of power to assure that this long-dead rivalry does not germinate again.

We had a definite sense of history in the making throughout the three-year preparation period, as we were the first 16 in the United States. The history of who the deacons were, what they did, and why they were disassembled was all a part of what we were preparing to do.

In 1968, almost 2000 years later, vestiges of that self-created priestly image remained. Into this circumstance, the permanent diaconate was reintroduced. I saw the entire program as an opportunity for me to be of service, to give something back to groups of people, many who would never be in a position to offer me anything but a "Thank you!"

I telephoned the Archdiocese on that day in late spring of 1968 and inquired about how to make an application for the program. I was told that the application process, which included a careful screening of the selected candidates, had already been completed. To my assertion that I had only just learned of the revival of the permanent diaconate (the program that started in January of 1968), the person on the other end of the line advised that the selection process was not conducted in public and was carefully structured.

Further, most likely there had not been any announcement of the permanent diaconate program from the pulpit either, as the Archdiocese was recruiting a carefully-selected class of about 25 initial candidates, probably no more than one man per parish, to be trained for this very specialized program. As best as I could determine, the targeted parishes were given a basic measurement criteria and directed to look within its active male membership, and then approach only certain men about considering the program. No one had approached me.

I was told that there was still a possibility that I could be selected for the second class and begin training in 1969, and that I could still make an application, if I wished to, for the class that was almost finalized. I was neither encouraged nor discouraged about the likelihood of my being accepted. Two significant points were not mentioned in that conversation. Through my own detective work, I later discovered and used both items as my trump cards.

First, there was no permanent diaconate candidate from Sacred Heart parish where I had been a member since 1949. Second, Auxiliary Bishop John Spence, pastor of Sacred Heart, was in charge of the entire program for the Archdiocese of Washington; and in the discharge of his many episcopate duties, he had not found the time to concentrate on locating a suitable candidate from his own parish. The time was ripe for a volunteer.

In a way this entire matter took on a life of its own. Everything was happening so fast, and I was caught up in it—with the need to make a life decision. Either way, I stood to both gain or lose something significant, but I viewed this potential opportunity as a chance to be of service to others; and in the process, I would likewise be rendering service to God by helping to care for some of His children in times of need.

My application was quickly processed. After a series of interviews, including a brief one with Pastor Spence, who also provided the mandatory letter of recommendation from the home church pastor, an evaluation of my credentials and fitness to serve was conducted. I was then selected as a qualified candidate, someone whom the church felt it could expect to carry forward the church's mission and many ministries.

Approximately 21 men were selected for the history-making first class, which convened in September 1968. Sixteen of us would later complete the three-year training program and be ordained in September 1971 at St. Matthew's Cathedral, located on Rhode

Island Avenue, in Northwest Washington, D.C. At the outset, I knew only two of the other candidates, Hiram Haywood and Joseph Curtis, both African-Americans.

Our class was diversified racially and ethnically. A carefully worded *Catholic Standard* article specifically stated that African-American and Hispanic men were encouraged to apply; and both groups were represented in the mix, which was made up of a majority of white males. As we introduced ourselves for the first time and got to know each other better, it became apparent to me that most, if not all of them, were younger than I was, and likewise had not had the cross-section of community involvement that I had cultivated over the years.

While my volunteer service was primarily focused on civic work—including the Cub Scouts, the Boy Scouts, my Omega Psi Phi Fraternity and its youth development organization, Les Jeunes Hommes, as well as significant participation in anti-racial discrimination activities like interracial home visits and other black-white focused activities—virtually all of the other men played intimate roles in their own parishes. Several were on their respective parish councils. Some were sacristans, lay readers, ushers, members of the Holy Name Society or choir, Knights of Columbus or Knights of St. John, or a combination of the above. I was none of those things. Yet, my credentials were no less impressive from my perspective and had earned me considerable recognition in the community at large.

Further, it certainly did not hurt that several of my fellow male Quander Family members were still maintaining active memberships in those same positions, and that several of the Quander woman were likewise serving in varied capacities at several of the other Catholic churches in the Archdiocese, and that the name "Quander" was viewed most favorably in the church's community at large.

Our primary focus was upon Bible study, homiletics (the art of preaching homilies), counseling, and Catholic dogma. We were given diverse assignments that focused upon those primary areas and often did role-playing as our fellow students worked cooperatively on certain projects. Frequently they were also our audience as we read and interpreted Bible passages, preached our fledgling sermons, did mock counseling, and explained the church's dogmatic teachings to inquiring minds which pretended not to fully understand.

In our many intimate sessions, we discussed several subjects, and sometimes I disagreed with the church's teaching and position. For example, I spoke out against celibacy as being necessary, which led to a big, heated discussion. I noted that it was married men, heads of households, who fathered potential priests; and that if everyone became celibate, pretty soon there would be nobody left. This led to huge guffaws. I emphasized that we all have different callings in life, and sometimes many callings within the same life; and the priesthood is but one of those callings. I also noted that celibacy is a man-made rule, not God's rule, as nothing in the Bible addresses that issue, other than the fact that Jesus was not married. I finished my point of the conversation by noting that we do not know if Jesus was celibate or not, as looking into the sex life of Jesus is something that just does not happen.

From the scowls on their faces, including several of the celibate priest instructors, this was a conversation that they wished did not take place, although there were continuing rounds of laughter. They wanted to shut me up, but considering that we were all adults, and at age 50 I was among the oldest students, they were not quite sure how to do it. So they let me finish but surely did not enjoy what I had to say on the subject.

Although we were all enrolled in the same first class, did the same work, and likewise were expected to produce a like end product, we each also had different goals that shaped how we individually focused upon certain aspects of the training. Some of us were targeted towards working with the poor, or the elderly, or drug addicts, or other social service components. Historically, deacons are men of service to others, more than focusing upon the formal structure of the church. However, knowing and understanding the structure is an invaluable component of understanding the deacon's role, which is to be delivered within the context of the church's overall mission.

During our training period, we were not expected to undertake any particular religious or social service assignments, as our time was limited due to three evening meetings per week already.

However, I knew from the outset that my primary focus was going to be with the elderly, and eventually I worked with the residents of the Stoddard Baptist Home where many Catholics were in residence, as well as other communities of elderly in the Archdiocese.

My challenge was to manage the program as a diabetic, work full time, go to class three evenings a week, and also complete out-of-class academic assignments. It took a lot of discipline, but with God's help, I managed. On school nights I moved fast after work—got home, took my insulin, ate my dinner and got to class on time. Class was from 7:00 p.m. until 10:00 p.m. I always carried my candy with me in the event that I had a diabetic reaction or low blood sugar coming on. Fortunately, there never was a problem because I always ate my dinner before class; and with the infusion of food just before class, there was no real need to be unduly concerned.

Although we were off in the summers, the overall class training was an accelerated program to get us ready in three years. I called upon my internal strengths of self-discipline that I had cultivated over the years as a juvenile diabetic, and these internal resources did not fail me.

I never wavered or thought for one minute that I would not complete the program. Becoming a permanent deacon and rendering service were goals that I set. I knew that completing the program was the only way to meet the goals. Because I was outspoken, especially on matters related to race and civil rights, I was referred to as a "black militant" by Bishop Spence on at least one occasion. Perhaps a few of my classmates held the same opinion.

I was not someone that the bishop knew particularly well, so he formed his opinions based upon a narrow slice of knowing who I was, or what my exposures had been prior to then. As well, being one of the oldest candidates and coming from a more secular world than most all of my class, I had had more exposure in certain areas. Of course, being African-American in this white man's world and church, any time I did not agree with them, they became inclined to attribute the difference of opinion to something of a racial nature. This was most unfortunate, as it skewed the equation and the ability to see a problem for what it really is.

The three-year training included several courses taught by different priest-lecturers. One of the primary lecturers was Rev. Eugene Marino who later became Archbishop of Atlanta. One of Marino's courses focused upon inward reflection, trying to better know oneself, and to be able to develop and use the power of prayer as a personal conversation with God. In addition to Rev. Marino, William Norvel, pastor of St. Benedict the Moor parish, was also one of our primary trainers.

Our training completed, we were ordained on September 11, 1971, at St. Matthews Cathedral located on Massachusetts Avenue, Washington, D.C. Our ordination was history in the making—a component of the revival of the Catholic diaconate after an 800-year hiatus. The first 16 to be ordained in the United States, this was widely reported in the print and video media; and it was seen as part of the church's long-term effort to share the religious and service responsibilities among a wider circle of men.

Upon graduating, I expected to be assigned to work in my home parish. After all, that was the parish that was responsible for my being in the program in the first place, and throughout our three-year preparation, our teachers routinely stated, "When you begin working and rendering services in your own parishes, ..." Naturally that is what I expected would happen. Still, the process of being formally placed required an interview and acceptance by the pastor.

By the time of my ordination, Bishop Spence had been reassigned, and he was no longer my pastor at Sacred Heart. I was directed to meet with Monsignor Martin W. Christopher, the current pastor, to discuss with him the parish's needs and how I might help to serve those needs. This was standard operating procedure. The pastors had every right to know in advance that a different type clergyman was coming to the parish; and the local pastor was expected to be fully cooperative with the arrival of this person and to find suitable responsibilities that the newly ordained deacons would provide in their home parishes.

To my surprise and anger, he rejected me out-of-hand, saying that he did not need nor want a deacon, questioning everything by asking, "What are those crazy people doing now?" referring to the archbishop and the clergy who were in support of the diaconate. Further, he mumbled something to the effect that the church was right some 800 years prior to disestablish the diaconate, because the deacons were really a fertile ground for breeding dissent within the church, since most of them thought that they were "little priests." He also questioned why the church felt the need to go back and restart the diaconate. Nothing that I said by way of explanation could placate him. Since he was newly arrived and did not know me, although we had met on an occasion or two, I never felt that his wrath was directed at me personally, but solely at the diaconate institution.

That language and attitude was shocking to me. Being a married man with four children, I never intended to become a priest, and for him to assert such was totally inappropriate behavior. After that encounter, I had no church placement and reported this experience back to the Josephite Seminary in Northeast Washington, D.C., where we had been training. Fr. William Norvel, one of my primary instructors and pastor of St. Benedict the Moor, immediately placated my concern and asked me to serve with him at St. Benedict, which had no one enrolled in the program.

Under these circumstances, I am happy that I was not assigned to Sacred Heart. While Bishop Spence and I had a difference of opinion caused by our vastly different backgrounds and experiences, we could have made it by working cooperatively. But this new man and his perceptions against the program—that would not have been possible.

Father Bernard Joy, a priest in residence at the St. Augustine rectory, was directed by the Archdiocese to confront the pastor about why he would not accept a deacon. Joy reported back that the same attitude displayed against me was likewise prevailing, although the negativity was directed at the church but not against me personally.

I interacted successfully with Fr. William Norvel on religious matters, but we had our differences over matters related to race and racial discrimination. He sometimes acted as if he believed that I did not know who or what I was, the exact opposite of what Bishop Spence meant when he called me a black militant. Norvel assumed that I was not a militant, and I had to tell him on more than one occasion, "Young man, before you were even born, I knew who I was. I've been fighting injustice against my race for decades. So

don't you tell me anything that implies that I'm not black enough."
He was about 30 years old at the time, and I was 53—old enough
to be his father.

Charles Quander and other Quanders and parishioners fell out
with him about that same issue. I think this was Norvel's first
encounter with middle-class African-Americans, and he thought
that we were not "black enough" or aware of who we were. He took
an approach to "teach us how to be black," and it created a
tremendous upset in the congregation. Charles, as one of the main
founders of St. Benedict in 1946, plus several others, simply
refused to accept Norvel's approach; and some of them even left the
congregation and went to other Catholic churches.

Norvel introduced the Gospel Mass and more Afro-centric
music into the church's religious programming. All the singing,
shouting, and swaying back and forth was not "Catholic" in the
eyes and minds of many of the parishioners; and it took a while for
this new approach to take hold among the congregation, several of
whom never accepted it. Norvel had one view of what being an
African-American Catholic was about in the 1970s; while the
overwhelming majority of the parishioners, most all of who were
"cradle Catholics" (a term we use to mean born into the faith), had
a vastly different view. They were not used to the Gospel Mass and
all of the charismatic features that were a part of that event. Yet St.
Benedict was founded in part upon African-Americans refusal to
continue putting up with racial discrimination and daily insults at
Holy Name Catholic Church, located at 11th and K Streets, N.E.
We were tired of sitting in separate seating and getting communion
after all of the white people had been served.

I reflected on that day in the mid-1940s when I went to
confession at Holy Name; and during the conversation with the
priest, I complained about racial relationships and questioned why
the Negro members of the congregation were intentionally
segregated from open access, and the church endorsed this
separation. The priest got agitated and only saw it in one
dimension. He asked me if I would ever marry a white woman,
since his only focus at that moment seemed to be black men
carnally desiring white women. I replied, "If I loved her, yes, I
would marry her, because that relationship transcends color and

racial divide." I was only about 26 years old, and I felt that perhaps the world was opening up to more equality among the races, including better opportunities for blacks.

Instead of continuing this conversation on an intelligent level and maintaining a civil tone in his voice, he got loud and started bellowing well beyond the confines of the confessional booth. There was a line outside waiting to come into the booth, and they certainly all heard him yell, "God put the races in different and separate places, and He intended for them to stay where they were put. If He had intended for them to mix, He would have made other arrangements." I was absolutely shocked at this comment and his behavior, and I quickly exited the confessional where I faced the quizzical stares of several parishioners who were waiting in line to enter.

I wrote a strong letter of complaint to Archbishop Michael J. Curley in Baltimore who oversaw the Diocese of Washington. Eventually an innocuous reply came from the Archdiocesan office acknowledging my complaint, but it did not address the incident and its long-term ramifications in any respect. It was only a short time after this incident that Charles J. and Alyce Quander, John E. and Helen Quander, and a host of other individuals, several of whom are officially credited with the generic title of "Founders," walked out of Holy Name and founded St. Benedict the Moor in 1946 in a surplus Quonset hut on Oklahoma Avenue, N.E. They too were tired and refused to take any more of this type of insulting behavior being visited upon them at the hands of our own clergy. Twenty-six years old at the time, I was also a member of the group.

This was the historic atmosphere and backdrop that I brought to St. Benedict in September 1971, 25 years after walking out of Holy Name. Norvel may not have known much about what we had gone through; and for him to actually assert that we were not black enough was a slap in the face to those of us who knew exactly who we were, where we came from, and had experienced the tribulations over time to get to the present triumphs. He was a bull in a china shop, and it took a while for him to learn and finesse the situation. To his credit, he worked hard, brought new insights to the parish, and by his Christian love and dedication to Christ and dogged determination to re-attract those parishioners who drifted away in dispute, he eventually prevailed.

Even Charles Quander, who had been the most stalwart person in opposition to him, eventually buried the hatchet and returned to the fold. So the story had a happy ending. But in the context of what had happened to us over the years, Norvel showed little empathy or understanding for that experience and my personal component in the larger picture; so I resented his initial approach toward me as not militant or not black enough. On more than one occasion, as he and I differed philosophically on what a "black Catholic church" was supposed to be like, he said to me, "You are just like your uncle Charles," although Charles was actually my cousin, and a distant cousin at that. Eventually, Norvel realized that I was not going to bend to his approach; and I was not about to give up all that I had learned in my 53 years to accommodate his new, "strange" and suddenly somewhat radical introductions into the church, which I had never been a part of or seen before.

Norvel was already in place as pastor when the diaconate program assigned me. Immediately, several parishioners bared their souls to me, complaining about how the Mass had changed and that they did not like "all that noise" that Norvel had brought to St. Benedict. But there was nothing that I could do about it, although I did carry the message to Norvel several times. But he was determined to "educate" the parish, whether they wanted to be educated or not. He held the line and eventually prevailed.

Although my wife and I had been among the founding group in 1946, we moved out of that area in 1949, so I really did not know its people or the area well. I learned the area though, and I was assigned to take the Eucharist to homebound parishioners, to visit them on other occasions, including taking some to the doctor when necessary. I also assisted at one or more Masses on Sundays, worked with the Confraternity of Christian Doctrine (CCD) classes, which are often called "Sunday School" (even if not held on Sundays). I also worked on various projects with the children in the parish school and the Oblates Sisters of Providence, the order that operated the school. There was always something to do; and since I was not yet retired from federal service, all of this activity was conducted in the evenings or on weekends.

I served at St. Benedict from September 1971 until 1973 and during that period switched my active church participation away from my home parish, Sacred Heart. While attending a citywide Catholic clergy activity, I met Rev. Joseph Ranieri, then pastor of Sacred Heart. He was not the pastor who earlier had rejected the opportunity to have a deacon assigned in 1971. Ranieri was shocked to learn that one of his parishioners was among the first 16 deacons ordained in the United States, and that the golden opportunity to have him serve his own people in his home parish had not been realized and appreciated.

He immediately requested that I be reassigned to Sacred Heart, and within 45 days I was—effective October 1, 1973. By then I was preparing to retire from federal service and would come out as of December 31st. I had far more time to devote to my ministry; and falling back upon the years of health discipline and strict regimen that I had followed since childhood, I found the demands upon my time and body to be agreeable.

I had already focused my efforts primarily upon the elderly, despite working with religious training for the children at St. Benedict's. Upon reassignment to Sacred Heart, the parish took immediate advantage of my knowledge of the area, having moved to 3714 13th Street, N.W., on December 3, 1949. I worked well with all of the staff at Sacred Heart, which included the clergy, parishioners, and occasionally with the school staff. I was assigned to take the Eucharist to about 50 people per week, the greatest number of whom resided in the Stoddard Baptist Home. The home was ecumenical, and many Catholics were in residence. I also arranged with the parish for a weekly Mass for the homebound to be celebrated on-site, with the parish sending a priest each week.

Historically, the deacons attended to the faithful people's personal needs, such as food, clothing, and shelter, while the priests attended to their spiritual needs, celebrating Mass, counseling the sick, delivering the last rites, performing marriage ceremonies, and the like. Eventually the lines blurred, and the deacons (in the eyes of the priests) became too powerful, since their roles were viewed more tangibly, while the priestly role was somewhat abstract.

The church observed that the congregation was more faithful to the men who arranged for food, clothing, shelter, and provided for widows and orphans than to the priests who emphasized prayer, fasting, sacrifice, and heaven. Eventually, this dichotomy resulted in the priesthood getting the upper hand and abolishing the permanent diaconate completely, with the priestly role expanding to accommodate more of the faithful people's personal and temporal needs.

Once the diaconate was reestablished after an 800-year hiatus, the duties that were assigned to me were the typical role that the permanent deacons were initially understood to assume. In addition to delivering the Eucharist at Stoddard and other locations, I took many parishioners to the doctor, bought groceries and delivered them, cleaned apartments for several elders, counseled young couples before marriage, assisted on the altar in weekly Masses, weddings, and funerals, and occasionally preached sermons at various Masses. I was also a regular for conducting graveside funeral services and accompanying the body to the cemetery for the church's final commendation.

Serving as the permanent deacon at Sacred Heart was a good experience, one that I discharged for 18 years, 1973 -1991. During that time I served under a number of pastors and worked with various clergy, not all viewing the permanent diaconate in the same light. Some still seemed to harbor the "little priest" mentality, while others opened their hearts and minds and considered me to be an integral part of the parish family. It made no difference to me: I knew what my responsibilities were and did them. There was nothing that anyone could say to reduce my workload. There are some things you don't say to a Deacon, such as: "Don't visit those sick people over there." "Don't take communion to Stoddard anymore." "We don't need you to conduct any more graveside commendations."

I have so many fond memories of this period. I cultivated many friendships, especially with older ladies, some who had been on faculty at Dunbar High School years before. I even assumed the presidency of the Young at Heart Club, a senior citizen group, comprised mostly of elderly widows. Over the years, several of these ladies were guests in my home on Christmas, Thanksgiving,

Easter, and other times as well. The opportunity to be of service to those in need was my greatest reward; and now in my twilight years, I am reaping the benefits of what I did for others, as many blessings continue to come my way, despite my now being homebound due to partial blindness, diabetes, and right leg amputation.

Regretfully, I also had a couple of particularly negative experiences in the early phase of discharging my duties. In the first situation, I had just been ordained and had struck up a friendship with Rev. Brown who celebrated the 12:10 p.m. daily Mass at St. Matthew's Cathedral, which was located on Massachusetts Avenue directly next to the Longworth Building where my U.S. Department of Labor office was situated. He offered me the opportunity to assist him at Mass several times per month. The lunch-hour Mass was short and particularly offered for the convenience of federal employees, many of whom worked in nearby office buildings.

One day one of my coworkers approached me and alerted me to what another coworker had been saying throughout the building— namely, that I was using government time for my private purposes—and that he was going to complain to the authorities to make me stop. I was not really using government time since I could assist at Mass, eat my lunch, and be back to work—all within an hour. But it still hurt and gave the unknowing the impression that perhaps his vicious gossip was somehow the truth.

I confronted the guy and told him, "You go the bar room at lunch and get several drinks, frequently staying for a couple of hours, return to the office with alcohol on your breath, unable to function well for the rest of the day, but now you're complaining because I do a short religious service. This is done on my time, not the government's." He had no real comeback for my remarks, but after putting him in his place I still went to the branch chief and told him everything. He too was Catholic and had even attended the 12:10 p.m. Mass on occasion. He approved what I was doing and simply told me to keep an eye on my time so that the falsely laid allegations would not stand up in the face of the truth.

The second experience also occurred at St. Matthew's. I had trouble with one of the priests there who had no appreciation at all for the permanent diaconate and openly questioned and resented my presence and my assisting at Mass; and he seemed equally disarmed by having a black man on the altar. He consistently and begrudgingly referred to me as "the deacon for the colored," and no matter what I said to rebuke him, initially in a friendly manner, and then later more directly, he consistently referred to me that way, "the deacon for the colored." He never altered from that attitude or position; and it was quite uncomfortable since I continued to assist at Mass quite regularly, and he was often either on the altar as well, or within the immediate location.

My only real regret is that my health failed me. Looking back, perhaps I could have done more. But I have a deeper religious feeling now, a spiritual rebirth as a result of directly doing for others. Perhaps my efforts were not on so grand a scale, primarily one-on-one, but it gave me a greater spiritual insight into who I am and what was and is expected of me. Now that my sight has even failed me, I see things differently, more spiritually than at any prior time. This means a great deal to me.

I am more conscious of the greater picture of what faith is about, which is decidedly separate and different from any particular religious sect. Faith to me is about ecumenism. I told that to someone recently, and they questioned whether that meant that I did not consider myself to be a Roman Catholic any longer. I said, "No, it does not mean that at all. I'll always be Catholic; after all the word means 'universal.'"

It has nothing to do with any particular sect or dogma but deals with a greater, broader sense of spirituality. That's it. A rebirth of the spirit is what it's about. Basically, all of our Christian religions have more in common, more similarities, than dissimilarities. That's been the whole problem. We need to accept and focus more on how we are alike and less on emphasizing our differences.

The same is true with our racial problems. We are all human and experience both good and bad times. We all experience pain and loss. We are far more alike than not. Yet far too often we do not look for the similarities.

One of the greatest highlights of my permanent diaconate service was the day that I personally assisted Pope Paul VI at Mass in Rome. Along with a group of other Americans from the

Washington, D.C., area, I went to Rome in September 1975 to witness the canonization of Elizabeth Seton as the first American-born saint. There were thousands of Americans in Rome for that event, and although the permanent diaconate program had begun to be more widely embraced by various Catholic archdioceses and dioceses around the United States, the concept of the permanent diaconate was still quite new to most.

Four years after I had been ordained, several U.S. Catholic communities still had no deacons, or their respective first group of deacons was either still in training or just recently ordained. I knew Cardinal William Baum, former archbishop of Washington, and had assisted him in the celebration of Mass in this city. He, appreciating that I was one of the original 16 permanent deacons ordained in the United States, as well an African-American, saw this as a good opportunity for some good public relations.

I had no connections to make it happen, but I was informed, once I was already in Rome, that I would be assisting Pope Paul VI at Mass. It was not a concelebrated Mass with a small army of priests on the altar. It was just a daily Mass offered by the Pope with me at his side. The Mass was celebrated in Rome, but not at St. Peter's. I do not now recall the name of the church. But, it was a great opportunity, and the church was full of American Catholics and other Catholics from throughout the world who had come to Rome for the canonization. It was a great experience, one that I will never forget.

I regret now that I do not have a photograph of the event, although several photographs were taken, some by people who had come to Rome in my group. Unfortunately, no one offered any of the photographs to me, and I did not pursue getting one from anyone in our group. I cannot track a photo down now, as many people from the group are dead, and I cannot now recall who the rest of the others were.

I formally retired from the active permanent diaconate in 1991, as my health increasingly deteriorated. I was experiencing diabetic neuropathy, extreme circulatory problems in both legs, and great difficulty in both walking and standing. My balance was going out of alignment, and I constantly felt that I might fall. This is a condition that often plagues diabetics, and it is especially the case for juvenile diabetics, like myself, who have lived with the ailment since early childhood. The body acts adversely to the long-term presence of varying amounts of sugar, sometimes rapidly increasing or decreasing naturally, or adversely affected by something eaten which had some sugar content in it.

# Chapter 14

# Managing Diabetic Health in the Twilight Years—Coming Out of the Diabetic "Closet"

My decision to retire from the active permanent diaconate service in 1991 was not reached lightly but deemed necessary by me due to certain adverse health conditions that I was experiencing. For 20 full years, and most specifically since I retired from federal service in 1973, I had actively and faithfully served the Archdiocese of Washington.

I worked under the coordinated supervision of the pastors at both St. Benedict the Moor (1971-1973) and the Shrine of the Sacred Heart (1973-1991). During significant portions of each location, I functioned semi-independently, discharging the church's mission of rendering service to those in need. At no time, beginning with my expedited application process in the late spring of 1968, through the effective date of my official retirement, was it reflected anywhere that I was a juvenile diabetic.

My life experiences on why this was the case have already been laid out in detail in the prior chapters, and it is simply sufficient to state here that, in my estimation, attitudes of discrimination against diabetics had modified somewhat towards a greater tolerance; but there was still a significant core of indisposition to people whose health circumstances were different. Jim Quander had always been "different," but the cause of why he was different, health-wise, had never been officially declared—until now.

I never made a conscious decision to declare myself as a juvenile diabetic. It just sort of happened. Further, at 73, my age in 1991, it occurred to me that if ever there was a time to finally talk about a health condition, one that I had survived since at least 1924, if not earlier, now was the time.

While I did not climb a mountain to announce to the world that I was a juvenile diabetic and was suffering sustained health problems related to that illness, I began to occasionally mention in conversation that I was a diabetic and had been one virtually all of my life, probably since birth. Although my 1991 letter of resignation to Cardinal James Hickey, Archbishop of Washington, simply stated that I was electing to retire from the active diaconate for "health reasons," I shared the nature of those health-related reasons with a number of the parishioners and my friends, the latter group of which already knew of my condition.

But surprisingly, there were several members of the parish who shared with me freely and openly that they too were diabetics, virtually all of the adult-onset group, or that they had close family members who were suffering from the ailment. Several parishioners shared with me their great surprise, and in a few instances, their actual shock at learning that I was a juvenile diabetic, and that I had managed to function so well for so long.

Belatedly, I found myself elevated to folk hero status in some circles, as the word spread that Rev. Mr. Quander, the deacon at Sacred Heart, was a juvenile diabetic, and that for all of these years he has functioned so well.

Prior to 1991, I began to experience lasting circulatory problems in both my arms and legs. Knowing the risk of limb amputation that diabetics often face, I was particularly concerned, since my life had always been a mobile, active one. Besides the permanent diaconate and the many church-related community events that flowed from that ministry of service, I was also active with several community and fraternal organizations, including the civic association, the Omega Psi Phi Fraternity, the Dunbar High School Class of 1936 Alumni, the M Club (Miner Teacher's College alumni association), the Optimist Club, and the Young at Hearts Senior Citizens Club.

Each of these groups had regular meetings and several activities a year. And as is so typical for retirees, I found myself more active after I left federal service than before and quickly asked myself, "Where has all the time gone?" But as I grew older and the brittleness of my diabetic condition started to push itself forward into having an increased effect upon my daily routines, I found it more difficult to manage all of these religious, community, and social obligations.

The level of my medical visits increased significantly, as I began to lose sensation in both hands and feet. Having lived with the potentiality of amputation since the 1920s, I naturally became alarmed in about 1990 when Dr. Susan Housman, my long-term physician, advised me that there were indications of decreased blood flow in all of these extremities, and that I would have to be extra careful in self-monitoring to observe whether I felt an even further decrease in sensation. She also advised that as a result of my having taken insulin for so long, there was most likely some damage to the nerves in my extremities, a term called "diabetic neuropathy," which is exhibited by a burning, tingling, and also periodic numbness sensations, especially in the fingertips and toes

She was calm in her conversations and explanations to my wife and me, but I could see Dr. Housman's concern in her eyes and on her face. I came to realize over the next couple of visits that she was telling me that after all of these years of my body having been exposed to diabetes, and the adverse impact that that condition imposes upon the body systems, my body was experiencing significant physiological changes. Further, the ultimate impact of what those changes would be was yet to be determined.

My diabetes could only be regulated by the introduction of insulin into my body, gleaned from a foreign source. It is a difficult and uncertain process, knowing exactly when to inject and in what quantities. Eventually the smaller, more extremely located blood vessels, like the capillaries, get clogged with thick, sugar-laden blood; and the blood flow slows dangerously, or may stop completely.

This most frequently occurs in the lower legs and feet, but sometimes in the hands as well, being the extremities located farthest from the heart. The heart has to pump harder to get the blood to the extremities; but with the smallest blood vessels clogged, neither blood nor oxygen can reach and enrich those areas. The tissue starts to die, and the nerves are starved for nutrients and likewise irritated by long-term insulin regimen. The nerves surely let you know how distressed they are on the pain register scale.

This was an extremely painful ordeal, one that I experienced for several years—between 1991 and January 1995. During that sustained period, several medical tests were run, therapies attempted, medications administered, and then eventually leg bypasses in both legs seeking to increase the blood flow to the lower extremities. The 1993 bypass worked in the left leg and is still functioning, although at times I am fearful that the blood flow might be slowing. The bypass raised my blood flow up to about a 60% of optimum capacity where the flow has been consistently maintained.

Unfortunately, this same surgical procedure worked for only a few months in my right leg before failing to maintain at least a 40% minimum blood flow. My medical advisors at Group Health, now a part of Kaiser Permanente and affiliated with the George Washington University Hospital, Washington, D.C., had always raised the specter of amputation, if the first right leg bypass failed.

After it failed, I was again counseled and advised that they could attempt a second bypass procedure, but that if it failed, amputation was the only remaining alternative. I elected to try one more time, and in late 1994 the second bypass was attempted. Unfortunately, it failed almost immediately. My heart, although apparently in reasonably good shape considering that I was in my 77th year, was not strong enough to pump blood back into those deprived areas. Within a matter of weeks I was back at George Washington University Hospital, and in January 1995 I was subjected to the final solution—amputation of my right leg just below the knee.

After a week in the George Washington University Hospital, I was transferred to the National Rehabilitation Hospital, one of the leading rehabilitative centers in the country. There I was immediately exposed to a totally different attitude. While the staff at G.W. was nice, professional, and attentive, the staff at National Rehabilitation had a "can do" attitude, which I had never before experienced. They were specially trained in all dimensions of rehabilitative therapy, and devote time and attention to getting their patients back up to speed quickly after sustaining a traumatic loss.

I was not the only diabetic amputee in my immediate group, and being located in the heart of Washington, D.C., which has among the highest level of diabetics in the nation, especially from among African-Americans, the staff was experienced in dealing with this population. Whether I felt up to it or not, and they never asked me, I had to move, move, move. Strength therapy was a part of everything that we did. Leg lifts, arm stretches, and learning to balance and walk on a combination of one leg and a prosthetic support device were all a part of the daily regimen.

As well, adjusting psychologically to the traumatic loss was also part of the program. It was formidable to face the loss of a part of your body that you have taken for granted and depended upon for 77 years. We saw films and had in-person lectures from individuals who had sustained a loss that required rehabilitative treatment. Some had lost both legs or an arm. Some were relatively young and managed to get about without the use of any canes or crutches. They counseled us, both individually and in groups, encouraging us that we could do it, and that age was not a barrier if we cultivate both a good attitude and physical strength to assist us.

I had a lot to address and overcome. No one else in the entire hospital had faced juvenile diabetes as long as I, and although they each had a story to tell, mine was unique in longevity, if nothing else. To have been so active throughout my life, to have exercised so completely in order to maintain good diabetic health, and now to look down and notice that my leg was gone, was a shock that I still have not fully recovered from. Yet, even now, in my 86th year, my "leg" still "hurts," despite having been removed in January 1995.

The pain centers in my brain are still regularly registering that I am suffering the pain incidental to poor circulation in my lower right leg. This is a sympathetic experience, as the brain remembers what happened and still aches due to the problem, despite the problem having been literally eliminated. This experience is generally called "phantom pain."

The attitude expressed by my son, Rohulamin, towards this situation perhaps captures it best. Constantly, he would say, "Dad, you are still here, so let's celebrate what left. Celebrate what's left of life and celebrate what's left of you. That leg had served you for 77 years, and now that it got tired and gave up, don't you give up. You still have another leg, all the medical support in the world, and a loving family that is going to help you get through this thing."

Those words brought tears to my eyes, and before I could say anything of a self-pitying nature, he added, "Those sure better be tears of joy, because there is no time for sadness today. We'll have sadness another time, but today we celebrate that you survived the operation and are here among us—a loving wife, children, grandchildren, and friends. No tears today, but tears of joy."

One of the tears of joy is my grandson, Alexander James, who was only two years old when I sustained my amputation. He came to visit me at the rehabilitation hospital; and on his first visit and upon realizing that I had lost my leg, he very cutely said, "Apah, where's your shoe?" After I explained to him what had happened and that my leg had been amputated, his only question was, while looking quizzically at me, "Will it grow back?"—a question that seemed far-fetched, but is not such anymore as medical science makes great strides in research to regenerate injured or lost body parts. I do not expect to see much progress on this endeavor in the remaining years that I have, but already I am aware of tremendous strides that have been made in this direction, and hopefully the mastery of regenerative surgery will also lead to significantly increased blood flow in diabetic limbs, which will make amputation unnecessary from the outset.

I would dry my eyes, and realize, even if only briefly, that he was absolutely right. It brought back memories of an old song, which I can hardly remember the words to. It went something like this:

*Save your sorrows for tomorrow.*
*Smile a while today.*
*If you cheer up, skies will clear up.*
*Laugh today and have fun.*
*Tomorrow never comes.*

I was measured and outfitted with two prosthetic devices at National Rehabilitation—one for everyday use, which was not designed to get wet, and another less formal device, which I could wear in the house and even take into the shower. Despite the costs (I never saw a complete bill since Kaiser Permanente paid most of the expenses), neither leg fit properly and had to repeatedly be adjusted. Eventually, I gave up on ever getting the so-called "casual" prosthesis to fit properly and kept it only in the event of an emergency should something happen to my "good" artificial leg.

I embraced what I thought were my final days on earth during the cycle of the leg bypasses and faced the amputation with a thought that I would never awake from the surgery. For all of my life I had been programmed to die. Dr. Wilder told my parents in 1924 that the prognosis for me was not good, and that there was a significant likelihood that I would be dead before my 10th birthday. I can still imagine Mama's changed facial expression as she was told that her youngest son was staring death in the face, and that it would, in all probability, not be too far away.

Now, 71 years later, that child, who was supposed to be long dead, is still here. But this time was different, or so I thought. I believed that facing the imminent loss of a limb, my life was pretty much over, and that it would only be a matter of perhaps weeks or a couple of months before I crossed over the River Jordan.

My family has heard me cry wolf before; and my oldest son, Rohulamin, had scolded me any number of times for referring to each Christmas as perhaps my last. But in January 1995, I truly believed that I had enjoyed my last Christmas and recall that that observance was anything but joyful. I was in constant agony and could hardly wait until the late January amputation surgery. I grew to hate that leg and asked God to just take me away from here.

But my family was unrelenting and refused to share in any aspects of my self-pity and grief. Oh they understood what I was going through all right, but they steadfastly refused to accept that I was going to die this time. They denied me any form of condolence or encouragement to feel sorry for myself. It is universally called "tough love." Joherra, my wife, was attentive as always, but she entertained no thoughts inconsistent with anything other than a complete recovery.

All four of my children, my ten grandchildren, daughters-in-law, and others were not only supportive but encouraging. When I attempted to be engulfed in self-pity, and I had daily bouts with it, they were always upbeat and encouraging. When I lamented about the things that I used to do, that I would never be able to do again, they sloughed it off, changed the subject, and started talking about when I was going to take my next trip to Barbados, referring to our annual trek to the vacation paradise nation that was my wife's birth land.

I never entertained the thought that I would see Barbados again, but fate would smile upon me several times: We resumed our annual trip in July 1995, just months after my amputation. The hotel had two barrier-free suites that had been retrofitted for disabled guests. The doors were wider too, easily accommodating a wheelchair. The bathing facilities had a shower chair and appropriate handles for added convenience; and the toilet had been raised, adjusted, and also had conveniently located handles for ease in access. These were features that I had never really paid much attention to before, but now that I was one of the "disabled," I appreciated the added convenience that these little features contributed to my enjoyment.

While I elected not to go into the Caribbean Sea, and I do think that getting down to the sea and up again would have been too physically taxing, I had the option of lowering myself down into the cool, shimmering water of the hotel swimming pool, using the steps and hand rail. Although I did occasionally enjoy the pool, my satisfaction was just to be in Barbados, sitting out on the ground-level sun porch, surrounded by the aromas of hibiscus, bougainvillea, crotons, and all of the other tropical floral ambiance.

I watched the sun rise and set daily, reading any number of books that I always took for the two-week sojourn, listening to the beat of the island music, both on the radio and from the nearby clubs in the evening, and receiving family and friends who would come by to stay awhile with us.

In addition to several of Joherra's family members still residing in Barbados, we also had cultivated Barbadian friends, some of whom we met in Washington, D.C., but who had retired and returned to the island. Others were people that Joherra knew from years ago, some from childhood, or that we met on prior visits. Whenever we were finalizing our annual trip, we would mail letters in advance to let them know that we were coming. Others we called upon our arrival, as they required less notice. Lunch and dinner invitations passed back and forth, sometimes to come to our place, or we were invited to dine with them.

Because of my newly acquired physical limitations, fewer invitations to homes were extended to us, as people appreciated that I could no longer climb the steps. But we continued with most of our socializations, as they came to dine with us, or at least to visit. As well, as you grow older and less social, there is a decreased emphasis placed upon always having to do something. Sometimes you can just relax and enjoy life a little more. That is what I learned as a juvenile diabetic in my twilight years.

I was never like my wife in this respect, anyway. She always had to have something going. A dinner planned. A dance scheduled. Another foreign trip. Some activity at the church. Something was always on her agenda. Do not misunderstand me. I wanted her to be happy and encouraged her to go to these activities. And I went to many of them, too. But I never had the need or the burning desire or curiosity that she did. Unlike her, I never took the many long trips to exotic places in other parts of the world. Instead, I satisfied myself with visits to Barbados, Jamaica, the Cayman Islands, and a trip to Rome in September 1975 for the canonization of St. Elizabeth Seton, the first American-born Catholic saint.

I also had another severe health crisis that many thought I would never recover from. On Christmas night 2000, after having enjoyed a very blessed Christmas, including a big dinner at the home of my son, Ricardo, I managed to climb up the front steps of my home, holding onto the hand railing. But that evening the climb was extremely taxing, and the eleven steps might as well have been a steep mountain incline. I managed to make it to the front door when suddenly I collapsed onto the porch floor. I did not appreciate it at the time, but I had badly splintered my left hip; and the fracture was so severe that the only solution was a total hip replacement.

At 82 years of age, and in my overall health condition, the last thing I wanted or needed was to have hip replacement surgery. At first I tried to convince myself that the hip area was only bruised, and I labored under that misconception and self denial for the better part of a week, taking pain medications, and hoping against hope that the problem was getting better. While it did feel better for a couple of days, and I really thought that I was getting better, as the new year approached, the situation suddenly crashed, and I had to be hospitalized. The diagnosis, in addition to a multiple compound fracture, was total hip replacement on the left side.

Reluctantly, I consented, and despite the many medical naysayers who questioned whether I would survive the operation, I not only survived the operation, the recuperation at both the hospital and a convalescent center, but I realized that the hip was significantly stronger than I ever imagined it would be. Further, I gained increased mobility due to my being able to place greater weight on that side when I walked. The biggest surprise of all is that I have experienced virtually no pain in that hip subsequently, despite the most inclement weather conditions.

Since retiring, I have become more reclusive, unable to go out on my own as previously, and especially more so since my amputation in 1995. But it is a case of gone but not forgotten. Because of my long permanent diaconate tenure at both Sacred Heart (1973-1991), the church we joined in 1949, and my shorter but no less enjoyable tenure in the same capacity at St. Benedict the Moor (1971-1973), there remains a residue of members of the church community who still keep in touch.

The telephone is a wonderful invention; and in addition to phone calls, I receive visitors on occasion to personally check on me and to share their love. I find that uplifting, as my one shoe is literally on the other foot. For years I was the one visiting the shut-ins, the homebound, and now I am the recipient of their love and affection. They say that what goes around likewise comes back around. I physically gave and shared when I could, and now it is their turn to do the same. Several of them are doing just that.

While I did not specifically set out to counsel my visitors from the perspective of being a permanent deacon, on several occasions my visitors have asked for my opinion on particular matters. Some have asked me to counsel them on marital problems they were having, sometimes with both parties present. People have sought my advice on diverse matters as different as drug problems, frustration in their careers, and educational objectives. Although I never proclaimed myself as anyone specially trained or experienced in crafting responses to these persons in need of assistance, somehow I found the appropriate words to counsel them, trying to really help them to help themselves.

Having been in the diabetic closet for so very much of my life, it would have been difficult to actively counsel anyone on the art of living with diabetes, since I had elected not to share with the world at large that I suffered from this ailment. However, as I got older and dealt more with the adult population, particularly at Sacred Heart, I came to a different realization. First of all, the world has changed in so many ways, far different from when I was born or a young person.

The ribald discrimination that people demonstrated against me as a juvenile diabetic has vanished, unfortunately replaced by other forms of discrimination. While racial discrimination is still very much a part of our daily lives, other discrimination is exacted against people based upon other health conditions, like AIDS. Discrimination is also based upon economics and class, religion, country of original, and the like.

At least by 1980, I noticed that diabetes and its debilitating effects are rampant in both the African-American and Hispanic communities, communities that comprise about 90% of the religious community at Sacred Heart. Although I had a language barrier with the Hispanic community and could not assess their health status and needs, my fellow African-American parishioners, many of whom contracted Type II adult onset diabetes in later years, would discuss that health problem quite freely. Without any inhibitions, they compared personal blood sugar levels, medical approaches, diabetic-related health problems they were experiencing, and diabetic recipes.

I would consider this openness and non-concern about being discriminated against as the result of two particular considerations. First, the success of the civil rights movement that this country endured for the torturous decades of the 1950s, 1960s, and 1970s has removed discrimination's sting from different groups.

The efforts of Dr. Martin Luther King, Jr., and others who led the way to the formal outlawing of racial discrimination in this great country has likewise led to tumbling barriers against women, older citizens, gay men and lesbian woman, Hispanics, Asians, Jews, and the disabled, to name several groups. And as these barriers fell, the hush-hush discrimination against diabetics and others classes with misunderstood medical problems has likewise fallen.

That leads to my second point. When I came along, many people did not know what diabetes was. In the vernacular, the victim often said he or she was "running sugar," or "I'm a little sweet, but I feel okay." These were ways of saying the same thing. But those terms were a euphemism for a ravaging and often unforgiving illness—diabetes. For someone who does not understand the ailment or what it can do to your body, it makes no difference whether you have Type I juvenile diabetes or Type II adult-onset diabetes.

All that significant percentages of the population knew was that you had a serious illness and were "strange" sometimes. And to this equation, they brought their own preconceived notions that more often than not, according to my experiences, resulted in the patient being discriminated against.

Coming from this mindset, it was difficult for me to open up and admit that I was a juvenile diabetic, let alone freely discuss it with anyone, or everyone. Yet that is exactly what happened. It was in the early 1980s, and I was sitting with a group of parishioners one day, talking about a number of parish-related issues that we were addressing. Someone made a reference to a parishioner who was suffering a ravaging and debilitating insult to his body due to diabetes.

He had sustained damage to his circulatory system that probably would result in double-leg amputations. His heart, kidneys, eyes, and other bodily systems all seemed to be failing and shutting down. The word around the room was that he was not going to be with us much longer, but still it was such a shame that someone who had been so active, and who had contributed so much to so many other people, should suddenly find himself on the receiving end, as he rapidly declined into almost total dependency and approaching death.

Along with the others, I expressed my sympathy and concern. Gradually, some in the room added that they too were diabetic, and that they have been able to hold the condition at bay, they thought, through a combination of prayer, diet, exercise, discipline and medication. A couple of others commented that they too were diabetics, and from that point the discussion took off. It became readily apparent that some of them had done their homework. They had studied the illness, knew fairly well how it worked, and what was required to control it, if only they were able to stick to the strict regimen.

Likewise, I suddenly and better realized that education is the key. These people were educated to what the ailment was about. In sharing their thoughts with us, as they had probably already done in other sittings with different groups of people, the overall population came to better understand. There was no more need to be hushed about the ailment. There was no longer a need to keep the "Big Secret," as it was called, because no one really cared anymore about discriminating against you because of diabetes.

Almost reflectively, I blurted out, "I'm a juvenile diabetic, and I've had the ailment since I was three years old." Incredulously, several of them stared at me in amazement. Someone said, "Deacon Quander, you did say since you were three years old, didn't you?" I answered in the affirmative, and at that precise moment, I came out of the diabetic closet.

They had nothing but question after question. How did you find out that you were a juvenile diabetic? When did you start taking insulin? Have you experienced any diabetic-related complications that resulted in hospitalization? How do your wife and family feel about your being diabetic? Have you participated in any of the long-term studies that are searching for the cure? Have you ever passed out and been taken to the hospital in an ambulance due to low blood sugar? A million questions, and I tried to honestly answer each one of them.

Suddenly, I was thrust into the spotlight, a place that I hardly wanted to be. But the subject was diabetes, and I slipped from my perch and joined the fray. And I never looked back. Since then, I have counseled innumerable people on learning to live successfully with diabetes.

Initially I was focused upon members of the Sacred Heart parish community who approached me and asked for diabetic health-related advice. Eventually, though, I found myself in an expanded arena, fielding occasional questions from strangers who, with my previously having given my telephone number to my treating physicians with permission to use it, called me on behalf of themselves, or about conditions that their young juvenile diabetic children were currently experiencing.

My condition, and especially since I was a juvenile diabetic who had survived for so many years, caught the attention of the news media; and in recent years I have been featured in the *Washington Post, Diabetic Forecast,* and innumerable other publications—all examining how I have managed to live such a diverse and enjoyable life for all of these years, despite the physical, emotional, and psychological toll that diabetes has taken over these now more than eight decades.

# Chapter 15

# Salute to My Wife, A Loving Tribute

I met my wife in January 1942, on a blind referral from Saxton Howard, a coworker in the U.S. Government Printing Office (the GPO). After graduating from college, I transferred my federal service from the U.S. Post Office, where I worked for a little over a year, to the GPO.

While performing printing-related job duties at GPO, Saxton and I were casually talking. I had mentioned to him that I was on the rebound, recently detached from the girl I had intended to marry when she declined the engagement ring. She and I parted as "friends," according to her perception; but in my own mind I was deeply disappointed and hurt by her dismissal.

He replied by telling me that he had met a real pretty West Indian girl who had just relocated from New York to Washington, D.C., a few weeks prior, to work in the War Department. He could not even pronounce her name, "Jo-something," he said, adding that she did not know a soul here in Washington. Although he thought that she was very nice, he noted that she perhaps was a little young for him. Besides, he was committed to his girlfriend, whom he planned to soon marry. He asked if I would like to meet her. She was his new neighbor in Ivy City.

My parents had only wanted the best for me, and they too ached because I did. Only after my old girlfriend dumped me did Mama and Papa share their concerns about her. First of all, she was not Catholic, and this immediately posed a dilemma, since mixed religion marriages in the early 1940s always seemed a problem. Further, she was not enamored with the Catholic Church as an institution. In fact, she was critical of it on numerous occasions.

Additionally, although I had met her mother and some other family members, her father, whom I never met, was not a part of her life. Apparently, she was the product of what we then called a "broken home," raising a question about her family's stability, something that both my parents and I prioritized. My health dictated that my marital relationship should be as smooth and non-stressful as possible, and starting off on a questionable footing did not fare well with them or me.

When she refused the ring, I thought that life had ended. Papa, being wise counsel, encouraged me to take several breaths of fresh air, close my eyes, envision something peaceful, and not let myself get all stressed out over this seemingly insurmountable crisis. He reminded me that new love comes into someone's life every day, and that perhaps I had just been blinded by my old love, who turned out to be different from what my blinded eyes had been seeing all along. He urged me to step back and pray, and let God help me through this "crisis." I followed his advice and simply let go. And when I let go, I found myself at peace rather quickly. This entire seemingly tragic incident occurred within a couple of months in late 1941, and just as suddenly as it came on the scene, it almost as quickly evaporated.

I was 23 years old, and although I was looking for a wife, I was by no means desperate. I had been out of college since June 1940, only a year and a half, and still had contact with most of my college-era and many of my high school-era friends. But there was still something missing. So when Saxton mentioned her name, which he could hardly pronounce, I said, "Yes, I'd love to meet her." He again repeated, "She's very pretty," to which I replied, "Pretty! That's enough to get started."

He brought her telephone number to work the next day. I still remember the number—*Lincoln 3531*. I had the number for a couple of days, as I fortified myself in anticipation of dialing her up. Finally, on that cold early January 1942 Sunday morning, after

I returned from Mass, I called her and introduced myself, advising her how I got her number. I asked if I could call on her later that day, in the early afternoon. I remember most vividly her reply, "Why, of course!" She was living at 1834 Capitol Avenue, N.E., near Gallaudet College (now University) in the Ivy City section of the city, an older part of town that was somewhat rural at the time. Many of the streets still lacked sidewalks, and some houses still had outhouses, despite the city's stated policy and efforts to eradicate all of them.

I had not yet laid eyes on her, and the most distinct and only characteristic then was her strong Barbadian accent, which is unlike any other accent in the Caribbean. Barbados is said to be the nation where the word pronunciations of a certain group of Irish meet the Yoruba language pronunciations from Nigeria, which has resulted in a distinct "Barbados brogue." Other than "pretty," the word used by Saxton, I had no idea what she looked like, and at that point it made no difference.

I found the house and rang the doorbell, waiting for what seemed like an eternity. When she opened the door on that cold Sunday afternoon, the warmth and smile that emanated from her Asian eyes took me in immediately. To say that I was "taken in" puts it mildly. It was not necessarily love at first sight, although perhaps close to it—from my perspective. From the outset, we came from completely different worlds. I was a Washingtonian of African-American background, having attended local, segregated schools, but graduating from the famous Dunbar High School and Miner Teacher's College. My world was an all-black world, and very limited, despite my residing in the capital of the nation. At that time, Washington, D.C., was still very much a sleepy Southern and much-segregated city. The U.S. Congressional overseers were all Caucasian Congressman, mostly from the Southern states, and they did not take kindly to the colored citizens of this city. The effect of that attitude severely limited my worldview perspective.

Conversely, Joherra was from some exotic island called Barbados. At the time I did not even know where it was, or have any knowledge of its rich history in the slave trade, sugar plantations, rum, and hot Caribbean music. As well, she had been educated in the British system until she immigrated to New York in

1934, and while there were some racial restrictions imposed upon her both in Barbados and in the United States, her society was far more open than mine ever was.

Ethnically and racially, her father, Mohammed, was an Indian Muslim cloth and jewel merchant who migrated to Barbados from Calcutta, India, in 1913. Her mother, Oquindo O'Brien Amin, was of mixed English, Irish, Scottish, and Afro-Caribbean ancestry. Therefore, the only thing to identify her as black within the racial confines and restrictions of this country at that time was the artificially created "one drop rule." Otherwise, she would not be considered a Negro. One point we had in common was religion. We were both Catholic, and that made an immediate positive impression upon me, as I could see the relationship building based in part upon the commonality of religion factor.

But none of that complicated stuff made any difference to me at that time. All I knew was that I was interested and available, and maybe she was, too. When we first met, we spent time in the parlor of the house where she was staying. She was 21 years old when she relocated to Washington, D.C., in December 1941, just a few days before Christmas. We talked about everything, and I found it most interesting that we had such a different view on a lot of things.

While I attempted to portray a worldview, I really did not have much of one, as my world was so limited by the above-referred parameters. In my entire 23 years, I had never been more than about 35 miles from home, to the beaches along the Chesapeake Bay shoreline in the Annapolis area. Yet Joherra had come from far away, and until shortly before we met, was a British subject, the term analogous for citizenship. She had a far broader view of the world than I, primarily still with a British-centered focus. She discovered that I could sing, and I discovered that she could play the piano; and with that we closed out our first meeting with music, entertaining ourselves until mid evening.

Because my work hours dictated my reporting to duty at GPO by 12:00 a.m. every workday, our relationship started as Sunday afternoons only. However, during the week, I would call and we would talk at length, getting to know one another better. The same streetcar that operated on U Street, N.W., also ran out Florida Avenue, N.E., depositing me in front of Gallaudet. From there I could take a bus or walk past the campus, up West Virginia Avenue and across Mount Olivet Road to Capitol Avenue in Ivy City. It was a fairly long walk, but consistent with my diabetic psychology of getting as much exercise as possible, I almost always elected to walk the distance.

Although I was smitten, I do not think that the feeling was mutual at that stage. But sometimes relationships grow slowly and require nurturing. Ours was no different. Because she was nonwhite, Joherra's on-job affiliations were all with the Negro girls who had migrated from all over the United States to work in the War Department or other federal agencies. Most all of them were like her in that they knew no one prior to their arrival in the nation's capital city. Undoubtedly, many of them were lonely and longed for back home. Being young and resourceful, these ladies were determined not to want too long. With Valentine's Day 1942 approaching, several of them got together and formed a social group for the express purpose of having a Valentine's Day party. Although Joherra had only been in Washington for two months and had only known the girls in the group for about one month or less, she embraced the group enthusiastically, and became a member.

I was her sole-invited guest for the party, but I declined her invitation on the basis that I had to report to work by 12:00 a.m.; and with my rest schedule prior to reporting to duty, it was not possible for me to attend the party. I did not want to be left out of the equation completely, so I arranged for my brother, Joseph Pearson, whom we universally just called "Pearson," to deliver a box of chocolates from me to her during the party. It came as a surprise to her when he showed up with the candy and started the other girls to gaggle on about how this relationship must be getting serious, since she was the only one who had a gift delivered to her by an absent suitor.

Laughing off their little friendly cupid-related jabs, she was further surprised when, despite my having to report to work, I suddenly showed up at the party for a few minutes to personally wish her a Happy Valentine's Day. Pearson drove me by the party for literally a few minutes, and then home to change clothes before reporting to the GPO. Because I wore workman's clothes while dealing with the dirty inking equipment and printing machines, I did not want to show up at the party not properly attired, including wearing a shirt and tie. Washington, D.C., in those days was a center for well-dressed Negroes. Much emphasis was placed upon fashion, and people dressed quite well and properly for each occasion.

Howard University professor, E. Franklin Frazier, would later point out in his acclaimed book, *Black Bourgeoisie*, that colored high and middle society around the United States dressed in the latest fashion and acquired the most expensive and up-to-date items, including clothing, as a psychological way of overcoming the stigma of second class citizenship. Frazier's observations in the 1950s were drawn in part upon what Washingtonians of color were wearing in the 1940s, and although I was not a part of the big social scene, I understood and appreciated that if I was going to the Valentine's party at the Phyllis Wheatley YWCA, I needed to be dressed in a certain way. My fate was sealed that night, only I did not yet know it. Joherra said to the girls, including Elaine Boyd, her roommate and in whose aunt's house they both resided, "You know, I don't particularly like him, but I think I've met my future husband."

By the time the comment got back to me, several weeks had passed, and our relationship was quickly cementing. Mama and Papa were curious about who this girl was. They too were very limited in their exposure. Papa, having migrated from Upper Marlboro, Maryland, to Washington, D.C., in about 1893, had never ventured beyond the Washington, D.C., area, except once, when he went to Philadelphia to retrieve my sister, Elvira, who had run away from home to join a theater group that had just passed through town. She was 15 years old. Mama had migrated from Walterboro, South Carolina, to Washington, D.C., in 1890, at age ten years, and had been nowhere as well, other than occasional trips back to her sleepy hometown of less than 1,500 people.

They knew nothing about this girl, except for what I had told them. Not that they were especially concerned, because I had told both of them that she was a person of high moral character, Catholic, pretty, and attractive in both her manner and values. The qualities that I wanted in a wife were exhibited in her personality, and I was determined to follow this budding relationship to wherever it carried me. I prayed on it, and my parents did likewise.

Finally, the time was ripe for Joherra to meet my parents. Mama was an excellent cook, and Sunday dinners on Seventeenth Street were a way of life. I had not yet elected to subject Joherra to that experience, as it could easily be intimidating. Native-born Washingtonians, then and still, have the reputation of not being particularly friendly to outsiders at the outset. It takes some time to warm up to them, as it does in other matters as well. But in this case, the fact that Joherra was from a different country, a different point of view, and in many an eye, a different race, although race is an artificial creation, caused me to hesitate before exposing her to the fray.

Would they be kind to her? I never thought they would be hostile. How would they accept someone who was foreign born, looked different, and "talked funny"? They had never been exposed to someone so "different," and my only real concern was that they kept an open mind about her, which they did. These were all valid considerations that raced through my mind for several weeks before I ventured to bring her home to meet my parents and whoever else happened to have their feet under the table that Sunday afternoon in late March 1942. Pearson had already reported to Mama and Papa that it looked quite serious to him, but they each kept their counsel, waiting for me to say something to them directly.

Everyone was on best behavior. Mama prepared the most delicious Sunday dinner—Southern fried chicken, light-as-a-feather hot rolls, ice tea, chocolate cake, and everything that went with it. She always did, but this Sunday seemed special. Maybe I was just in love, and for that reason everything tasted better, looked better, and was more promising in every respect. But what counted most of all were the favorable reactions, the approval if you will, that I immediately got from Mama and Papa. Mama was never one with a lot of words, and this occasion was no different. Knowing her as I did, however, I could tell that she was most favorably impressed.

Conversely, Papa had a lot to say. A very wise man was he, and an excellent judge of a person. After spending several hours with her in our family's context, before I took her home, he pulled me aside and said, "James, this is the one. She's what you have been looking for, and if this relationship continues as it seems to be developing, I believe that she's an excellent choice for your wife."

I was elated. I had not yet ventured to ask Papa for his opinion, although I intended to ask him for it at a later time. His suitability seal of approval meant a lot to me, and cleared the path from what could have been a major obstacle. From that Sunday afternoon forward, the budding relationship blossomed forth. Some weeks before, when it was clear to both of us that this relationship was developing into a serious romance, she returned the engagement ring to her old Jamaican boyfriend, "Smiley," to whom she was betrothed when she relocated to Washington, D.C.

She had come to realize that her words uttered at the Valentine's Day party were prophetic, and that indeed, she just might have met her future husband. Not being a person who would unfairly and improperly string someone else along, she realized that the right thing to do was to release herself from any commitment to Smiley, to allow him to get on with his life, too. Years later, when we were visiting New York, she and I bumped into Smiley on the New York subway. The introduction and brief encounter was most cordial.

Up to this point, I had not confided in Joherra that I was a juvenile diabetic. My health secret was still part of the baggage that I had been carrying since childhood, and I was hesitant to bring the subject up, as I did not know how she would react to discovering why my eating habits were so strange, so different from what other people were doing. Up to this point, she never once asked me about it, although I am certain that she wondered.

For the balance of 1942, I squired her about town. Washington being a Jim Crow town, we attended the colored only cinemas and ate in Negro-owned restaurants, mostly located along "Strivers Row" and "Black Broadway," the names we attached to U Street, N.W., the primary center of entertainment for black Washingtonians in the 1940s. I took her to more than one fraternity dance at the Lincoln Colonnade, a couple of formal affairs where we were really dressed up. We routinely visited high school- and college-era friends' homes on the weekend, getting there by bus and often leaving by taxi.

The word got out that Jim Quander was squiring someone new about town, a foreign girl from "the Islands," and she was quite nice, both inside and out. Although I never desired to get even with my old fiancée, as she was yesterday's news by then, a number of the persons we visited were also her friends; and I know that the word got back to her that I had gotten over her and moved on with my life.

By now, spring was well in the air, and with it, young love. While everyone she met was cordial and gracious, the true sentiment was sometimes not expressed. Joherra seemed to be quite "OK" with the guys, several of whom were likewise smitten by her physical beauty and her beautiful ways—nice and sweet to everybody. Many of them knew of my being on the rebound, and they wished me well, without limitations.

On the other hand, many of the girls, while nice and polite to our faces, were also expressing negative sentiments to others that I apparently did not consider them good enough for me, since I had gone elsewhere in search of someone from a significantly different background. I sloughed off the sentiment from within my own racial group, thinking that their negative comments were insignificant, and made my plans to move this relationship forward hopefully to marriage.

I had not anticipated then that the sentiments expressed by not just a few of my contemporary female friends and acquaintances would likewise and far more adversely be later expressed by their own mothers, upon learning that I was planning to marry Joherra: "What's the matter? One of our own is not good enough for him?" "Why did he have to go looking in some strange place for a wife, and then take up with an Asian girl at that?" These remarks were typical. Other sentiments included: "Careful boy, do you know what you're doing? Those West Indian women are dangerous. Cross one of them, and they'll cut you for sure." "Don't marry her. She doesn't understand our ways. There'll be nothing but trouble between the two of you, and it will never work."

I did not listen to any of this naysaying and focused in my mind how I was going to ask Joherra to marry me. The months had flown by quickly, as April gave way to May, and May to June. By June the time seemed right to ask the question. We had been seeing each other since January 1942, less than a month after Joherra migrated from New York. By now the romance had developed to a point where logic dictated that some definitive permanent action must occur, or the chance of a lifetime might be lost and never presented again.

I collected my thoughts and calmly wrote a "Will you marry me?" speech. As the days had grown longer, and the sun was setting later each evening, we had acquired the habit of taking long Sunday afternoon into evening walks through the neighborhood. Gallaudet College (now University) was the cornerstone of the area, having been initially established as the Kendall School in 1856 by Edward Gallaudet, Amos Kendall, and several other persons dedicated to educating children who were deaf, hard of hearing, or who could not speak. The buildings were stately, many ivy covered, and the lawn and gardens a great attraction and asset to the entire neighborhood.

It was only natural that Joherra and I would be drawn to the heavy shade trees, the well-manicured property, and the total ambiance of the site. As well, many in the neighborhood gravitated towards Gallaudet as a place to put down stakes and rest on the lawn or a bench for a while, regardless of whether you had any academic connection to the institution.

Having written down what I wanted to say, and planning to also tell her that I was a juvenile diabetic as an extension of the marriage proposal, I rehearsed my speech for several days, including while riding the street car out Florida Avenue. This was to be the day when I would learn whether this relationship was permanently going forward or not. I picked her up at the house, having checked my pocket for the hundredth time to make certain that the ring was securely tucked away, and we walked towards Gallaudet.

By then she had moved to the home of Rev. and Mrs. Haywood Threlkeld, he a local minister in the Colored Methodist Church (since 1956 called the Christian Methodist Church), and she a school teacher and church musician, who also gave private piano lessons. In later years, Mrs. Threlkeld would teach all four of my children. The Threlkelds lived on G Street, N.E., closer to the college than the Ivy City location.

Recalling the steps of how I attempted to get engaged the first time, I initially assumed that I should use the same approach. Only this time it was different. And when the time came to essentially state in words all that I had thought about and written down on my outline, everything went wrong. All the words flew out of my head, and I was momentarily tongue-tied. After starting with something formal, like, "Jo, we've been seeing each other for some time now, and …," fully expecting to carry that same level of presentation, my mind went blank. After this awkward pause, she looked at me as we walked arm in arm past the college's main entrance on Florida Avenue and said, "Well, is there more?"

I never stuttered, but on that occasion my mind did, and after what seemed like an eternity, I blurted out, "Joherra, will you marry me?" Although I know that it seemed like an eternity waiting for an answer, she looked me in the eyes and said, "Why, of course!"—the same three words she uttered on that cold day in January when I called her on the telephone for the first time and asked to call on her.

I immediately recalled that up to that point in our conversation that early Sunday evening, I had said nothing to her about juvenile diabetes and the many health problems that I had faced my entire life because of it. I did not want to enter marriage under false pretense, and I needed to make certain that she knew exactly what she was getting into from the health perspective as a potential long-term caregiver.

After regaining my composure in response to her affirmation of marriage, I slowly began to explain exactly what diabetes is and how it affects people. My explanation was far too academic and medical and went right over her head. It was pretty clear to me that not only had she never heard of diabetes, she had no idea what I was talking about. Her mind was someplace else, and as I explained the disease, its characteristics, symptoms, and my daily regimen to her, she nodded her head, smiled, and absorbed my words, not letting on that she was not really too concerned about it.

While no one ever sets out in a relationship to become a dependent invalid, I was in essence telling her that this is exactly what might happen, as I explained how excessive sugar in the blood can eventually clog the vessels, lead to great pain, and even result in amputation—all of which eventually would occur in my later years. I had witnessed this exact scenario at Freedmen's Hospital during my several periods of hospitalization as a youth in the 1920s and 1930s.

I also explained the relatively complicated process of daily monitoring both my blood sugar and insulin intake, and how I measured and administered insulin to myself. In the recesses of my mind, I was afraid that once she heard all of these things, she might be hesitant to continue our relationship for fear of the possible complications and seriousness of the undertaking, if she elected to become my wife.

But Joherra was from a totally different place, not just geographically, but spiritually and emotionally. She had been born in a place and raised in a culture where family took care of its own, and even other people in need who were not actually part of the family. Barbados then was an economically poor place, but the notion of taking care of each other was deeply ingrained. So she never really thought much about the potential gravity of what I was explaining to her, and likewise never entertained the thought that maybe she did not want to be potentially involved with diabetes or me over the long term.

After my long explanation of what diabetes was all about, including that there was no cure for the ailment at the time, although research for a cure was underway, she summarily dismissed the entire conversation with, "So what difference does that make between two people who love and really care for one another?" And that was it. Dismissed!

What neither she nor I knew at that time was that her own father, Mohammed, who remained in Barbados when her parents separated and her mother immigrated to the United States in 1929, had become an adult onset diabetic. Quite probably due to a lack of good medical care as well as a questionable diet, he sustained a poor circulation-related double-foot amputation in about 1944. In those days, few people in Barbados actually used the terms "diabetes" or "diabetic," simply dismissing the ailment as "running sugar," which had the unfortunate effect of not adequately explaining the seriously debilitative nature and long-term adverse effects of the ailment.

As previously explained in detail in Chapter 11, *The Gifts of Marriage*, Joherra really never understood at the outset what was in store. She never anticipated the number of late-night and early-morning diabetic reactions that I would encounter, with her having to get out of bed in the middle of the night to give me orange juice, and during the most severe insulin reactions, having to pour syrup down my throat to achieve the fastest injection of pure sugar into my blood stream.

On that Sunday evening, as the sun set on Florida Avenue, she never appreciated that there would be times, and indeed many times, and at all hours of the day or night, she or someone at work would have to summon an ambulance because I had slipped into a severe insulin reaction, or was dangerously close to a diabetic coma. More than once my blood sugar slipped below 20, and the medical experts were confounded that not only did I survive, but I fully recovered and was functional within a day or two.

No, she never could have known that in saying, "Why, of course!" to Jim Quander on that Sunday evening, as the sun was setting on one of the longest days of the year, that she was entering into a covenant that would last for 60 years, that her patience and loving kind manner would be tried on several occasions, and that even her own health would be placed in jeopardy.

Yet, with eyes open, she embraced me, loved me, gave me four devoted children and likewise ten attentive grandchildren, all of whom have made me exceedingly proud. There were so many myths about diabetics, largely the result of ignorance and preconceived notions, all of which were wrong. Diabetic women were routinely told that they could not have children, when instead doctors should have told them that their pregnancies needed to be carefully monitored. Diabetic men were likewise told that they could not father children due to erectile dysfunction and therefore should not marry.

If I had listened to all of the "You cannots ..." expressed by my family, and even some of my treating physicians, I never would have accomplished anything. All of my life, I yearned to be a complete person, to throw off the yoke of health disability, and in my dreams I am often "whole." But for me, and like in a game of playing cards, life never dealt me a hand that was without a handicap, and a significant one at that.

In January 1942, I was looking for something—for someone who would help me realize my whole self, someone that I could confide in, and who would not tell me that I could not do this or that. I found that someone in Joherra. She was not the least bit pretentious, had no "airs" about herself, and was not concerned with being the most glamorous or the fashion plate in Washington's colored society; although I did help her to become such to a certain extent, due to my own fashion sense and knowing that I wanted my wife to convey a particular aura and appearance about herself.

She was certainly up to the task. Smart and adaptable, she dressed well and had a sense of the latest fashion, making most of her own clothes, another skill that she brought from Barbados. As well, her mother, two aunts, and other relatives all worked as seamstresses in New York factories; so Joherra had been exposed to that discipline and likewise developed the skill. It was nothing for her to put the extra leaf in the dining room table on Saturday morning, lay out a new dress from a pattern she had just purchased, and make and wear the dress to a dance that same evening. As well, on occasion she sewed without a pattern: she was accomplished to the point that she did not always need to use one.

But all of these appearances, while genuine, were also superficial, as the real person lay beneath. Resourceful and energetic, she took on many tasks, often keeping several things going at the same time. From the outset of our marriage, she voluntarily took it upon herself to learn from my mother how to cook American style; only she did not fully comprehend the distinction between Southern and "American" cooking. But quickly she became an excellent cook, and likewise adapted to the regimen of preparing an additional menu to accommodate my diabetic food needs while serving something else to others in the family.

From the beginning, and initially unknown to me, she was a saver. People in the Caribbean were always struggling, it seems, and learning to put a few dollars away until a more crucial time became another of her hallmarks. It was a genuine surprise, and likewise with a sense of pride, that I learned that she had saved enough money to pay my graduate school tuition as I enrolled in Howard University in January 1944, in pursuit of my Ph.D. degree in economics. Having then recently relocated to our own apartment at 1631 Montello Avenue, N.E., and with the arrival of our son, Rohulamin, on December 4, 1943, two days before our first wedding anniversary, she was on maternity leave, and we only had one income at that time. How she managed to save enough money before temporarily leaving her job as a clerk in the War Department still confounds me. But this too set a tone in our marriage, as she was brought up to always set something aside and save it for a rainy day. And because we did not have too many rainy days, those set-asides accumulated, and in later years were also helpful in making our lifestyle more comfortable.

For 60 years, Joherra was my partner in life. She loved me, just as I deeply loved her. She made things possible for me that I never would have otherwise known. And most significantly, she made me realize, understand, and appreciate that the limitations that were imposed upon me as a juvenile diabetic were mostly self-imposed. All of the "cannots" that I grew up with, all of the "do nots" that were a part of my daily early life, even from my own parents and treating physicians, all were replaced with "why nots" and "you can."

She had such a positive outlook on life that everything she undertook was always approached in that manner. We never jointly went into any endeavor with a thought that it might not work. And on the occasions when I had self-doubts, and these occasions were not just a few, she always countered me with something positive, even if only to say, "Well Jim, if it doesn't work, we've at least learned a lesson and can profit from it."

But at the same time, she was always realistic, having her feet firmly grounded, even when our heads were in the clouds. This grounding contributed significantly to every phase of our married life. Initially starting in a one-bedroom apartment, we saved enough for a down payment and purchased our own house in 1949, 3714 Thirteenth Street, N.W., where I still reside today.

There we raised and educated four children, all of whom have two degrees, good careers—a judge, a social worker, an environmental scientist, and a veterinarian—and families with children, ten grandchildren in all. Knowing my situation, I doubt that I ever could have accomplished all of this but for Joherra.

She was the light of my life. She illuminated an otherwise uncertain path for this poor 1930s-era boy from sleepy town Washington, D.C., to get to know that there was much beyond the limited confines of the totally segregated world that was all that he knew. She introduced me to people from different backgrounds, caused me to travel to places that I might never have seen otherwise, and gave me hope that there was always a brighter tomorrow.

Although she suddenly left me on that bright sunny day in early December 2002, when God, our beloved Father, called her to be with Him, she also left a legacy that will never be forgotten. And it is to that memory, to the appreciation, that I celebrate our life together and am eternally grateful to God, who, in His infinite wisdom, saw that I needed someone very special and He sent her to me.

In my early grief and shock at what had occurred, I was at a loss to understand why this happened. Dying suddenly on December 3, 2002, three days before our 60th wedding anniversary, I just knew that I would not survive, that I could not cope with this catastrophe. Through the years I had lost both parents, all of my siblings, my personal friends, and several of my treating physicians who had become like family. With each death there was a sense of sadness and loss, but I always felt that I had enough strength of character and mind to carry on, relying upon the God within me to make it. And each time I was right and survived quite well.

But this time was different. My first thought was anger. I was angry with God initially because He had taken her from me. Yes, but more so because He had called her home, and not me. I have always prayed to die first, because I wanted Joherra to have some years when she was free of the stress, strain, and obligation of taking care of a sick old man—me. I thought that if I died first, she and my daughter, also called "Joherra," could have some quality mother-daughter time together. I thought that if I died first, then my wife could enjoy the company of our three sons on trips and enjoy spending more time with our ten grandchildren.

But God's plan was otherwise. As my son, Rohulamin, so fittingly said at the funeral, "God, in His infinite wisdom, lent

Joherra to us for 82 years, and to our father, James, for 61 years, January 1942 to December 3, 2002. Now, He has called for her to return to Him. We are deeply saddened at the sudden loss, and ask ourselves, 'How will we ever get over it?' Well, we will never get over it. Never! Mom was our light, our love, our counsel and true friend; and her loss will always be deeply felt. But we are not forever saddened, as much as we are grateful.

"For He lent her to us, and we feel very special at having been selected to receive His beneficence. So this is an occasion of thanksgiving at her having passed this way, and for her having been a part of our lives for this long. Many families do not have the benefit of a loving wife and a caring mother, grandmother, and friend for as long as we, and so we give a special thanks to God Almighty for being among the chosen, to receive the many gifts that she bestowed upon us while she was on loan from heaven. Go Mom, and return to the Father who sent you. We will always love you. Rest in Peace!"

And that is my exact sentiment. While she laid unconscious on her deathbed at the Washington Hospital Center, my four children, Rohulamin, Joherra, John, and Ricardo, told her to go home to God, to let go of everything here in this temporal world, and to trust Him who sent her. They also promised to take care of me for the remainder of my days, and I am pleased to note that they are well meeting that commitment. No, it is not the same without her, but the values she instilled in each of them sustain me. And I too am thankful indeed.

*Rest in Peace my Love, until we're together again. And I trust it will be soon.*

James

# Post Log

On October 9, 2004, James W. Quander died as a result of the long-term effects of diabetic-related complications. His death was not treated by his family as a moment of sadness, but rather as a time to rejoice and be glad in knowing that his entire life, and life contributions, were lessons well taught in how one can live with great health-related physical adversity, yet persevere, accomplish, and even triumph.

Dad and I spent a great deal of time writing this book, researching facts, date checking, and discussing several aspects of his story with my siblings, his health professionals, classmates, family members and friends. We took great pride in structuring the most accurate, yet interesting story that we could, and in March 2004, we completed the first draft of the manuscript.

In his old age, Dad became more determined in everything that he did, and he insisted that his story must be told and widely disseminated to all who would listen. He believed that no diabetic or family member of a diabetic should ever again think of the ailment as a curse. Rather, diabetes, and especially juvenile diabetes, is a life challenge that must be met head on, and that is manageable if the diabetic is truly forthright in his or her intentions to handle the situation in the best possible manner.

Dad always recognized and underscored that each person's diabetic story is unique, and that the ailment is more virulent in its toll in certain people. He recognized that no matter how prepared an individual is to meet the challenge, in some cases the outcome is going to be very disheartening. Still, his message and mine today is that the earlier in life the diabetic comes to grip with the ailment, the sooner he or she sets about to adopt the appropriate food, exercise, and disciplinary regimen required, the greater the likelihood that the ailment will be under relative control.

Perhaps "control" is not the right word, as Dad's diabetes never was under true "control" and flipped out of alignment several times a year, resulting in very high or very low blood sugars, adjustments of insulin and food intake, and even an occasional hospital visit. Yet he never lost faith in himself, his family, and, most importantly, his God. Yes, there were times when he was depressed, and asked, "Why me?" But those occasions were quickly met with self-assurance, a reflection upon all he had done in his life, and the many, many "Firsts" that he accomplished in education, race, employment, religion, and history.

He always said that although he lost the gift of good eyesight in his last couple of years, the loss of physical sight gave him great spiritual and emotional insight into who and what he was. It gave him a better understanding of where he fit into God's plan and the message to go forth and share the good news of what he had accomplished, despite the debilitating circumstances. As well, he frequently mentioned that the loss of his eyesight was compensated by recalling the 60 years of happy marriage to Joherra and all of the associations that came with that relationship, the many places he had traveled to, the people he had met, the events he participated in, and how he felt a strong sense of appreciation that God allowed him to accomplish these diverse and exciting things.

Having attended the renowned Dunbar High School and then graduating from Miner Teachers College, both in Washington, D.C., he appreciated how much his parents, who did not have the benefit of much formal education, had sacrificed to make his accomplishments possible. He was especially grateful how they supported his health needs as he reached out in many directions in the 1920s and 1930s, in search of how to survive and monitor himself as a young healthy diabetic child and adolescent.

This book could not have been written much earlier, for it took years of tempering, sober reflection, and unique experiences to meld my dad into the person that he became at the end of his life. For much of his life he was angry, hostile with some of his peers, both black and white, and carried the air of a man who was supremely disappointed in how his fellow man had hurt him by not being honest in addressing several relationships and instances where injustice had been done.

A good example of what I speak is the entire story surrounding the circumstance of his sudden retirement effective December 31, 1973, in which he was the scapegoat for several people who made a great tactical error; but they were not honest enough to own up to their superiors that they had made a mistake, only compounding the problem with a cover-up of lies and collective amnesia.

Yet with time and a good loving relationship from his devoted wife, he learned to let many things go, coming to realize that there are things in life that you cannot do much about, and that in the end much of the "stuff" of life is just that—"stuff" about which we need not inordinately concern ourselves. His adult life was divided into three essentially equal time frames—33 years of federal service (1940-1973), 33 years of religious service as a permanent deacon (1971-2004), and 31 years of formal retirement (1973-2004) from the federal government.

Despite getting out and working every day, I deem that some of his most productive time was spent after he left the federal government and likewise after 1991, when he became inactive as a deacon due to health limitations. For in his true senior years, he acquired a new attitude. He was surrounded by a new atmosphere in which many of his former peer group belatedly and finally came to a realization of what he had endured on their behalf for so long. Many of them grew into their own maturities and came to appreciate what it meant to be a trailblazer, what it meant to not follow a path, but rather to create a path for others to follow. It was this courage that at last became appreciated, and with it came "elder statesman" status, which he was not only well entitled to, but had earned one difficult day at a time—PEACE.

Rohulamin Quander
July 19, 2005

Rohulamin Quander is currently working on a book about the
Quander Family's distinguished history, documented in the
American Colonies from 1684. Here he contemplates the family's
historical relationship with George Washington at the Mount Vernon
Plantation where many Quander ancestors were enslaved.